A PREFACE TO LITERATURE

By Edward Wagenknecht

PSYCHOGRAPHY: THE MAN CHARLES DICKENS (1929); JENNY LIND (1931); MARK TWAIN, THE MAN AND HIS WORK (1935); HENRY WADSWORTH LONGFELLOW, AMERICAN HUMANIST (in preparation)

CRITICISM: VALUES IN LITERATURE (1928); UTOPIA AMERICANA (1929); A GUIDE TO BERNARD SHAW (1929); CAVALCADE OF THE ENGLISH NOVEL (1943); CAVALCADE OF THE AMERICAN NOVEL (1952)

ABOUT THE THEATER: LILLIAN GISH, AN INTERPRETATION (1927); GERALDINE FARRAR, AN AUTHORIZED RECORD OF HER CAREER (1929)

ANTHOLOGIES: THE COLLEGE SURVEY OF ENGLISH LITERATURE (with others) (1942); SIX NOVELS OF THE SUPERNATURAL (1944); THE FIRESIDE BOOK OF CHRISTMAS STORIES (1945); THE STORY OF JESUS IN THE WORLD'S LITERATURE (1946); WHEN I WAS A CHILD (1946); THE FIRESIDE BOOK OF GHOST STORIES (1947); ABRAHAM LINCOLN, HIS LIFE, WORK, AND CHARACTER (1947); THE FIRESIDE BOOK OF ROMANCE (1948); JOAN OF ARC, AN ANTHOLOGY OF HISTORY AND LITERATURE (1948); A FIRESIDE BOOK OF YULETIDE TALES (1948); MURDER BY GASLIGHT (1949); THE COLLECTED TALES OF WALTER DE LA MARE (1950); AN INTRODUCTION TO DICKENS (1952)

INTRODUCTIONS by E. W.: THE CHIMES, BY CHARLES DICKENS (LIMITED EDITIONS CLUB) (1931); LIFE ON THE MISSISSIPPI, BY MARK TWAIN (LIMITED EDITIONS CLUB) (1944); A TALE OF TWO CITIES, BY CHARLES DICKENS (MODERN LIBRARY) (1950)

A
PREFACE
TO
LITERATURE

by EDWARD WAGENKNECHT

HENRY HOLT AND COMPANY

NEW YORK

KRAUS REPRINT CO.
New York
1969

Reprinted with the permission of the original publisher
KRAUS REPRINT CO.
A U.S. Division of Kraus-Thomson Organization Limited

for
ROBERT

"Look, here, this garden of exhaustless delights!"

Contents

To the Student

~~~~~~

Forget, if you can, that this is a "schoolbook." Dismiss from your mind the idea that you are preparing a "lesson." You will get more out of this book if you begin reading it in the spirit in which you go to the "movies"—or even pick up the comic section—that you will if you go at it in the manner in which most of your "assignments" are (very properly) prepared.

On your program card, "English" is a "subject," just as history and science and mathematics and perhaps a foreign language are "subjects." And so long as the English language and literature are going to be studied in our schools and colleges, this is inevitable. It may, nevertheless, lead to very serious misunderstandings. It will almost certainly do so unless you understand that "English" differs from your other studies in at least two important particulars.

The first difference is this: Practically everything that you will read in your "English courses" was written for the purpose of giving its readers pleasure. It was written to be enjoyed. Some of it, to be sure, was directed toward the enjoyment of a special audience. But some of the greatest literature of all—Shakespeare's plays, for example—was addressed to the people, the same kind of people who go to the "movies" and other forms of popular entertainment today.

Moreover, whatever the intention of the author may have been, no work of literature ever established itself and became, through its survival value, a "classic" except by pleasing its readers. Readers, not critics. Not schoolmasters. There are books published every year which please the critics greatly but still fail to please sufficient numbers of those who read for enjoyment to ensure their survival. These books (and some of them are good books) do not get into the anthologies, not even into anthologies intended primarily for school use. They disappear and are forgotten. In the long run, critics no more control the development of a literature than grammarians control the development of a language.

Now why is all this important? What does it mean? And, by the same token, what does it not mean?

Well, it certainly does not mean that "English" is the only course in college that it is going to be possible for you to enjoy. It is quite possible to enjoy history and science and mathematics and foreign languages. There is nothing "wrong" in such enjoyment. On the contrary, it is very desirable that such courses should be enjoyed. But they are enjoyed differently from the way literature is enjoyed. The subject-matter of these courses was not created to give pleasure. They belong to other aspects of human experience altogether.

Neither are you going to enjoy all the literature that you read, either in college or elsewhere. Reading is a matter of personal taste and judgment. Not all the books in the world were meant for you. All men do not fall in love with the same book any more than all men fall in love with the same woman. And in the last analysis nobody else can choose your best book for you any more than anybody else can choose your best girl for you. But in both fields of choice, a certain amount of helpful guidance can be exercised.

To take a very simple illustration, it is impossible to fall in love with a girl you have never met. Neither can you discover whether or not a given book was intended for you if you do not know that it exists or if it never comes into your hands. Those young people who, 150 years ago, grew up in small villages and never, or hardly ever, stepped outside of them, were very limited in their choice of life-mates. In many cases they must have married people eminently unsuited to them, and whom they would never have dreamed of choosing, had they enjoyed the comparatively wide and varied contacts of the young people who attend large city universities today. Similarly, many a potentially good reader has got stranded on the shallow reef of the Bobsey Twins, or the comic books, or the machine-made detective stories—all of which have their place—or, worse still, has decided that he did not enjoy reading at all, simply because nobody came along to make the proper introductions in the right place and at the right time. Such introductions it is, among other things, the function of school and college courses in literature to make.

Of course it is clear that special disciplines are involved in the study of literature for those who would "specialize" in it: as teachers, as professional scholars, or as creative writers. The man who takes his Ph.D. in English may be presumed to work quite as hard as the man who takes his Ph.D. in chemistry. This book will probably fall into the hands of a good many persons who are planning to specialize in English. I hope that it may be useful to them. But it will certainly fall into the hands of a much larger number of people whose basic professional interests will lie in other fields. I am addressing myself quite as much to the second group as to the first. I presuppose no special interest in the technical aspects of literary study on the part of the readers of this book. And this brings me to the second aspect in which your "English course" differs from your other "studies."

"English" addresses itself primarily to human beings as human beings. It deals with matters of fundamental human interest. Its stock-in-trade comprises those basic concerns which all men share with all other men, and which one cannot be a human being without possessing.

I am not trying to make my line of demarcation more definite than it actually is. Few persons would deny that some knowledge of history and of science is necessary for all. And students who do not understand while they are still in school why it is important for them to learn something about figures generally discover the reason not later than the first time they try to make out an income tax return! Many disciplines, on the other hand, *are* specialized, and *their value lies not in themselves but in the use that is going to be made of them.* Even when this is not true, they may still be concerned with some particularized, limited, comparatively narrow phase or aspect of human activity. "English," on the other hand, addresses the whole man. And this is how it may come about that while nobody except lawyers knows very much about the law, and nobody knows much about medicine except physicians, yet there are lawyers and physicians—and bankers and journalists and labor leaders—who possess as fine and discriminating a taste in literature as any college professor.

What I am trying to say, in other words, is that *"English" is about you!* Unless you are going to follow it professionally, I hope that you will try to think of it not as·an academic subject but simply as a matter of human interest.

To say, therefore, that you are "not interested in English"—or even, as students have sometimes been heard to say, that you "hate English"—is virtually equivalent to saying that you are not interested in life, or that you hate life. Unhappily there are some psychopaths about who could honestly make that statement, but it is very unlikely that you are one of them. If you think you "hate English," it is much more likely either that you have not yet found what really belongs to you in this incredibly vast field, or else that you have been made the victim of stupid, unsympathetic, or unimaginative teaching. Henry James said that when Tennyson read his poems aloud, he took more out of them than he had put into them when he wrote them! Unfortunately it is also true that a sufficiently bad teacher can take more out of Shakespeare's plays than Shakespeare put into them when he wrote them, or than any playwright could put into any play. And the tragic thing about bad teachers of English is that their influence is likely to exert itself in the most baleful manner upon the very people to whom their subject in itself could mean most. One of the best writers of our time, Willa Cather, nearly had "English" destroyed for her by the overformalized method of teaching it that was followed at her alma mater in her time.

The accumulation of human knowledge has proceeded at such a bewildering rate during the last 100 years that professional specialization has become increasingly necessary for us all. Gamaliel Bradford used to be fond of saying that our age was outstandingly the Age of Ignorance. Simply because the race knows so much more than the race ever knew before, the individual knows less. We are buried under the accumulation of our own knowledge. We can no longer, like the Renaissance humanist, take all knowledge to be our province. Will Rogers came much closer to being our spokesman when he said, "We are all ignorant—only on different subjects."

Yet concerning the fundamental aspects of human experience none of us has a right to be ignorant. Nor can we be if we know ourselves. It is incumbent upon us to understand these matters clearly, so that we may have a sense of union with our fellowmen, who are like us fundamentally, in spite of all the bewildering surface differences between us. If this does not happen, then we shall soon find ourselves in a position where it is impossible for us to communicate with anybody who does not belong to our own little group. It was the wife of a recent president of the United States who once inadvertently remarked that her husband always found it difficult to achieve a meeting of minds with anybody who was not his social equal.

Against all such dangers, literature—art in all its manifestations—forever stands a barrier, forever enters its protest. This is what John Galsworthy had in mind when he called art "the one form of human energy in the whole world that consciously works for union and destroys the barriers between man and man." It is very important that the boy who is preparing to become an engineer should realize that he is also preparing to become a man. It is the function of his college to prepare him not only to make a living but also to live a life. An education directed toward what man does in his professional aspect only is at best an education for one-third of life. And the art of living is by all means the most difficult art there is, and the one in which we encounter the highest percentage of failures. It is because they realize these things that the faculties of engineering colleges require their students to take some work in "liberal arts subjects," of which they will never be able to make any professional use.

"Cannot a man live, then, without literature—without art?" Certainly, and a man can also live without love. A man can learn to live, if he has to, without a surprisingly large number of things. A man can live with one leg, one lung, one kidney, but not so well as he could live with two. This book is based on the assumption that literature contributes for those who use it wisely to the enlargement and enrichment of life. It is intended to serve as a map, as a guide, as a key to unlock priceless treasure houses. Education itself has been defined as a process of opening blind eyes and unstopping deaf ears, and the definition is a good one. But it applies in a special way to the field with which we are here concerned. A man who did not know how to use a can opener might starve to death in a food warehouse. And there are many people who are starving to death intellectually and spiritually because they have never learned how to make their way to the treasures that are hidden away in books.

What you have learned in geometry will probably be equally useful to you (should you ever be engaged in an occupation which permits you to use it at all), whether you were bored or enthralled while you were learning it. But if you did not enjoy reading *Treasure Island*, then it will do you no good whatever to be able to tell, after you have finished it, whether it was the right leg or the left one that John Silver had lost, or how many men perished during the cruise of the *Hispaniola*. And this book of mine, which is not a work of literature but simply a preface to literature, can never be of any value to you in and for itself. Its usefulness must be measured by what it contributes to all the other books you read after it. Simply to "learn" its contents, as you might learn the contents of a textbook in American history, would be worse than useless.

From the stress laid in this introduction upon the idea that it is the function of literature to give pleasure, it must not be inferred that this is all it does. Literature is something much larger than either an entertainment or an emotional orgy. (If these things are not clear at this point, they will be made clear, I think, as we proceed.) But the element of aesthetic pleasure must be there. It is not the end of reading, but it *is* the beginning, and it is indispensable.

I have, I dare say, raised other questions which I have not

yet answered. After all, this *is* the introduction; if I could say everything I need to say here, there would be no need to write the book! Our method of procedure will be very simple. We shall begin by considering the reading process itself—not the reading of literature specifically, but just reading—the newspaper as well as the Bible. From here we shall proceed to differentiate between literature and non-literature and to define the qualities which belong to literature in general. We shall distinguish, as best we can, between good literature and bad, and try to define the relationship between the printed page and the rest of life. Finally, we shall concern ourselves with the definition and discussion of the various kinds of literature and literary types.

E. W.

Boston University
August 1, 1953

CHAPTER ONE

Black Marks on White Paper

Language, a Form of Communication

Language is a means that human beings have devised to assist them in communicating with one another. It is not, of course, the only means of communication. Animals communicate without language: dogs bark, whine, and wag their tails; cats miaow and purr. Nor do human beings themselves rely upon language exclusively, even in their loftiest and most formal utterances, as we may see by reference to the fact that literature is the only art which is dependent upon it. Painting and sculpture employ other means altogether, and the music arts make use of language only in such hybrid forms as song and the opera, which are half literature. Outside the arts, too, feeling and emotion may often be more powerfully expressed than by words: love, for example, by a glance, a smile, or a caress; hate, by a frown or a blow. The children recognize this very clearly when they chant

> Sticks and stones will break my bones,
> But names can never hurt me!

Furthermore, even when we use words, freely and abundantly, their meaning may be profoundly modified, or even completely transformed, by their inflections and by

1

the gestures, or even the cast of countenance, that accompany them. "You old rascal, you!" is often spoken with real affection, while words of endearment may be uttered in so sinister a manner that they seem more malevolent than a curse. The whole art of acting consists in the reinforcement of a playwright's language by the actor's movements, personality, presence, and mode of utterance. The words Hamlet speaks are quite the same whether they are uttered by the high-school student who encounters the play for the first time or by John Gielgud or Laurence Olivier. But the effect may well be altogether different.

The whole vast subject of the origin, growth, and development of language is beyond our scope in this book,[1] which is concerned simply with the way language is used by writers and readers. In order to understand this, however, it is necessary to pay some attention to the basic conditions under which communication through language exists.

The Need for Communication

The basic necessity for communication needs no argument. No creature is wholly sufficient unto himself, and the more highly developed he becomes the more does he require other creatures—to minister to his necessities, to supplement his powers, even to provide him the means of self-expression. A very large share of human energy is enlisted in this struggle to put off solitariness, to escape from the maddening loneliness of the ego and achieve a harmonious adjustment with life: in this task, the lover, the scholar, the artist, and the religionist are all (each in his own way) engaged. It is also true, to be sure, that much human energy is expended in the assertion of the ego, in

[1] Interested readers are referred to Otto Jespersen, *Language: Its Nature, Development, and Origin* (Holt, 1924), especially Chapter XXI, and to Edward Sapir, *Language: An Introduction to the Study of Speech* (Harcourt, Brace, 1921), especially Chapter I.

maintaining the "rights" or exerting the will of the individual against the group. This, however, becomes necessary only when the balance between the group and the individual has been disturbed, so that the latter has come to feel oppressed. The ideal society would be that which should allow the individual the maximum amount of freedom and also the maximum access to the resources of the group. Defoe's story of *Robinson Crusoe* is not only one of the classics of Western individualism; its universal vogue (which few books have ever equalled) testifies eloquently to the depth and power of the appeal it has made to fundamental human needs and hungers. But for all Robinson Crusoe's ability to live alone and like it, it is very clear that he was the product of a social group. It was his triumph that when he was cast upon his desert island, he was able to make use of the skills which he had learned from association with his fellows in England, and which he and they had inherited from their ancestors. A Robinson Crusoe cast away before he had acquired such powers from his contacts with others must infallibly have perished.

Sound and Symbol

Primarily language is sound, addressing itself to the ear rather than to the eye, and men may be presumed to have communicated with each other by word of mouth long before writing (and, much later, printing) existed. Even literature was originally oral. Ultimately, however, it was discovered that it was possible to make black marks on white paper—or parchment or papyrus, or to carve symbols in stone—which the human brain would have the power to translate into the equivalent of the spoken word. "These little symbols, made up of fleeting sounds and insignificant impressions on the printed page," as Gamaliel Bradford calls them, "can flood the human spirit, your *I* or mine, with the richest ecstasy of hope and the deepest horror of despair."

This was one of the most wonderful of all human achievements. It made it possible for man to take a very long step in the direction of conquering both space and time. So long as language could only be spoken, a man's communications were necessarily limited to those within the natural range of his voice. Writing made it possible for us to speak to those far away from us—(how important this was will be fully realized by anybody who has ever waited with longing for a letter from home)—and even to those whom we had never seen and never would see; it even made it possible for us to address posterity. And as soon as the first writing generation had passed, men found themselves in possession for the first time, through written records, of a far more accurate and useful kind of racial memory than had hitherto been available, thus greatly increasing their power to stand on the shoulders of their predecessors instead of standing beside them. Through writing, in other words, man had extended his power of coöperation with other men indefinitely, backward and forward through time and to distant places.

Like all great human accomplishments down to and including atomic fission, the coming of language, and later of writing, opened up great possibilities, for good and for evil alike. As the Captain puts it in Charles Rann Kennedy's play, *The Terrible Meek:* "There is great power in words. All the things that ever get done in the world, good and bad, are done by words." After the invention of printing, mankind began to grow more and more eye-minded,[2]

[2] Of late years, the ear has again begun to be more important. The telephone extended the range of the human voice in space, the phonograph in time and space alike. These wonderful inventions were followed by radio broadcasting and the addition of sound to the already-existent motion picture. Now with telecasting replacing or supplementing broad-

and it is often said and believed that the art of oratory now belongs altogether to the past. It is probably true that what such men as Edmund Burke and Daniel Webster thought of as oratory would be listened to with extreme impatience today and exercise very little influence on human conduct; yet nobody can study the careers of such diverse political leaders of the twentieth century as Woodrow Wilson, Winston Churchill, Hitler, Mussolini, and both the Roosevelts without realizing that the spoken word is still a great power among men. Hope girdled the earth with Wilson's promise that "The world must be made safe for democracy," and when the bitter aftermath of the war into which such idealism led us had created a cynical and disillusioned public to such an extent that no such slogan could be employed again, still words were not robbed of their power, for Churchill made the horrors of the hour themselves attractive and craftily appealed once more to human heroism when he held up for our adoration his famous "blood, sweat, and tears."

There is a sense, too, in which the children are wrong when they boast that

> Sticks and stones will break my bones,
> But names can never hurt me!

Names—name-calling, which is one of the principal occupations of the twentieth century—*can* hurt you much worse than sticks and stones if the conditions are right. It can hurt you if the people who listen to it are persuaded in sufficiently large numbers that you deserve the label that has been attached to you. And it can hurt you even more if it penetrates a weak spot in your own armor to such an

---

casting, the eye is again involved, though the TV-viewer uses his eyes very differently from the reader. All in all, it is much less difficult for a blind man to live abundantly now than it was fifty years ago.

extent that a doubt is planted in your mind, so that you yourself begin to wonder whether you may not be something like that.

The Conventional Character of Language

But the problems created by the deliberate misuse of words, whether written or spoken, are not the only problems that we have to face, nor are they the most perplexing. Attempting to describe the relationship between literature and the other arts, my old teacher, Professor Albert Harris Tolman, of the University of Chicago (to whom my thinking about literature is indebted not only here but elsewhere), used to group ARCHITECTURE, SCULPTURE, and PAINTING together as

1. Originally and still united
2. Arts of space or surface
3. Relatively permanent.

All three, for example, exist in the design and decoration of a great building, and though that building may, of course, be destroyed, it is still true that if we trust it to the forces of nature, it will last much longer than the time it takes to perform a dance or to sing a song.

In his second group he placed DANCE,[3] MUSIC, and POETRY as

1. Originally and still united
2. Temporal, rhythmic
3. Transitory, though readily reproduced.

Really to have seen The Last Supper one must have gazed upon the actual wall-painting that Leonardo created, and to have done so, moreover, before time robbed it,

[3] In his fascinating book, The Dance of Life (Houghton Mifflin, 1923), Havelock Ellis presents the dance as the basic art form, out of which the others developed.

through deterioration, of half its beauty. But the loveliness of Keats's "Ode on a Grecian Urn" does not reveal itself only to those who have handled the original manuscript. Neither could it be impaired by the loss or destruction of that manuscript. So long as one copy of the poem survives in the world, even if it should have been printed with crooked, broken type in an obscure country newspaper, the full power of those verses can still make themselves felt among men.

But the groups in which the six arts arrange themselves are not symmetrical from every point of view. All the arts in the first group, *plus the first art in the second group*, are visible, while the other two are audible. And all the arts in the first group, *plus the first two in the second group*, are natural or sensuous. Poetry, alone, is not natural but conventional. Poetry, in other words—literature in all its aspects, reading matter in all its aspects—alone makes use of materials whose meanings are determined not by their own character but by general agreement.

For example, there is nothing in the word itself, or in the sounds which compose it, to make it necessary that "good" should mean whatever we understand by goodness, nor is there anything in the word "evil" to necessitate its meaning the opposite of good. It is true that the word "little" suggests what it indicates by the mere fact of being itself made up of little sounds. But it is also true that the word "small," which means exactly the same thing, is not a little word at all; it is a good large, mouth-filling word, quite as large, indeed, as the word "large" itself. And if we look at this word "large" we at once perceive that it means the same as "big," yet "big" is made up of no larger sounds than those which compose the word "little." [4] Thus the

---

[4] The ideas suggested here will be discussed more elaborately in the chapter on poetry. What I have said is true, but it is also true that literature (and language) are forever chafing at their limitations.

German composer can speak directly to the English listener without intermediary, and the Italian painter to the Japanese viewer. Painters and composers use a natural or universal language which, within limitations, all men understand. But the German or the Italian poet cannot speak to those unfamiliar with their language until their work has been "translated" into another language, for their medium is not natural at all; it is conventional.

The Difficulties of Reading

But we are not primarily concerned in this chapter with the use made of language by literary artists; our business at this moment is the process of reading itself. Man becomes accustomed to his own achievements very quickly. Many of us can still remember how wonderful it seemed the first time we heard a phonograph, first saw a motion picture, first heard sound coming to us over the airways. It did not make any difference what we saw or heard; the fact that sound or movement had been created was the essential, the miraculous thing. It was not until movement in itself had ceased to thrill us on the screen that the pioneer film-makers were obliged to give attention to the quality of their product, or that anybody became aware that there was a distinction to be made between "good" pictures and "bad" ones. What we see and hear in these media today is far more wonderful mechanically than any effects that were produced then, but unless we ourselves are concerned with production, we rarely pause to consider this aspect.

Reading has been with us much longer than any of these things; reading, therefore, is likely to receive even less analysis. An inevitable consequence is that we both fail properly to appreciate our achievements and adequately to assess our limitations.

Small children preparing to leave home for their first

day at school have often been heard to say, "Now when I come back, I shall be able to read." And though they are generally disappointed in this, probably most of them would still feel insulted if anybody were to suggest that they had not yet learned how to read when they had finished with the elementary school. The United States is so proud of its high literacy rate that I actually find myself somewhat uncomfortable when I sit down to write a book which has no purpose save to teach grown-up people how to read, and not only that but find myself writing under the conviction that the number of people in this country who really know how to read is most dangerously and uncomfortably small.

I comfort myself, however, and I try to comfort my readers too, by remembering that probably nobody who encounters this book will claim that he has a better mind than that of the greatest German writer of the nineteenth century, Johann Wolfgang von Goethe. Yet when Goethe was eighty, he lamented that the dear, good people did not know how difficult it was to learn to read, and he added that he himself had been at it all his life, and was only beginning to master the art now. Robert Louis Stevenson was no notorious incompetent in this field either, yet it is Stevenson (speaking, to be sure, this time, of a highly specialized type of literature) who tells us that it is as difficult to read a play as it is to read score.

Some Difficulties of Reading the Bible

But, after all, why should we be dismayed by these circumstances? So far as we know, man is the only being in the whole universe who knows how to read at all, and it has only been during what we may describe as the last few moments of cosmic time that man has been able to do so. Let us look, by way of illustration, at the book which has come closer than any other to achieving a universal circulation in the Western world—I mean, of course, the Bible. And let us center our attention upon just two of the writers whose work has come down to us in the Bible: the Prophet Isaiah, say, in the Old Testament, and Saint Paul in the New.

Saint Paul lived in the first century of the Christian era, Isaiah in the eighth century before Christ. Paul was a Jew, a native of Asia Minor who was also a Roman citizen; his travels covered the whole eastern half of the Mediterranean world, as far west as Rome. Isaiah lived long before the Roman Empire was ever dreamed of; Assyria was the power he had to face. He inhabited the Northern Kingdom of Israel in the days of King Ahab, a small world compared to Paul's and a far more Oriental one. Yet both these men had something to say to us.

"To us" I say because, as a matter of fact, what they said changed our world, exerted such an important influence upon Western civilization that we can hardly think of it as existing without them, or without what they stood for at any event. So they set down their thoughts, each in his own way, one in Hebrew and the other in Greek. No minutest trace of either's manuscript has survived. What we have comes to us through a succession of scribal copyings and translations, rolled at last off a printing press, a contrivance which neither of these men ever saw, and which both, probably, would have had considerable difficulty to understand.

What a gulf between the North Israelitish prophet of the eighth century B.C. and the American college freshman of the mid-twentieth century, A.D.! Is it surprising that the freshman should fail perfectly to understand Isaiah? Is it not far more surprising that he should be able to understand him at all? or even to read him without understanding? And if he fails to understand him, is he not entitled to all the comfort he can get out of the reflection that Isaiah would probably not be able to understand him much better?

What Reading Is

Ordinarily (though not invariably) the literature of our own people and our own time is easier for us to understand than ancient or very foreign literature can be. You cannot read the Bible as you would read the morning newspaper, and you would be a fool to try. But whether you are reading the Bible or the newspaper or anything else, this is still true: *You have not really read any piece of writing until you have got out of it just what the writer put into it.* Writing is communication. If it fails as communication, it does not succeed as something else—unless maybe it is mumbo-jumbo. It simply fails.

Now in the absolute sense, nobody has ever succeeded in getting out of a piece of writing exactly what the writer put into it. This is another way of saying that in the absolute sense nobody has ever really read anything. Probably no writer has ever succeeded in getting down on paper everything that was in his mind. However skilful he may be, there will still be something that eludes him. And what does not get itself down on paper naturally does not reach the reader at all. But that is not all. For no reader has ever perfectly succeeded in understanding everything that the writer has expressed.[5]

Why the Writer May Fail

The writer may fail for any number of reasons. Sometimes, especially in the higher branches of literature, he

[5] This idea, and others related to it, are developed at considerable length in a stimulating and amusing book by J. B. Kerfoot, *How To Read* (Houghton Mifflin, 1916).

may fail because he lacks a technique which is adequate to his conceptions. Sometimes, too, he fails because he is lazy, will not take the trouble to bridge the gulf between his mind and the minds of his readers. Some writers have made a cult of obscurity. Sometimes, even, a creative writer may begin a story with no very clear idea in mind of how it is going to develop; it chooses, as it were, its own line of development, and it may seem to the writer that he has little command over what comes and little to do except to record it. Most honest writers will testify, too, with varying degrees of shame, that they have sometimes been obliged to modify an idea in the interest of literary form or effectiveness of expression. What you really "mean" cannot be made to "sound" nearly so well as something that you do not quite mean! We realize what a very great poet Dante was when he tells us that though he wrote *The Divine Comedy* in the difficult and intricate verse form known as *terza rima*, he was never betrayed into saying anything he did not mean to say, or would not have said in prose.

Why the Reader May Fail: Prejudice

There are many reasons, also, why the reader may fail. Some readers do not wish to understand what they read. They do not care what the author is saying: they merely wish to read their own ideas back into him, to make him their mouthpiece. For centuries, various religious bodies have used the Bible as a hunting-ground for evidence to support the special tenets they hold, quoting these passages quite out of context and completely without reference to the general, over-all meaning of the book to which they belong. So, also, twentieth-century readers have found the Kaiser or Hitler (or whoever the current political villain of the hour chances to be), in the Book of Daniel and the Book of Revelation, or interpreted *Hamlet* in terms of a psychology which Shakespeare lived 300 years too early to become familiar with. When Herman Melville was rediscovered in the 1920's, a good many critics interpreted his works in terms of their own post-war disillusionment. There is an English Marxian writer named T. A. Jackson who has a genuine affection for the novels of Charles Dickens. He loves them so well indeed that he cannot bear to give them up. At the same time, he cannot bear to accord high rank to a *bourgeois* writer! He solved his problem triumphantly by writing a book in which he proved to his own satisfaction that Dickens came very close to anticipating some of the major tenets of the Gospel according to Marx![6]

For such readers, unfortunately, one can do little. We get enough wrong when we are trying to get things right. If we will not begin with the postulate that the reader's first job is to determine what the author is trying to say, then no book can ever be anything more to us than a divingboard into a world of dreams, and though we may deceive ourselves that we are listening to a great writer, we shall never really hear anything except the murmur of our own subconscious minds.

Why the Reader May Fail: Ignorance

When Dr. Johnson was asked why, in his dictionary, he had defined "pastern" as "the knee of a horse," he replied, "Ignorance, Madame, pure ignorance." Ignorance, pure ignorance of the meanings of words, either in themselves or in the particular context in which they are encountered, is the most obvious cause of misunderstanding in reading. In the old song, Yankee Doodle

[6] See T. A. Jackson, *Charles Dickens, The Progress of a Literary Radical* (International Publishers, 1938).

> Stuck a feather in his cap,
> And called him macaroni.

If the only meaning you know for "macaroni" is something to eat, how will you understand that Yankee Doodle is priding himself upon being a dandy? If you think of "corn" only in terms of the American Indian corn, what will you make of the early Victorian agitation looking toward the repeal of the "Corn Laws," which regulated not what Americans call corn at all but rather wheat. In a well-known passage in "L'Allegro" Milton tells us that

> . . . every shepherd tells his tale
> Under the hawthorn in the dale.

Many readers of these verses get a lovely, idyllic picture of the shepherds sitting about under the trees telling each other stories. This is probably far more "poetic" in the ordinary sense of the term than what Milton wrote. Only, Milton did not create it, and when we conjure up such a picture, we are not "reading" Milton at all! For Milton is using the expression "tells his tale" in a now obsolete sense. His shepherds are engaged, quite unromantically, in counting their sheep.

Occasionally, it must be admitted, even ignorance can be creative. No reader of the fairy story would willingly relinquish Cinderella's glass slippers. We all know that she would never be able to walk in them, to say nothing of dancing; but, no matter, they are an incomparable romantic property. But Charles Perrault never gave Cinderella glass slippers. He gave her slippers of fur. The English translator of the tale misread the French word for "fur" (*vair*) for the French word for "glass" (*verre*), and it was thus that our heroine acquired the glass slippers she has worn ever since in English-speaking countries. The results were less happy, however, when a well-known but unmarried actress was spoken of by an enthusiastic reviewer as "pregnant with all the passion and power of her race," and some of her less erudite admirers proceeded to proclaim far and wide that they had "seen it in the paper" that she was going to have a child. These were close relatives of the countryman of whom James Freeman Clarke tells, who, having heard John Brown's action at Harper's Ferry described as "dropping a match into a powder magazine," carried through the rest of his life the firm conviction that Brown was hanged for trying to blow up the arsenal. In both these instances, the cause of the misunderstanding was a failure to realize that the words employed had been used not in their primary, literal sense but in a derivative, figurative sense.

That "seen it in the paper" or "read it in a book" suggests another problem. "Somebody said in *Harper's Magazine*" is a form of reference sometimes encountered even in print. But who cares what "Somebody" said in *Harper's Magazine*—or anywhere else? No statement has any greater authority than the man who made it; neither does a lie become the truth simply because somebody has had it set up in print. A book is the projection of a human being; it deserves no greater respect than can be commanded by the man who wrote it.

Why the Reader May Fail: The Problem of Associations

Another difficulty is that words are exactly like people: what they mean to us depends upon the associations we have had with them. There was the old lady who called "Mesopotamia" "a blessed word." It was blessed for her because she associated it with her beloved Bible; she forgot, for the time being, that it was the name of the country where the children of Israel were enslaved. The word "mother" is rich with tender associations for most readers, yet there are some to whom it is a blank ("Judy, what's a mamma?" asked the little girl in the orphanage in Mary Pickford's production of *Daddy Long-Legs*), and to those prime unfortunates who have had unworthy mothers, it is something even worse than that. After hearing an eloquent sermon on the Fatherhood of God, a young lady told her pastor that unless he wanted to turn her against God forever, he had better stop talking about that; if God was anything like her father, then she wanted nothing to do with Him!

Such highly individualized reactions the writer can do little or nothing to control. He does need to remember, however, that there are many words which are nearly synonyms, so far as their actual definitions are concerned, yet whose connotations are altogether different. (A half-hour with *Webster's Dictionary of Synonyms* will make this point clearer than pages of discussion could make it.) The connotation of a word might be described as the atmosphere it carries with it, and in any of the higher branches of creative writing a piece may be made or marred by the connotations of the words employed in it. A physician may quite safely speak of one of the commonest of bodily functions by its Latin name, but if he were to employ the French word whose denotation is exactly the same, most of his patients would feel gravely insulted. For in this country the French word is, for some mysterious reason, obscene. Again, "snake" and "serpent" mean exactly the same thing, but to people who have a horror of reptiles, the first is inexpressibly the more affecting, partly because it is in itself one of the ugliest words in the language, and partly because "serpent" has both lofty and dignified Biblical associations and a sinister beauty of its own. Even the shape of the letters on the printed page exercises its effect on the reader's mind. These lines from Ralph

Hodgson make up one of the most serpentine passages in English poetry:

> Mute as a mouse in a
> Corner the cobra lay
> Curled round a bough of the
> Cinnamon tall.[7]

And here, surely, there can be no doubt that the shape of those four "c's" is one element in a baleful power. Nor can one substitute either a more general term or the name of some other particular snake for "cobra" in that passage without spoiling the poem. Dr. Hayakawa is as accurate as he is amusing when he points out, in his *Language in Action*,[8] that, so far as their denotations are concerned, "I have the honor to inform your excellency" means the same thing as "Cheez, boss, git a load of dis," and that "finest quality filet mignon" equals "first-class piece of dead cow."

An Exercise in Connotations from Wordsworth

One of Wordsworth's best-known poems is the tribute to his wife which the poet called "She Was a Phantom of Delight":

> She was a Phantom of delight
> When first she gleamed upon my sight;
> A lovely Apparition, sent
> To be a moment's ornament;
> Her eyes as stars of Twilight fair;
> Like Twilight's, too, her dusky hair;
> But all things else about her drawn
> From May-time and the cheerful Dawn;

---

[7] Ralph Hodgson, "Eve," *Poems* (Macmillan, 1917). Reprinted by permission of the publishers.

[8] S. I. Hayakawa, *Language in Action* (Harcourt, Brace, 1941). A revised edition was published in 1949 under the title, *Language in Thought and Action*.

A dancing shape, an Image gay,
To haunt, to startle, and way-lay.

I saw her upon nearer view,
A Spirit, yet a Woman too!
Her household motions light and free,
And steps of virgin liberty;
A countenance in which did meet
Sweet records, promises as sweet;
A Creature not too bright or good
For human nature's daily food;
For transient sorrows, simple wiles,
Praise, blame, love, kisses, tears, and smiles.

And now I see with eye serene
The very pulse of the machine;
A Being breathing thoughtful breath,
A Traveller between life and death;
The reason firm, the temperate will,
Endurance, foresight, strength, and skill;
A perfect Woman, nobly planned,
To warn, to comfort, and command;
And yet a Spirit still, and bright
With something of angelic light.

The first two stanzas of this poem indicate the response of the poet to Mary Hutchinson's individuality: (1) when he first encountered her as a girl; and (2) after he had won and married her. The third stanza gives his interpretation of the meaning of her spiritual nature. The contrast is strongly indicated, and the division of materials is logical and well-planned.

The particular idea which Wordsworth wishes to communicate in the first stanza is that he was completely overwhelmed by Mary Hutchinson's girlish, unearthly beauty, the first time he saw her. To use a current slang expression, he thought she was "out of this world."

But even that slang expression, hackneyed as it has become, is considerably better than some of the words Wordsworth uses. For the poet has been very careless indeed about his connotations.

> She was a Phantom of delight

Why "Phantom"? A phantom is a ghost, a wraith, an apparition. The connotations of all these words are sinister or frightening or weird or gruesome. To most readers they suggest either the terrors of ghost stories or the phenomena of the séance room. Furthermore, phantoms are not commonly associated with "delight." Neither do they "gleam." Obviously, "Phantom" is the wrong word. "Vision" would have been better. Incidentally, one of Wordsworth's great successors among the English poets, Alfred Tennyson, was to make a much better job of it impromptu when he met his wife-to-be, Emily Sellwood, for the first time, in the Fairy Wood. "Are you a dryad or an oread wandering here?" he asked her.

In the third line, Wordsworth reinforced "Phantom" with "Apparition," which has all the same unfortunate connotations. But the next line is even worse:

> A lovely Apparition, sent
> To be a moment's ornament;

Why "a moment's ornament"? Apparitions are not ornaments; moreover, the expression introduces inappropriate suggestions of trifling. No man thinks of the girl he wishes to marry as an "ornament" merely, nor surely could he wish to confine her share in his life to a moment. This expression would have been more appropriate if the poet had been planning to seduce the girl, like the villains in the old melodramas.

The next five lines are better, but with the last line we are lost again:

To haunt, to startle, and way-lay.

The sinister, supernatural quality is getting worse instead of better, for "haunt" is the third ghostly word that has been employed, and "startle" goes well with it, and reinforces it, much better than "delight" and "gleamed" ever reinforced "Phantom." Finally, the last word, "way-lay," introduces a whole new set of connotations, and these are quite as unfortunate as any that we have been struggling with hitherto. Poor Mary Hutchinson! It is highwaymen that "way-lay."

The other two stanzas are less unfortunate in their connotations, though there are other faults, which need not be considered in detail here, where no complete analysis of the poem is called for. The worst words, from the point of view of our interest here, are "records" and "machine." However interpreted, "records" are surely prosaic and unimaginative articles for a lovely lady to carry in her face, and though "machine" (corporeal being) was not so bad in Wordsworth's time as it would be now, the Industrial Revolution was already under way, and the expression, therefore, considerably less suited to love poetry than when Hamlet had written Ophelia: "Thine evermore, most dear lady, whilst this machine is to him. . . ."

Meeting the Author Halfway

So far we have concerned ourselves mainly with the necessity of reading carefully and critically. And in a world in which a good many of those who address us by way of the printed page want to get something from us, ranging all the way from the money in our pockets to the possession of our minds and souls, we can hardly guard ourselves too carefully. But simply to stand guard against the author is not enough; neither is this the frame of mind in which the most rewarding reading is done. For reading is a meeting of minds; it depends for its highest success upon effort exerted from two directions; the author cannot give a good performance unless the reader will perform also. "To have great poetry," said Whitman, "you must have great audiences too."

Barrie is very clever in *Peter Pan* when he tricks the audience into committing itself to a belief in fairies by applauding at a crucial moment in order to save Tinker Bell's life. ("She thinks she could get well again if children believed in fairies.") For the audience which has applauded has not only proclaimed its faith; it has acted upon it, done something about it, and it is going to be very hard to renege on that. Of course this does not mean that, in order to enjoy *Peter Pan*, one must "believe" in fairies in the sense in which one believes in God or in democracy. The gambler said that religion was "betting your life on the existence of God," and *Peter Pan* audiences are not, in that sense, going to be asked to bet their lives on anything. It is necessary, however, that, for the purpose of the play, the audience should be brought to accept the basic postulates upon which the play rests. This is what Coleridge, in a famous phrase, called "that willing suspension of disbelief for a moment which constitutes poetic faith."

In other words, there is no sense in going to see *Peter Pan* if you are going to spend your two hours in the theater assuring yourself that this is all nonsense because "there ain't no such animal as a fairy." Or *Hamlet* or *Macbeth*, for that matter, if you are going to meet the ghosts and the witches in the same spirit. You may possibly think yourself very "wise" when you do something like that; actually you will only be proving that you have no imagination, that you are ignorant of the way in which a spell is created in the theater. There is a difference between being a bright young man and being a "smarty pants."

It is necessary to take the limitations of an author's range into consideration when forming a critical estimate of him, and placing him in the hierarchy in his relationship to other writers, but it is not sound criticism to refuse to admit the value of what he has done simply because you wish he had done something else. Every teacher who has ever asked a class to point out flaws in any work of literature knows how many students who would have been quite unaware of any shortcomings in the work in question, had they been left to their own devices, will forthwith proceed to apply utterly unreasonable and irrelevant tests to it, finding multitudinous shortcomings where they do not exist, and, as likely as not, overlooking the essential weaknesses altogether. The present writer has often had this experience with "She Was a Phantom of Delight." And even now there are probably readers of this book who think that the author is "down" on Wordsworth, or considers him to have been a "rotten" poet, and that he included a discussion of "She Was a Phantom" in this volume because he wanted the satisfaction of "taking him down." As a matter of fact, he considers Wordsworth to have been a very great poet indeed—one of those rare writers who have enriched us all, not only by the beauty which they themselves have created in their writings, but also because they have taught us to see more beauty in life itself than we should, in all probability, have perceived if they had never wrought.

Hazards and Rewards

By this time, it may perhaps be clear that so far from being the simple process that many of us have imagined, this business of reading, of interpreting the meaning of black marks on white paper, is so complicated, so varied, and so many-sided that a very large part of the educational process is concerned with teaching people how to read. I have already remarked that one does not read the Bible as one reads a newspaper. One does not read lyrical poetry as one reads a novel either, or if one does, one either refuses to pause long enough and respond deeply enough to savor the passion that the lyric poet strives to communicate, or else one slows down the novel to such an extent that one loses most of its continuity. Special techniques are required also for special forms of scientific and report writing and for many other forms of communication too numerous to mention. When Professor John Livingston Lowes, of Harvard, used to caution his graduate students always to scrutinize the quoted matter in any piece of scholarly writing they might encounter with great care, *and to be sure to consider what was left out of the quotation*, he was trying to teach them how to read a particular kind of material.

At this point, the reader may well be forgiven if he begins to be impatient with the author for having overwhelmed him with an oppressive sense of intolerable difficulties. "But I never knew that reading was so difficult!" I can hear him say. "You've put me back in the first grade. I thought I knew how to read. I've been reading all my life. Now you come along and insist that I must learn all over again. If the game is as difficult as you say it is, I don't see how I ever *could* win! Why, then, should I even try to play?"

The answer, of course, is simple: If you would live in our world, you *must* play. You can no more escape from the game of reading than you can escape from the game of living—of which it is, for people like you, a very important part. It is much too late in the day now to withdraw from either game. As Samuel Butler used to say, the question "Is life worth living?" is a question for an embryo, not for a man.

Moreover, if the game is hard, the stakes are correspondingly high, and the rewards—for those who win—are very great. Here, as in any art, those who achieve the very highest prizes are few, though you should certainly not assume at the outset that you will not be among them. On the other hand, this is not a game in which any person of normal intelligence who is willing to put his powers to work need ever go away empty-handed. Whoever you are, you will be given as much as you are able to carry off, and that is as much as anyone can reasonably ask for.

Hunger for life is planted deep in the hearts of all normal men and women, and it is this hunger which reading seeks both to cultivate and to satisfy. "What did you do in the war?" the inquisitive lady asked the refugee, and after a long pause for thought, he replied, "I survived." In itself this may not seem like a great achievement, but it is basic because no other achievement is possible without it. The old saying to the contrary notwithstanding, the blood of the martyrs is not the seed of the church: it merely watered that seed. Faith is the seed. The church survived in this world not in those who died but in those who managed to stay alive, and if all Christians had been martyred, there would have been no church. Perhaps that is one of the reasons why theologians have always rightly insisted that despair is a mortal sin. And Emerson asks impatiently why so many people desire immortality when they do not know how to make profitable use of one hour of time here!

Tennyson made Ulysses, in his great poem about him, a type of the pioneering spirit who sails out in search of new adventure even in his old age:

Life piled on life
Were all too little, and of one to me
Little remains: but every hour is saved
From that eternal silence, something more,
A bringer of new things.

So Gamaliel Bradford began the study of Portuguese when he was on his death bed.

It is probably no exaggeration to say that the man who has learned how to find and employ the treasures locked up in books can live more life in a normal lifetime than he could if he were permitted to remain upon the earth a thousand years and not permitted to read. He can enter all lands and mingle with all peoples. (The reader of Charles Doughty's *Arabia Deserta* knows much about Arabia that most Arabs themselves will never know.) He can travel backward in time to any age of which written records have been preserved. He can think the thoughts of the wisest men after them. And if he is willing to use his imagination, then he may embrace literally everything that the human mind has ever been able to conceive. Men are just now beginning to talk in earnest about going to the moon on rocket ships. But men have been going to the moon on the wings of the imagination for many centuries[9] —and incidentally probably "seeing" much more and enjoying themselves far more hugely than any actual voyagers, if such there are to be, will ever be able to encompass.

So far, though we have taken many of our illustrations from creative writing, we have been primarily concerned with the process of reading itself, the problem of translating into meaning the black marks on white paper that act as a surrogate for the spoken word. It is time now to try to distinguish between that printed matter which is literature and that which is not.

[9] See Marjorie Hope Nicolson, *Voyages to the Moon* (Macmillan, 1948).

CHAPTER TWO

But Is It Literature?[1]

~~~~~~

A Semantic Difficulty

"Excuse me," said the Young Lady—there was a great deal of noise and confusion in the bus terminal, and she had to talk very loud—"excuse me, but do you have any literature covering your excursions to Mount Vernon and Alexandria?"

"The reason I am asking you about this novel in advance," said the Earnest Seeker—he had made a special appointment to see his "English teacher" for the purpose— "is that I am very busy this term, and I do not want to waste my time on anything that is not literature."

"The trouble with most of the people who talk about 'literature,'" declared the Visiting Lecturer, "is that they do not know what it is." He was a heavy-set man, and it was very warm in the lecture room; people in the front rows could see the perspiration standing out on his forehead. "The truth of the matter is that literature is not necessarily good writing, nor is non-literature necessarily bad

[1] Chapters Two, Three, and Four of this book traverse ground which I have already been over once before in a book of mine called *Values in Literature*, which is now out of print. Though a number of the same topics have necessarily been considered in both productions, not many paragraphs from the earlier work have been reprinted in this one, even in a modified form. *Values in Literature* was copyrighted by Edward Wagenknecht, 1928, 1935, 1937, and 1941.

writing. After we have distinguished between literature and non-literature, we shall find that we must next distinguish between good literature and bad. Unfortunately, there is much more bad literature in the world than good."

At this point, he looked up and glared at the audience, as if he expected somebody to contradict him and was determined to make that contradiction as hazardous as possible.

It sounds—does it not?—as though the gentlemen and the lady were talking about entirely different things.

The Young Lady, of course, is using "literature" in its broadest and most general sense. All she means, really, is "printed matter." She wants information. Presumably she is either planning to visit Mount Vernon and Alexandria, or else she is depending upon the "literature" she is asking for to help her make up her mind whether she wants to go or not. She is certainly not expecting to be much interested in the quality of that "literature"—its goodness or badness as writing. Nor will she attempt to differentiate it as to type from other things that she has read.

Probably the Young Lady is not old enough to remember *The Literary Digest*, but that periodical—the *Time* or *News-Week* of its day—carried a title which fairly well illustrates her conception of literature. *The Literary Digest* was not particularly concerned with what either the Visiting Lecturer or the Earnest Seeker would call literature. It was a weekly summary of what was taking place in all fields of human interest and endeavor. It attempted a kind of summary of newsprint for its readers.

Our second speaker has very different ideas about literature. So far from being disposed to fling the word about loosely or cavalierly, he is very austere in his employment of it. He scrutinizes all the books which present themselves before him with extreme care, and unless their credentials are unimpeachable, he will have nothing to say to them. In his present stage of development, however, he has no confidence in his own ability to distinguish between a counterfeit and the genuine article. That is why we find him in the act of going to his teacher for a guarantee of excellence, in much the same spirit in which a different kind of snob might wish to determine whether his new neighbor was listed in the blue book before making up his mind whether to speak to him.

To the Earnest Seeker literature is something rare; it is also something holy. Only one other word has the same hypnotic and ennobling effect on him: that is the word "art." That either art or literature is something to be enjoyed has hardly occurred to him. He might even be shocked at the suggestion: it would be rather like laughing out loud in church. But if he were told that there was no difference in kind but only a difference in degree between, say, Keats's poems and the newspaper rimes of Edgar Guest, or between a painting by Michaelangelo and the rude sketches which the caveman scratched on the walls of his dwelling, he would be almost as horrified as the first aristocrat was when he heard the first democrat proclaim that all men are brothers, or as a conventionally-minded religious man might be if a pantheist were to tell him that the marketplace is as holy as the chapel because God is everywhere. The Earnest Seeker, I fear, would not like the Visiting Lecturer's discourse, and he may not like this book either.

There are times when it is convenient to use the term "literature" as the Young Lady at the bus station used it. There may even be times when it is convenient to call a book "literature" as a tribute to its quality. Here is an extract from a current review of Conrad Richter's novel, *The Light in the Forest:* "Mr. Richter makes us realize again," says the reviewer, "the truth of the old saying that it takes a great deal of history to make a little literature. That this book *is* literature there can be no question at all." Accurately employed, however, and in the strictest sense, the term "literature" does not, as the Visiting Lecturer has already informed us, indicate a *quality* of writing. Neither is its use a guarantee of quality. Rather, it indicates a *kind* of writing. And that *kind* is a very difficult and complicated thing to attempt to define.

By this time you will have gathered that though the Visiting Lecturer may be a rather tense and difficult man, he is essentially right in what he says.

"Story-Books" and Others

If we are to understand the differences between literature and non-literature, we shall have to begin very simply. We shall have to go back to the beginning. I hope you will not be insulted if I ask you to return, through your imagination, if you are a girl, to the time when you played with your dolls, and, if you are a boy, to a corresponding stage in your development.

If you will give a moment's thought to the matter, you will realize that you already know quite well that not all the books in the world are at all like what you used to call, when you were little, your "story-books." When did you first find out that not all the books in the world were intended for your enjoyment? Was it, perhaps, the first time somebody, your teacher probably, required you to read a book, not for enjoyment, as you had always read your "story-books," but in order to "learn something" out of it? Many people can remember how disappointed they were the first time they received that kind of book as a gift, instead of the "story-book" which, so far as they had known up to that time, was the only kind of book there was. That was almost as bad as the Christmas when you got shirts and socks and ties instead of the toys you had been expecting. Here is the Spring Announcement Number of the *Publisher's Weekly*. Turning to the index, which lists most of the books that will be published in America from January through May, and choosing six titles at random, we note *The Story of the Metropolitan Opera*, by Irving Kolodin; *Men Like Shadows*, by Dorothy Charques; *Auditing*, by Walter B. Meigs; *The Collected Plays of W. B. Yeats; A Public School for Tomorrow: A Description of the Matthew F. Maury School, Richmond, Virginia*, by Marion Nesbitt; and *Kingfishers Catch Fire*, by Rumer Godden.

Would you like to try guessing which of these books are literature and which are not? Unlike the sponsors of your favorite radio program, I cannot offer sixty-four dollars to the winner. But if you say that Items 2, 4, and 6 are literature and that the others are not, you will have the satisfaction of knowing that you found the right answers.

But at this point I always want to wave a red flag. For you must be very careful to note that this does not mean that these books are "better" than the others, or even, necessarily, that they are "better-written."

It would be a very easy thing to define the *purpose* for which any of the non-literary works in the *Publishers' Weekly* list were written. And the same thing may be said of any other non-literary works that you may care to name, for example:

The Origin of Species, by Charles Darwin
Studies in the Psychology of Sex, by Havelock Ellis
The American Language, by H. L. Mencken
A Natural History of Western Trees, by Donald Culross Peattie
America First: The Battle Against Intervention, 1940-1941, by Wayne C. Cole

But for what purpose did Dickens write *David Copper-field?* Or Longfellow, the *Tales of a Wayside Inn?* Or James Joyce, *Ulysses?* Or Ernest Hemingway, *The Old Man and the Sea?*

These books are literature. And you will perceive at once that it is much more difficult to answer such a question about them than it was in the case of books written to convey information, or to propound a theory, or to advance an argument. Indeed, it is more than difficult. It is impossible.

Literature an End in Itself

"The genus Literature," said John-Burroughs,[2] "includes many species, . . . but our business with them all is about the same—they are books that we read for their own sake. We read the papers for the news, we read a work of science for the facts and the conclusions, but a work of literature is an end in and of itself."

Indeed, if you can define the purpose of your book, then you do not read it for its own sake, and your reading is not in itself an act of life; you merely use your book as a means toward an end. "Delight," says Dryden, "is the chief, if not the only, end of poesy." And Coleridge adds that as "the proper and immediate object of Science is the acquirement or communication of truth," so "the proper and immediate object of Poetry is the communication of pleasure." And this is true not of poetry alone, in the narrower sense of the term, but of all literature.

Let not such words as "pleasure" and "delight" mislead us into thinking literature a trifling thing. It is dangerous to sneer at "mere literature." "I suppose," says Woodrow

[2] The quotation is from an essay called "Literary Values" in John Burroughs's book, *Literary Values and Other Papers* (Houghton Mifflin, 1902). This is a very stimulating collection of discursive essays on various aspects of literature.

Wilson, "that in Nirvana one would speak in like wise of 'mere life.' " But I think it somewhat more accurate to say of the creative writer, the producer of literature, that what he is seeking to do is to share life. Not to teach, to argue, to persuade, to convince, but to share life, to communicate a sense of experience, for its own sake, and with no ulterior end in view.

This may be a very high order of experience, as in the great literature of the world, or it may be a low order of experience, as with most of the material in the dime novels and the pulp magazines. It may be something that has happened to the writer, or it may be something that he has dreamed or imagined.

These distinctions are not in themselves important. The fundamental, experience-sharing, outgoing impulse is. Literature, like language itself, is (I must repeat) communication. The "poet-talking-to-himself" may or may not be a lunatic, as those critics who are most hostile to the cult of obscurity which has grown up among modern poets insist. One thing is certain: he has failed as an artist.

The impulse to share experience is universal: we all know that joys increase and sorrows decrease in proportion as we are able to share them with others who are sympathetic toward us. The artist, however, communicates not with an individual alone but with the world. Goethe said that whenever he had a sorrow he made a poem of it. And one critic says of Byron that "his writing was merely a means of telling his . . . secrets to the whole world and making that world know him and remember him."

Of course, this does not necessarily mean literature. The artist may be a painter, a musician, or even an actor or a dancer. But the basic urge to communicate, to make beauty out of emotion, is the same in all types of artist, and in some human beings it is so strong that it becomes incomparably the most powerful force in life.

The Neurotic Artist

Artists are ordinarily more than commonly sensitive people, and, other things being equal, they are likely to live more intensely than most people do and to experience more difficulty in achieving an harmonious adjustment between themselves and their environment. It is not surprising, therefore, that many people should believe that all art takes on a kind of compensatory character. Who needs to read a love story while experiencing an actual love affair? Who could interest himself in the enthralling adventures of another when he might be having enthralling adventures himself? Denied fulfilment in his own living, the artist projects pictures upon the screen of his imagination, living vicariously in this imagined world, he fulfills the needs which experience itself leaves unsatisfied. In Bernard Shaw's utopia, *Back to Methuselah*, the Ancients, who represent the goal of Creative Evolution, have outgrown their need of art.

This theory is suggestive and seems superficially plausible. One may be quite sure that this element has been important in the lives of many artists. But it is well to shy away from over-simplification in these matters and to beware of theories which try to explain too much. As Oscar Wilde once reminded us, life imitates literature quite as often as literature imitates life. There would be much less romantic love in the world if Shakespeare had never written *Romeo and Juliet*. Furthermore, one may read—and, one would think, write—*The Three Musketeers* with breathless interest, without having the slightest desire to go through the adventures related at first hand. The caveman's wall-paintings, already referred to, and the tales which primitive people whispered about the campfire of a winter's night both tend to indicate that if maladjustment is the root of all artistic achievement, then being maladjusted and being alive are very much the same thing. In a sense, no doubt, this is quite true, but if everybody is maladjusted, then nobody is maladjusted, or, at any rate, maladjustment is a much less terrifying thing than the horrible sound of the word might indicate. Finally, we must remember that many of the most seriously maladjusted people never turn toward aesthetic expression. However important maladjustment may be as a contributing factor, it does not seem likely that we shall uncover the basic root of aesthetic expression by exploring maladjustment.[3]

Art and Technique

Sensitiveness to experience—and the ability to penetrate more deeply than most people can into the meaning of experience—this, then, would seem basic to achievement in any art. But sensitiveness to experience is not enough. Equally important are the ability to express what one feels or perceives and the possession of some adequate means of expressing it; this last is what is commonly meant by the artist's technique.

In the most popular poem in the English language, the "Elegy Written in a Country Church-Yard," Thomas Gray declares provocatively that

> Full many a gem of purest ray serene,
> The dark unfathomed caves of ocean bear:
> Full many a flower is born to blush unseen,
> And waste its sweetness on the desert air.

Is it, truly? There is no a priori difficulty involved in con-

---

[3] The idea that art is basically unhealthy was stated, many years ago, in a more extreme form than has appeared here, by Max Nordau, in his *Degeneration*. Bernard Shaw's devastating reply, *The Sanity of Art* (1895), was one of his most exhilarating performances.

ceiving the possibility of a fair number of human beings having existed on this planet whose sensitiveness and understanding were as great as Shakespeare's, but who, because they lacked technique, never made themselves felt in the world. In that enchanting feminist document, *A Room of One's Own*, Virginia Woolf has imaginatively described the sad fate of a feminine Shakespeare in an age in which women were not granted the privilege of self-expression. Virginia Woolf found the right way to consider the matter: it is impossible to be dogmatic about such things, for the evidence is lacking. We do know that a related proposition is true: There have been many writers who possessed magnificent gifts of expression and a dazzling technique whose work was hollow and unimpressive because they could neither think nor feel deeply. They had nothing to say to us; neither were our contacts with them emotionally fructifying in any way. They were at best "clever" writers, and in a few years they were forgotten.

On the other hand, it must be admitted that since, in a wholly successful work of art, idea and expression are inextricably welded, the Shakespeare who lacked means of expression died a potential or embryonic Shakespeare only: that which remained unexpressed never really existed, for the gifts of a Shakespeare come into being only through exercise and expression. Is this, perhaps, what Croce meant by his somewhat cryptic saying that technique either does not exist or else it coincides with art itself?

Genius, too, is a much hardier plant than most of the people who theorize about it have any idea: the many would-be artists who assure us that if only the conditions of their lives were changed, they would be able to accomplish wonders, are probably mistaken. Very few of the great books of the world were produced under ideal conditions, and many of them have been produced under impossible conditions. Jane Austen wrote her novels in the family sitting-room, stopping whenever a visitor entered and pushing her manuscript hastily out of sight. "Grandma" Moses became a famous painter in her 'seventies, without having had any contacts with the world of art. Had she grown up in a different environment, she would probably have painted from her youth, but all we can be sure about concerning the pictures she never gave us is that they must have been very different from what, as it is, she produced. Technically they would probably have possessed many good qualities which the work of "Grandma" Moses now lacks; on the other hand, she might very well, under these different conditions, have completely failed to capture that endearing strain of the "primitive" which now seems her most precious contribution to American painting.

Literature and Imagination

But what, you may ask, has all this to do with the "storybooks" with which you began? If this is how literature comes into being, why do critics always put the emphasis on such things as novels, poems, and plays? If creative writers are primarily concerned to communicate experience, why do they not turn first of all to the essay and the autobiography?

Well, the essay *is* a form of literature, and we shall have to deal with it before we have finished. As for the autobiography, it is not literature if it merely sets down the record of a man's life, but it may very well be if the writer's imagination has operated upon his experiences toward the end of achieving realization and interpretation.

I may seem to be suggesting, at this point, that a literary man must falsify his materials, but actually this is not the case. Henry James raises nice questions when, in his autobiographical works—*A Small Boy and Others* and *Notes of a Son and Brother*—he actually rewrites not only his own early letters but those of William James as well, in order to bring them more into harmony with the "tone" of the book. *The Education of Henry Adams* is one of the greatest of American autobiographies. That it tells us a good deal about its author's life-experience admits of no doubt. But it also imposes a pattern upon that experience of which the author can hardly have been conscious at the time. It leaves out the whole tragic story of his marriage, which broke his life in two. It selects its materials in accordance with a carefully preconceived theory concerning the meaning of Henry Adams's life.

Writers differ notably as to just what self-expression means to them. Middleton Murry tells us that "To know a work of literature is to know the soul of the man who created it, and who created it in order that his soul should be known." Willa Cather, on the other hand, described her writing as a means of losing, of being delivered from, her individuality for three hours a day. But even amateur writers know, or soon learn, that it is not always the material we have "lived" that we are most successful in making seem real and convincing on the printed page.

"I can believe everything else in your story," said the instructor in "Advanced Composition: Narrative" to his star pupil, "but you fall down in this incident on page fourteen. This is completely unbelievable."

But the student triumphantly moves up into the driver's seat.

"Why," he exclaims, "that is the one thing in the story that really happened. It was my last year in high school. I described it just exactly as it took place."

And the instructor is supposed to be crushed.

But he isn't—not if he knows his business. On the contrary, he realizes that it was precisely because the thing did happen that the student failed to get his imagination to work on it. It seems the one unreal thing in the story because here alone the writer was content to transcribe. And transcription does not make literature. That, in fact, is precisely the difference between literature and reporting.

It has often been pointed out that many of our best novels deal not with the affairs of the passing hour nor yet with a time so remote that the author can know about it only through books, but with a period, roughly speaking, about a generation back from the time of writing, so that their materials, while still fresh enough to be held in living memory, are far enough away to fall into perspective. Sir Walter Scott's *The Heart of Midlothian* is a better novel than *Ivanhoe,* for one reason, because in its composition these conditions were fulfilled.

There is, therefore, no requirement that an author should use what are generally called fictional materials in a work of literature.

Pepys [says Edith Rickert] apparently intended his *Diary* as a record of fact; but few persons would deny that much of it is literature. The *Anglo-Saxon Chronicle* covers centuries with records of fact; then breaks out into something like literature when it tells of the fight between Cynewulf and Cyneheard. The truth is that all records of fact are subject to incursions of realized experience, which lift them for the moment into literature, and all literature is subject to incursions of fact, which reduce it for the moment to record. Over against the cases of Pepys and Cynewulf and Cyneheard, we have the famous Catalogue of Ships in the *Iliad.*[4]

On the other hand, I think it must be admitted that, other things being equal, the writer's imagination is more likely to operate effectively when not tied too closely to

[4] Edith Rickert, *New Methods for the Study of Literature* (The University of Chicago Press, 1927), pp. 3-4.

the world of fact. Art is always much simpler than life and much less chaotic also. There may, indeed, be a "pattern" in life itself, but so to affirm is an act of faith, not knowledge; for such a pattern would be too vast for the mind of man to be able to grasp it; the pattern, let us say, is clear only to the eyes of God. For this reason, among others, we need art; for art, though based on life, is not life; the artist chooses such aspects of experience as he can understand (or finds them chosen for him by his temperament and experience), and presents them in a pattern of his own devising, drawn from his mind and incarnating his values. From one point of view, the sculptor does not "create" the statue at all. The statue was always there, in that block of marble, from the foundations of the world. What the sculptor did was to cut away those parts of the marble that he did not want; then the statue, which until now only his eyes had been able to see, became visible to all men. I am not speaking now of didactic literature; didactic literature is a special subject, to which we shall need to give our attention at a later stage of our inquiry. But it is not only in didactic literature that the author must take up an attitude toward his material. This is necessary in all creative writing, and when it does not occur, the reader is vaguely dissatisfied, often without knowing why. The story is interesting enough; the people are well characterized; there is nothing wrong with the actual writing. But it does not seem to mean anything. When you have finished you ask yourself what was it all about? and what difference does it make?

"Faithfulness"

A few simple illustrations may make all this clearer. Early in his career, James Branch Cabell wrote a story in which part of the action took place in Tunbridge Wells. Mr. Cabell had never visited Tunbridge Wells, and in writing this story he found himself somewhat embarrassed by his ignorance of the local geography. Then and there he made up his mind that never again, when he could possibly avoid it, would he lay the scene of one of his stories in any actual place. "I needed in my own little world to be omnipotent, and to move untrammeled by historic facts that any demiurge other than I had brought into being." So he proceeded to create an imaginary country which he called Poictesme, the scene of most of his subsequent books.

This is an extreme case. Not all writers can either find or create a Poictesme, nor could they all solve their aesthetic problems by so doing. Mr. Cabell himself did not become a permanent resident of that realm. But in one form or another, the kind of problem which he faced here is encountered by all writers of historical fiction. A different type of novelist—Kenneth Roberts, for example—would have solved the difficulty by setting to work to learn all about Tunbridge Wells! But there are problems in this area which cannot be solved by learning all about anything.

Suppose, for example, that you are writing a novel which involves a well-known historical character, and that the plan of the book requires that character not only to do something which he never did in life but to do something which is at variance with what he is known to have done and out of harmony with the kind of human being he is known to have been? Marjorie Bowen, who wrote so many fine historical novels, proceeded on the principle that if the writer alters fundamental matters, she has no right to employ the actual, historical names. In the last scene of his *Abraham Lincoln*, John Drinkwater found it convenient to put into his hero's mouth a speech which included quotations from both the Gettysburg Address and the Second Inaugural, and to permit him to deliver it from his box in Ford's Theater, just before the assassination. This deviation from historic fact was accepted by the audience. But the audience would not have accepted the play if Drinkwater had falsified Lincoln's moral nature, if he had made him, for example, a man like Adolf Hitler.

Even this, however, does not touch the heart of the matter. Basically the creative writer is not concerned either with "faithfulness" to his materials nor with making changes to show how "original" he can be. Both Chaucer and Shakespeare, who lived early enough to escape the silly accusations of "plagiarism" which would have been hurled toward them at a later period, took what they wanted wherever they found it, apparently without ever giving a thought to whether it came from direct experience, from oral tradition, or from another writer. They knew that all literary material belongs to the writer who uses it best.

What the writer needs essentially is to be free. You cannot put him into a straightjacket and then tell him to create. That is why so little literature of quality is produced in totalitarian countries, and that is why even good writers are likely to write badly when they try to create to order, producing not out of their own inner creative impulse but in response to the "demand" of this editor or that producer. It is easy to make fun of the writer who must have "conditions" right before he can produce—the classical example is the German poet who could write only with the odor of decayed bananas in the room—but though a great deal of nonsense has been talked along this line and a great deal of self-indulgence displayed by the writers themselves, there is no denying that the creative imagination is very capricious and manifests many idiosyncrasies.

James Branch Cabell is, as already noted, a highly individual artist, but he speaks for all artists when he expresses his need "in my own little world to be omnipotent." Omnipotence implies freedom, and it is of the essence of freedom that you must be at liberty to use actualities when they serve your purpose and to discard them when they do not.

"Real" People in Literature

This principle applies to more than the treatment of history in fiction or the novelist's use of written records. It explains why, in spite of all the agitation that individuals have shown from time to time over finding themselves portrayed in a novel, as a matter of fact there are very few portraits of actual people in fiction. The world of fiction is not the world of actuality, and actual people cannot breathe in it. They have to be transformed into characters of fiction.

An actual man or woman whom he has known may indeed serve as the novelist's point of departure; some novelists even seem to require such contact with reality to set their powers in operation. But the point is that having been brought into operation, these powers do operate, and the character who finally comes to life upon the printed page will find himself profoundly affected by them. Hugh Kingsmill says of Dickens that his father was Mr. Micawber and his mother Mrs. Nickleby. On the contrary, Dickens himself was the father of both these characters. John and Elizabeth Dickens set his imagination going—that is all. One does not need to study John Dickens in order to understand Mr. Micawber. Nor will one learn much about Harold Skimpole, of *Bleak House*, by studying Leigh Hunt, who suggested him. Dickens admitted that he had taken some aspects of Skimpole's character from Hunt, but he was genuinely (though somewhat naïvely) distressed over his friend's displeasure at being thus indirectly associated with a character who was, in some of his aspects, something of a "dead beat." It had simply not occurred to the novelist that Skimpole would be regarded by his public as all of a piece.

Changes in characterization may be consciously or unconsciously wrought; sometimes they are effected in order to bring the character into line with what the author is trying to say, and sometimes the modification is due to the needs of the story. "My notion always is," said Dickens, "that when I have made the people to play out the play, it is, as it were, their business to do it, and not mine." When Thackeray was taken to task for having "made" Henry Esmond marry the mother of Beatrix Esmond after the girl herself had eluded him, he declared, "I didn't make him do it; they did it themselves." And Charlotte Brontë's people move, under the galvanizing influence of her powerful imagination, with a freedom and a passionate intensity that that extremely "proper" lady would never have thought of allowing herself in "real" life.

The relationship between art and life is much more complicated, then, than anything that can be expressed in a formula. Art is, in the larger sense, "true to life," but it is not bound, in any literal sense, to the "facts" of experience. Neither is it a form of lying upon this account. The detailed discussion of just why this should be so will have to be postponed to the next chapter. Here it must suffice to say that the trouble with the people who do not realize it is that they have never learned how to distinguish between truth and fact. A sufficiently great book may sum up the meaning of an age as history itself cannot do it. And life itself, in any age, is so multi-sided that books which are not at all like each other may offer very different summaries or interpretations, all of which may be equally true. The soul of the Middle Ages is in Dante's *Divine Comedy*, but *The Divine Comedy* does not touch at all upon those aspects of mediaeval life which are reflected in the *fabliaux*. We go to Whitman for an impassioned vision of the burgeoning, teeming life of the great American democracy of his day. But the people who made that democracy refused to read Whitman. Instead they read Longfellow, whom we too must read if we would understand their tastes and their aspirations (which made up a very important part of their lives), and whom, we might do well to remember, Whitman himself read and relished.

Residuum in Literature

Reference was made, a few pages back, in the quotation from Edith Rickert, to the way in which predominantly factual material is subject to "incursions of realized experience" which turn it, for the moment, into literature, and to how, by the same token, literature may sink momentarily to the level of record. It is important to remember that a complete assimilation of his materials by the imagination of the creative writer is the exception rather than the rule. The percentage is higher in poetry and in the poetic drama—in brief lyric poems it may often approximate one hundred per cent—and considerably lower in types like the realistic novel in which an actual picture or impression of the surface variety of life fails to be indicated.

Poe denied the term "poetry" to anything but the short lyric poem because he could not consent to apply it to any work with a considerable unassimilated element in it. Some novelists succeed in assimilating a larger proportion of their materials than others: thus the percentage is higher in Hawthorne, James, and Conrad than it is in Bennett, Wells, or Dreiser. In an age in which many novels become best-sellers not because they give their readers an aesthetic experience but because they are supposed to shed light on some aspect of contemporary civilization, this point is worth making, and the reader who understands it is less likely to be confused about classifications than he would otherwise be.

Dickens's novel, *Bleak House*, contains an attack upon "the law's delay," as manifested in the workings of the Court of Chancery. The reader of Scott's *Kenilworth* learns something about Elizabethan history. Such material can be assimilated, or it can remain an extraneous element, as when Victor Hugo stops the story of *Les Misérables* to argue at length in favor of the use of human ordure as fertilizer, or again when Dreiser breaks in upon *Sister Carrie* to describe the workings of a department store. But not even the presence of unassimilated materials alters the fundamental character of the book in which they are contained. The mere fact that you "learned" incidentally about the Court of Chancery from reading *Bleak House*—and you could have learned much more from a legal work—will no more take that book out of the novel category than the fact that you enjoyed reading Havelock Ellis will remove his work from the category of scientific discussion.

The Girl Who Married an "English Teacher"

But why, it may be asked, should there be all this to-do about what literature is—or isn't? What difference does it make if the Young Lady uses the term carelessly or the Earnest Seeker is priggish about it?

I am afraid it makes all the difference between understanding and misunderstanding, between realizing that art is a basic form of human activity and viewing it as something with which only a few abnormal, or very highly developed, human beings have anything to do. We are living in a universe, not a multiverse, and we cannot understand anything unless we see it in its relationship to everything else. As Tennyson tells the "Flower in the Crannied Wall":

Little flower—but *if* I could understand
What you are, root and all, and all in all,
I should know what God and man is.

A current newspaper supplement contains an article by a young lady who writes to explain how it feels to be married to an "English teacher." The point seems to be that she is very glad she married him because whenever she wants to know the origin of a word, or what it means, he is always able to tell her, and she not only finds this very useful but extremely interesting as well.

All this proves the husband to be a very unusual "English teacher" indeed. It may also be said to have established, on the part of the wife, the strangest motive for marriage that has ever been known. Only, one is left wondering why she did not set up housekeeping with a copy of *Webster's New International.*

The implicit assumption underlying the article, of course, is that "English teachers" are freaks. They do not marry for the same reasons as other people do. Presumably they do not behave in marriage like other people. They are interested, in fact, in only one thing: words. Evidently this idea is entertained not only by the woman who wrote the article but also by the editor who printed it, or else he believes it to be held by the majority of his readers. Otherwise it is difficult to see why he wasted space on such idiotic drivel.

It seems a safe assumption that nobody who thinks about "English teachers," or "artists," or "authors," or "actresses," or any other class of people in this way, will ever, on God's earth, really find out anything about them, not even, one might add, if they should marry one. Edward Johnson, former director-general of the Metropolitan Opera Company, once overheard a woman's remark, "That man doesn't look in the least like a singer!" To which he very properly replied that though he had no idea what "a singer" looked like, he was nevertheless very thankful that he did not look like that!

John Livingston Lowes had all these things in mind, on a much higher level, when in his great study of the workings of Coleridge's imagination in *The Road to Xanadu*, he wrote that

it is of the utmost moment to more than poetry that instead of regarding the imagination as a bright and ineffectual faculty with which in some esoteric fashion poets and their kind are specially endowed, we recognize the essential oneness of its function and its ways with all the creative endeavours through which human brains, with dogged persistence, strive to discover and realize order in a chaotic world.[5]

But that poor girl who married an "English teacher"! Every woman is at least entitled to marry a man. God knows that is little enough!

A Glance at Some Youthful Connoisseurs

Here are Tom and Jack Mulligan, aged six and eight— neither of them can really "read"—having a battle royal of a Sunday morning over who is to have the first chance at the "comic section." And here is Sophie Klotz, who is seven, shedding bitter tears because she has been a bad girl, and to punish her, her mother is not going to let her go to the "movies" this afternoon.

These youngsters have never heard the word "art." They are quite indifferent to the social or intellectual or even moral prestige which, in some quarters, devotion to art is popularly considered to involve. Yet they are all passionately devoted to the thing itself, so enthralled by it, indeed, in the only form in which it has come their way, that at the moment they are indignantly rejecting every comfort

[5] John Livingston Lowes, *The Road to Xanadu: A Study in the Ways of the Imagination* (Houghton Mifflin, 1927), p. 433.

and solace and interest which life has the power to offer them at first hand, simply because art is being denied them. And if some well-meaning idiot of a grown-up should happen along at the moment to tell them that they must not mind their deprivation because "there are so many other things they might do that would be equally enjoyable," they would all bawl that "That's not the same thing!" And about that they would be perfectly right and a good deal more perceptive than the learned people who write about art have often been.

Indeed, much of the distress which cultivated adults often manifest over the tawdry quality of the art which enthralls the children might easily be avoided if these critics possessed a more adequate understanding of the strength and power of the child's imagination. Some years ago, I encountered an old collection of early *Katzenjammer Kids* cartoons which I had first read when I was five, and which I had never come across since I grew up. I was amazed to discover how many of the stock "properties" of romantic literature—pirates, cannibals, desert islands, the sea, and many more—I had first encountered in this strip. And I should be very ungrateful if I failed to acknowledge the tremendously stimulating effect which Rudolph Dirks and his Katzenjammers thus exercised upon my imagination! Similarly, I shall never know how many of the basic characters and great stories of literature and history first became my mental property through the early one-reel "movies," where, sooner or later, in the absence of adequate copyright regulations, everything was filmed. It is a stupid and unimaginative adult, indeed, who supposes that because the Star of Bethlehem must be painted by a Botticelli before it can take hold of his imagination, the same must be true of a child. The world is new to him, and everything is wonderful. Take a piece of cardboard, and cut a five-pointed object out of it with a pair of scissors. That will suffice.

The difficulty, then, with the boy who is still "stuck" with comic books or "horse operas" when he ought to have gone on to something better is simply that he has failed to grow. You cannot solve his problem by telling him that these things are bad in themselves, or that they are not "real" or important. "Don't get excited; remember it's only a picture!" If he were silly enough to follow such advice, he would be poorer, not richer: the world of the imagination would be closed against him forever. As it is, he has really got into that magnificent mansion, though unhappily only, through the servants' entrance, into the basement. Your job is not to kick him outside again. It is to lead him upstairs.

That can be done only through the development in him— or in yourself—of needs which the basement cannot satisfy. If you actually cannot see any difference between what you could pick up at a fire sale and what you have to go to the "28 Shop" for, why on earth should you pay the higher prices which the "28 Shop" demands? And if you have no needs which "swing" and the "pulps" cannot satisfy, why should you bother about Beethoven or Shakespeare? Only, you should remember this: that great art, great music, and great literature developed in this world not because anybody thought they "ought" to be here but because people themselves developed in such a way that the humbler forms of art no longer satisfied them. So Virginia Woolf speaks of "the seasoned and the fastidious, who in process of time have eaten their way to the heart of literature and there turn over and over a few precious crumbs."

Like lightning, genius often strikes in unexpected places: you can never be sure that a great story will not appear in one of the pulp magazines; neither can you be sure that the great writer will never let you down. "God was there" was the phrase Sarah Bernhardt applied to those performances— there were not many of them—in which she had really satis- fied herself; when God stayed away, she had only her technique to fall back on. But it was not only at such theaters as the Comédie Française that God might choose to manifest Himself; you might catch a glimpse of Him in very unexpected places, as Yvette Guilbert's café audiences sometimes discovered. Nevertheless there is a difference between the Comédie Française and the Moulin Rouge, and normal people, with the right kind of reading habits, do develop as Virginia Woolf has indicated, though not many of them arrive at the place to which she herself at last attained. By and large, we do find the books that were destined for us. But we read them because we need them and because we want to read them. You can no more relish a book because you think you "ought" to than you can love—or even like—a person for the same reason. In both cases you can pretend that you do, but that is a very differ- ent thing. As long as he lived, Bernard Shaw did his best to keep his plays out of the school books. He didn't, he ex- plained, want young people to come to hate him as they hated Shakespeare!

Artists in general have always been "yes-sayers to life," in James Huneker's fine phrase, and their eager responses have often shocked or repelled colder and less sensitive people. Eagerness, appetence are required, too, for the ap- preciation of art, for though art is not life, it is the distilled essence of life; as J. B. Kerfoot said, "Reading is a form of living."

Three Functions of Reading

Kerfoot and others have shown, too, the intimate connec- tion between reading and the reader's own past experience.

You may enjoy a book because it recalls experience. You may enjoy it because it deepens your experience, by interpreting it to you in some aspect that you had not previously considered. Or, finally, you may enjoy it because it enlarges experience for you by introducing you to some new phase or aspect of life. But, in any case, the only means you have of savoring the book is to apply the yardstick of yourself to it—your background, your comprehension of life, your capacity for responding to life.

No human being's experience has ever been exactly like that of any other human being; consequently, no book has ever meant quite the same thing to any two readers. Sir Herbert Tree used to be fond of saying that "Every man has the God he deserves." It is also true that every man has the book he deserves, and there are as many editions of every book as it has had readers. But to say that you are unlike everybody else, though it is true, is only half the truth; the other half is that you are also like everybody else. And for this reason, this key to literature to which you possess a clear title in the mere possession of your own humanity will, if you use it wisely, come in time to unlock many doors. For as the Roman dramatist Terence long ago perceived, you are a human being and nothing that is human can be alien to you.

Of course the same book may recall for one reader, deepen for a second, and widen for a third. Take, for example, Betty Smith's popular novel, *A Tree Grows in Brooklyn*. It deals with the world of childhood; in this aspect it performs, in some measure, a recollective function for every reader who has ever been a child, that is for all readers. But it also has a locale: it deals with childhood in a particular place and time—lower- and middle-class Brooklyn, a generation ago. Clearly, then, the recollective function will be performed over a wider area for the reader who grew up in Brooklyn than for one who grew up, say, in Missoula, Montana. For the Montana reader, on the other hand, *A Tree Grows in Brooklyn* will have a widening function which will not exist at all in the case of the Brooklyn reader. But the deepening function may operate with equal force for both, depending not upon the accidents of geography but rather upon their own sensitiveness and depth of understanding, as readers and as human beings. For unless Miss Smith was able to perceive something in her childhood experiences which most of her readers did not discern in theirs, then she will not, after all, be able to give them very much. They may enjoy her book, but it will not, in that event, be a means for them of growing deeper into life. And here we come back to the author himself, to the author's presentation of life in terms of his own personality, and to his addition to the stuff of experience of something which does not, essentially, belong to the material at all, but which he has added to the material by means of passing it through his own heart and brain.

G. K. Chesterton once wisely reminded us that as a bad man is still a man, so a bad poet is still a poet. The self-righteous snobbery which results from failure to heed such counsel is as devastating in criticism as it is in morals. Neither the author nor the readers of this chapter have, as I conceive it, been particularly interested to describe or to understand the conditions under which they think art "ought" to be created. Our concern has been simply to describe that which is. Man, as he has grown up on this planet, is a very complex creature who has developed manifold needs. Some of these he has tried to satisfy by creating pictures or images of life by means of the pen or the brush. Such productions, be it repeated, are not life, but in a sense they often seem more vital than life itself. As Conrad Richter's reviewer pointed out, it takes a great deal of history to produce a little literature. Hamlet never lived, yet he has outlived many generations and bids fair to outlive many more. No man was ever quite like him, but few men are altogether unlike him. Through literature man interprets man to himself, and through literature men interpret themselves to each other. Sometimes they do it very badly. Often they do not do it very well. Perhaps it has never been done with complete success. But it is wonderful that it should be possible to do it at all.

CHAPTER THREE

Of Choosing and Judging

~~~~~~

Why Criticism Is Necessary

Having established what literature is, we must next attempt to determine the difference between good literature and bad, to set up some standards for evaluating literature. But we ought first to establish the necessity for doing this, for it happens that the importance of criticism is greatly over-estimated in some quarters and greatly underestimated in others. Moreover, a great many people have completely erroneous ideas as to what criticism is.

To begin with, it should be understood that criticism has only a secondary, never a primary value. President Coolidge once made the penetrating remark that the United States was not maintaining an army and navy primarily for the benefit of the supply concerns. By the same token, the great writers of the world have not created their immortal works in order to provide schoolboys and girls with the materials for a series of exercises ingeniously designed to take as much joy out of their lives as possible. It seems a pity that some teachers have never grasped this profound truth.

Unfortunately there are some reviewers for the public press who have not grasped it either. Judging them by their performances, one would suppose them often to have their minds centered upon themselves when they should be thinking about the book or the play which they have under consideration. They themselves have no reason for being except to inform the public concerning the content and the merits or demerits of this work. But their own notion seems to be that the author's job was simply to furnish them with a point of departure for demonstrating how clever they can be.

In "A Gossip on Romance," Robert Louis Stevenson goes at the matter from a very different angle:

In anything fit to be called by the name of reading, the process itself should be absorbing and voluptuous; we should gloat over a book, be rapt clean out of ourselves, and rise from the perusal, our mind filled with the busiest, kaleidoscopic dance of images, incapable of sleep or of continuous thought.

This is a very high ideal, and one which assumes great gifts, both in the author and in the reader. It can hardly be necessary to point out here that it resembles most ideals in that considerable difficulty would be encountered by anyone who should attempt to apply it literally in a very imperfect world. Dr. Walter Russell Bowie writes of a friend, a clergyman, who, instead of telling the young couples whom he marries that he hopes they will be very happy—an amiable but essentially witless sentiment, since everybody knows that marriage, like everything else which widens and intensifies the range of human experience, must necessarily increase our opportunity and capacity for both pleasure and pain—simply tells them, "I hope you will be alive all your lives." This, too, is a very high ideal, but one fears that it might be rather wearing in practice. Says Browning, in "Christina":

Oh, we're sunk enough here, God knows!
But not quite so sunk that moments,
Sure tho' seldom, are denied us,

When the spirit's true endowments
Stand out plainly from the false ones. . . .

And Shelley, in his "Hymn to Intellectual Beauty" is quite in accord with him:

Love, Hope, and Self-esteem, like clouds depart
And come, for some uncertain moments leant. . . .

All sensitive people agree about this. We live on the heights only for moments, but we may spend years preparing for these experiences and weeks in recovering from them. So is it, too, with reading. A voracious reader, a professional critic or scholar, who should react to all his reading so intensely as Stevenson demands would, I fear, soon find himself in a mental hospital. But in spite of these reservations, we must all realize that when we are at our best as readers, we do respond to the printed page in some such fashion as Stevenson has described. Essentially, all our reading is a search for these moments. And no reader has really discovered literature until he has had such an experience.

But if that is so, why not leave it at that? Why bother with all this troublesome business of judgment and evaluation? There are, I believe, a number of very convincing reasons.

"Is It Any Good?"

The first reason, and in a sense the best, is that we cannot avoid it.

Whether the development of human consciousness upon this planet is, as we generally assume, the crowning achievement of the cosmic process, or whether it is, as weary and disillusioned spirits sometimes tell us, the disease of which this earth is destined at last to perish, the fact remains that it is here, and we cannot do away with it, even by the process of taking thought itself. For better or for worse, man is the thinking animal; at this stage of the game, the question is no longer "To think or not to think"; our only choice is between thinking well and thinking badly. You can no more avoid passing judgments, tentative though you know them to be, upon what you read than you can avoid "judging" the people you meet: you "like" this one, and you "don't like" that other.

"Where were you last night?" Jane asks her "girl-friend" over the telephone.

"Oh, I went to the 'movies.' We saw *The Story of Three Loves.*"

"Oh, did you?" replies Jane. "Is it any good?"

"Be sure to look at *King Aroo* today," says Henry to his brother Philip. "It's 'swell.'"

"Well," says Philip, looking up from the other paper. "I'm glad something is good. *Mutt and Jeff* is 'lousy.'"

These people are not professional critics, and they would be very much surprised if anybody were to tell them that they were engaged in aesthetic evaluation. Jane wants to know about *The Story of Three Loves* so that she can make up her mind whether to go to see it or not. Henry tells Philip about *King Aroo* because he wants his brother to share the pleasure he has found in it. And Philip is spontaneously giving vent to his feeling of disappointment in *Mutt and Jeff.* But in every case, what we call "judgment" is unavoidable. Henry could not read *King Aroo* without either enjoying or failing to enjoy it, and if he enjoys it, then he cannot help feeling that it is "good."

This does not mean, of course, that any of these people are necessarily "right" in their judgments. Suppose Mildred did not enjoy *The Story of Three Loves.* Jane will be very unwise to stay away from it on that account, unless she has already very carefully tested Mildred's judgment on other films. Perhaps Mildred does not like this kind of film.

Perhaps she was so much more interested in the boy who took her than she was in the picture that she did not pay sufficiently careful attention to what was happening upon the screen to be able to find out whether she enjoyed it or not. Or she may even be jealous because neither she nor her "boy-friend" could help realizing that both Moira Shearer and Pier Angeli, whom they saw in the picture, are prettier than she is. Again, Philip's unfavorable reaction to *Mutt and Jeff* may have been caused not by any fault of Bud Fisher's but simply by the fact that he does not seem to be in a very good mood this morning. If this is the case, then, likely as not, he will toss *King Aroo* aside, having examined it at his brother's instigation, with a contemptuous "I don't think that's so 'hot,' " while, simultaneously, Henry may be remarking of *Mutt and Jeff*, "But I don't think that's so bad."

This apparently trifling discussion contains a number of clues which we shall wish to pick up and examine before we have done with this matter of criticism. For the moment, however, let us content ourselves with having established the fact that criticism in some form is inevitable. If we must have it, then, it is surely desirable that it should be competent, intelligent, open-minded, and well-informed, a criticism based upon principles, not prejudices, upon knowledge and not upon ignorance.

Of Aims and Methods

Yet this is only one aspect. However brilliant it may be in itself, criticism still fails absolutely unless it contributes to a fuller understanding and a richer enjoyment of the work to which it is applied. Understanding cannot be achieved without sound critical principles and, in some cases, solid historical knowledge. There is a great deal in Shakespeare's plays, for instance, which must be seriously misunderstood by persons incapable of visualizing the outdoor theater, with a platform stage, for which Shakespeare wrote, and unable or unwilling to follow the reasoning and responding processes of the Elizabethan mind to which he addressed himself.

Wordsworth believed that poetical works "contain within themselves all that is necessary to their being comprehended and relished," but he knew, too, that every writer who is not content merely to follow in the footprints of his predecessors must, in a measure, create the taste by which he is understood. So he found it necessary to furnish a lengthy Preface to the second (1800) edition of his and Coleridge's *Lyrical Ballads,* in which he very carefully explained just what he meant by poetry and what, in these poems, he had tried to do.

Many readers of 1800 were still bound by neo-classical ideals in poetry; what poetry meant to them was essentially what it had meant to Pope. The so-called "pre-romantics" had, in a measure, broken the mold, but neither Thomson nor Gray nor Collins had departed so boldly or so radically from previously formulated ideals as to make comprehension impossible for reasonably open-minded and intelligent readers. But this is exactly what Wordsworth fears that he and Coleridge may have done. If they are to be judged by the standards which most contemporary readers of poetry have in mind, they will be misjudged altogether. He writes his Preface, therefore, to try to teach his readers how to read him.

This shows that it is not always true that we need more help in reading ancient or very foreign literature than we need to read the literature of our own time. Those who dislike "modern," or *avant-garde,* or experimental art are always being told by its admirers that the fault is in them: they "do not know how to look at it." After the world has lived with a new kind of art for a reasonable time, it apparently becomes easier to understand, even by those who have never made any serious or direct approach to it. It acclimatizes itself, so to speak, becomes a part of the atmosphere in which we breathe. Joyce's *Ulysses* is still a very difficult book, but it is less difficult for us than it was for those who attempted it when it was first published. And Meredith and James, who, in their time, were often considered almost as difficult, now lie comfortably within the range of the intelligent reader. In short, we need to be equipped with historical knowledge, and to possess ourselves of the fruits of historical scholarship, if we would read the literature of the past with maximum efficiency, but we feel the need of a new reading technique primarily in our attempts to grasp the more "advanced" writers of our own time.

Moreover, criticism is quite as necessary for enjoyment as it is for understanding. It is odd that this fact should so often have gone unrecognized:

... it is generally recognized that in the art of painting or of music a thorough understanding of the methods by which such art is created not only does not destroy appreciation but is the only way to attain full appreciation. Who would argue for a moment that a painter who can explain the perspective, composition, brushwork, and color in a painting and can tell precisely how such an effect was produced is prevented by his technical understanding from feeling appreciation of the picture? Or who will defend for a moment the view that the musician who can analyze a fugue or a symphony cannot feel the beauty of the music? Why should literature be on a different basis?[1]

But there is yet a third reason why criticism is necessary. Criticism and creation are mutually interdependent. With-

[1] Edith Rickert, *New Methods for the Study of Literature*, p. 20.

out creative work, the critic would have no materials to work with; on the other hand, the critic develops standards and sets up goals by reference to which the work of the artist himself is importantly conditioned. The art of the western world would have been very different if Aristotle had never lived, or if the standards which he promulgated had not for centuries been accepted, virtually at face value.

> 'Tis hard to say, if greater want of skill
> Appear in writing or in judging ill;
> But, of the two, less dangerous is the offence,
> To tire our patience, than mislead our sense.[2]

The bad poet creates a bad work, but the bad critic (let his false doctrines be widely enough accepted) may pervert the standards of a whole generation to such an extent that everything which appears may be judged amiss and false or irrelevant standards applied to it, until at length it becomes impossible for any work based upon sound principles to obtain a hearing. In "The Function of Criticism at the Present Time," Matthew Arnold, though perceiving clearly "that a free creative activity is the highest function of man," guards carefully against underestimating the value of the critical power, as tending "to make an intellectual situation of which the creative power can profitably avail itself." Sound criticism, he argues, "tends to establish an order of ideas, if not absolutely true, yet true by comparison with that which it displaces, to make the best ideas prevail." The "creation of a modern poet," he goes on, "implies a great critical effort behind it."

Criticism Not Faultfinding

The most basic misunderstanding concerning the nature of criticism is that which conceives of the critical activity

[2] Alexander Pope, "An Essay on Criticism."

as identical with faultfinding. If Johnny were to come home from school and report that "My teacher criticized me" or "my composition," there would be no doubt in his mother's mind that the judgment expressed was not a favorable one. Actually, however, the word "criticize" means to judge or to discern. A judgment or an evaluation which finds only merit in the work under consideration is not necessarily less "critical" than one which should result in outright condemnation.

It is true, of course, that unmodified praise may easily spill over into gush. And gush is foreign to the critical spirit. But, then, it is also true that unmodified faultfinding may easily take the form of spitefulness and backbiting. And that is foreign to the critical spirit also.

There are faults—or, at any rate, there are limitations—in everything that human genius has created, and a reasonably keen mind, applying itself systematically to the examination of a work of art, is fairly certain to come up with some realization of these limitations. But even when the critic is quite correct in his observations—when it is not, in short, simply his taste against the writer's taste—this is still the easiest part of his task.

Amateurs in all the arts have always been notoriously keen in analyzing the faults and shortcomings of their betters; what they generally fail to do altogether is to explain why the artist in question is a world figure while they themselves have never been heard of outside their own communities. Petty, carping critics do fairly well with the ordinary run of books. On bad books they are often much better than very fine critics. But when it comes to really great literature they are helpless, for the just evaluation of great art calls for two apparently contradictory qualities— humility and the great attitude—and there is no trace of either of these in them. We do not, any of us, judge the really great art of the world half so much as it judges us; we measure ourselves against it, and generally we discover that we are much smaller than we thought they were. Now, a certain kind or quality of mind, infuriated by this perception, protects itself against recognizing the truth by discovering at the same time that, after all, the work in question is not much. Shakespeare did not know that Bohemia had no seacoast. And Chaucer made the Second Nun call herself an "unworthy son of Eve," which, incidentally, may have been quite in harmony with contemporary religious practice. It would be too much to say that this kind of thing is not criticism. But certainly it is not a very lofty or difficult form of criticism. It is not like entering into the mind and heart and soul of a great writer, thinking his thoughts after him, understanding the character of his created world upon his own terms, and then explaining what he has done to others, in words so perceptive and so provocative that through your criticism men shall be able to understand something about that writer which they might never have perceived so clearly without you.

Toward Standards

But what, then, *are* the standards to be applied? The extraordinary range and complexity of creative activity in all the arts makes an answer to this question very difficult. One might, perhaps, be brave enough to try to describe the qualities which a good ballad must possess, or a fine sonnet, but who could be brave enough to concoct a "shotgun prescription" for literature in general?

Moreover, the creative spirit is an extraordinarily free spirit.

There are nine and sixty ways of constructing tribal lays,
And every single one of them is right.

Who shall prescribe the artist's mode and method of creation? The shores of criticism are strewn with the hulks of those voyagers who have attempted it. And one thinks of John Jay Chapman's witty remark about the much-vaunted "laws" of dramatic composition. There is, he declared, but one such law. And it is very simple. Something must be going on on the stage which interests the audience. Otherwise they will go away.

Some things, perhaps, may be taken for granted. One generally takes a certain measure of sincerity for granted. It is difficult to take a work of art seriously if we do not believe that the author took it seriously, that he did not mean what he said. There is the famous legendary sermon which the devil once preached, with overwhelming power, against all the hosts of darkness, but which won no converts because the speaker himself did not believe in it. When the writer condescends, when he "writes down" to his audience, you do not get literature: you only get journalism, and not journalism at its best, but at its worst. The artist need not live in an "ivory tower," but he is not generally considered to be functioning most effectively when too much concerned with "playing to his audience." ("From my point of view," said a famous actress, "the perfect audience is the audience which allows me to forget that it is there.") Tennyson wrote *In Memoriam* to solve for himself the pressing human and religious problems posed by the death of his friend, Arthur Henry Hallam. Readers, bending sympathetically over his shoulder, thought his thoughts after him, and because his problem was nearly a universal problem, in "solving" it for himself, he performed an important service for them also. Even so, one does not demand quite the same kind of "sincerity" from an artist that one expects from a preacher, and perhaps it might even be said that sincerity as such is a moral rather than an

aesthetic quality. Certainly its absence would be a much
more serious fault in some types of literature—the religious
lyric, for one—than in others—such as *vers de société*.

Clarity

Again, one might say that a certain skill in expression
might well be postulated as a *sine qua non* in any type of
literary work, but this again will not take us far, for we
shall still be obliged to define the constituent elements of
that skill, and these requirements will not always be the
same. It might seem that clarity would be a universal requirement, but this is not actually the case. There are some
types of writing—stories involving the supernatural, for example—whose power may even be increased by the absence
of clear referents. The Old Man in Chaucer's "Pardoner's
Tale"—the first great short story in the English language
and still one of the greatest—teases the imagination because
he is obviously something more than just an old man. But
what? Death? Old Age? The Devil? The Wandering Jew?
All these and others have been suggested, but it is because
he cannot be certainly identified with any of them that he
continues to hold such a powerful purchase upon our
imaginations. When the vampire and serpent-woman of
Coleridge's "Christabel" disrobes, the poet does not tell us
what was revealed. Instead he whispers awesomely:

> Her silken robe, and inner vest,
> Dropt to her feet, and full in view,
> Behold! her bosom and half her side—
> A sight to dream of, not to tell!
> O shield her! shield sweet Christabel!

The advantages of this line of procedure are obvious.
Instead of limiting the reader to some one particular horror
which is named upon the printed page, the poet forces him

to collaborate, as it were, in telling the story. He enlists our imagination, stirring us up to recollect all the horrors we have ever experienced or conceived, terrors all the more menacing because we cannot be really sure that any of them are here! Other good examples of this kind of thing in more recent literature may be found in the writings of such men as Arthur Machen and Walter de la Mare, notably in the latter's tale, "The Riddle," and in his famous poem, "The Listeners." Here the theme of the broken tryst is presented with great power, and we get a very vivid picture of the Traveler coming alone to the ghost-infested dwelling, untenanted by any living soul—

> "Tell them I came, and no one answered,
> That I kept my word," he said—

but who the Traveler is, and what the tryst was to achieve, and why the pledge was broken—all this we never learn, and the marvelous atmosphere of the poem would be spoiled if we did.[3]

So far we can hardly pride ourselves on having achieved any extraordinary success in setting up criteria for the evaluation of literature. Perhaps we had better try going at the matter in a somewhat less authoritarian manner.

What Was the Author Trying to Do?

Let us go back, then, to the beginning, that is to say, to the author. The book, as we have already observed, is the author's expression or projection of himself. Only a human being can produce a book, and (since water cannot rise higher than its source) no book is wiser or better-informed than the man who wrote it, and no book has any grace or

---

[3] For a fuller discussion of these matters than can be given here, see Edward Wagenknecht, "Walter de la Mare's 'The Riddle': A Note on the Teaching of Literature with Allegorical Tendencies," *College English*, XI (1949), 72-80.

beauty that is not a reflection of the author's own spirit.

Furthermore, nobody can know better than the author what he was trying to do. For while all literature, as distinguished from non-literature, proceeds from the writer's desire to communicate his sense of human experience, the circumstances under which the communication is made vary widely from book to book and are profoundly modified by many different conditions.

The beginning of all sound criticism, then, is here: First of all, you must determine what the author was trying to do. Not until you have done that, and done it right, can you go on to the next point (which many people find much more congenial and attractive), that is, to determine whether or not he succeeded in doing it.

Let us go back, for the moment, to Wordsworth's Preface. As we have already seen, he was trying to teach his readers how to read him. He knew that the application of conventional standards to his very unconventional verses must result in a critical verdict which would be not only unjust but incompetent.

The unguided reader might, for example, expect to find conventional poetic diction in Wordsworth's poems—as many personifications, say, as in Collins's odes, and an abundant use of metaphor and various rhetorical devices. Being unable to find these things, he might conclude that Wordsworth was an incompetent poet. He would be wrong, since a writer cannot fail with something that he never attempted.

Wordsworth explains, therefore, that he is not trying to use the conventional poetic diction. He is writing about everyday people, involved in incidents and situations of common life, and he is describing their doings in the real language of men. He believes that simple language is better for poetry than the language of cultivated society, because it arises out of permanent and regular feelings and is untouched by fad or affectation. He believes that if the poet would speak for humanity, he must use the language of humanity. The employment of a special form of language would thrust the poet himself between the poem and the reader, centering the reader's attention upon how cleverly the poet expresses himself at the expense of what he is saying.

Wordsworth believes, further, that it is very important that his readers should be made sensitive to the beauty and the passion which exist in quiet lives, and the cultivation of sensitiveness along this line seems to him particularly desirable in an age in which too many people tended to demand, or to depend upon, an excessive emotional stimulation. And if you ask him why, holding such views, he has chosen to express himself in verse rather than in prose, he will reply that it is not a prose effect that he is after. Furthermore, he desires to enlarge the scope of verse, and to show that poems written in a comparatively naked and simple style can be successful.

It must be clear that an intelligent reader of Wordsworth's Preface would, other things being equal, be much more likely to understand what the poet was trying to do, and to decide intelligently whether or not he succeeded in doing it, than a reader who should, as it were, go at the *Lyrical Ballads* "cold."

Naturally this does not necessarily mean that such a reader will necessarily "like" Wordsworth's poetry. We need not like a thing simply because we understand it. We may even dislike it *because* we understand it. But when we understand and reject, we reject intelligently. When we reject without understanding, we do justice neither to the writer nor to ourselves. Strictly speaking, the question whether we "like" a work of art or not is of autobiographical, rather than critical, interest. Though immensely important to us, it is no overwhelming importance to the cosmos. Many critics have never made this distinction clearly, even in their own minds.

The classical example of the critic who disregarded the procedure here outlined was the man who condemned the dictionary for its lack of continuity. It was, he said, impossible to get interested in the "darned book" because it was forever changing the subject. Do not be too sure that this man was a fool or too hasty in condemning him. You may find that you have condemned yourself.

What about the reader who dismissed *The Travels of Baron Munchausen* because it was "unconvincing," or Gorky's *The Lower Depths* because it was "depressing"? Were these works meant to convince and to exhilarate? Have you ever condemned a fantasy because you "like books that deal with 'real' life"? or a story of the supernatural because it is your conviction that "ghosts and all that business are 'hooey' "? Conversely, have you ever refused to accept a tragedy because "when a person goes to the theater he wants to be amused"? or a novel involving an honest picture of a social evil because you "prefer not to think about things like that"? Have you, perhaps, even disliked some particular novel because it is long and you "like short books," or, on the other hand, neglected a gifted writer of short stories because when you read, you want "something a person can stay at"? Have you dismissed Longfellow because he is wholesome, or Oscar Wilde because he is not? *Have you?* Then who's the fool now?

A Reader Protests That His "Rights" Have Been Invaded

"But wait a minute," cries an indignant reader. "Do I 'have to' like stories of the supernatural? Is there any obligation upon me to read long novels if I don't want to? Was the book made for the reader or the reader for the book? You began by stating that the function of literature is to give the reader pleasure. Haven't you forgotten that? And aren't you trying to make a worse 'job' out of reading than anybody has ever made of it before?"

No, I don't think so. Of course you don't "have to" like stories of the supernatural, or any other kind of stories, for that matter. Nor is there any moral obligation resting upon you to read anything that you don't want to read. But if you do read, and if you desire to read intelligently, so as to derive the maximum satisfaction from it, then there are certain conditions which you must be willing to fulfill. These conditions have not been created by my fiat, nor by anything that either readers or writers have decreed. They have been determined by the nature of literature and the character of the human mind.

"No, I don't like Dickens," said the Dignified Elderly Gentleman. "I like Thackeray." Or the other way around. To which James Branch Cabell retorts that it would be equally reasonable to decline to participate in a game of billiards on the ground that one was fond of herring. The ideal reader, of course, would be he who should have an equal appreciation of every kind of literary excellence. Naturally, the ideal reader exists only in theory. By the natural bent of our temperament and training, we are all so constituted that we find realism more congenial than romanticism or vice versa, prefer the freer or the more rigid forms in versecraft, read with greater relish novels in which human conduct is keenly scrutinized on the everyday level or those in which it is idealized. There is no more sense in arguing over such differences than there is in arguing over whether blondes are more or less beautiful than brunettes. But it *is* possible to admire both blonde and brunette beauty, and he would certainly be a very stupid gentleman who, because he "preferred blondes," should therefore dismiss all brunettes as ugly. In our family lives, monogamy has long since justified itself by its practical utility; fortunately we are much freer in the life of the imagination. Only very narrow-minded readers are wedded to one author, or even to one type of author. When this does occur, it deserves to be called less faithfulness than a fixation.

The author of this book spent a good many years writing the history, first, of British, then, of American, fiction. In the course of this work, he found it necessary to read or to re-read most of the important novels that have been written both in England and in the United States. There were not many authors involved whom he had read more than partially before; some he had not read at all. Some of these last he dreaded reading. Either because of their subject-matter, or their style, or some point of view that he attributed to them, he expected to dislike them and find them a task.

Among the scores of writers considered, he could now count upon the fingers of one hand the names of all those in connection with whom his fears were fulfilled.

Naturally this does not mean that all the novels he read were found equally enjoyable. But it does mean that he found very few among the many novelists who, since the sixteenth century, have acquired sufficient fame and influence to make it at all reasonable that they should be considered in a history of the novel, who had nothing to say to him, and none who, for one reason or another, were not worthy of his attention. He even found some special friends in unexpected places. If he had been left to his own devices, it would never, I fear, have occurred to him to read a novel by R. S. Surtees, for he would never have supposed that stories of the English hunting-field could possibly make any appeal to him. Yet when he read Surtees, he found him a thoroughly delightful writer, though his convictions on the subject of hunting as a pastime remained entirely unmodified by this experience.

Where Do We Go from Here?

We have begun, then, by asking ourselves, What was the author trying to do? and on the basis of all the information we could gather on that point, we have tried to make up our minds whether or not he succeeded in doing it. Do we stop at this point?

A purely historical type of criticism might be willing to do just that. For we could, upon this basis, understand the nature of the work under consideration and define its relationship to its age. But we should not really have entered any qualitative judgment concerning it. We should not have raised any question of values, or assessed either its human or its aesthetic worth.

If we stop at this point, indeed, it is difficult to see how we are to avoid giving the "artist" who has built a replica of Cologne Cathedral with match sticks (provided only he has succeeded in his task) the same rank which we assign to the author of *The Divine Comedy*. Suppose you have achieved what you aimed at. If your aim was frivolous and unworthy, your results will still be contemptible. Indeed a rigid or consistent or unimaginative application of this test would give the advantage to the artist of mean aims and petty aspirations and the disadvantage to him who tries to scale the stars. It was Browning's conviction that no great artist ever stops working until he has reached his point of failure; that was why he praised "the glory of the imperfect."

Troublesome questions of evaluation plague us here, and they do not cease to plague us when we leave the contrast

between worthy and unworthy behind and confine ourselves to the stars alone, for one star differs from another
in magnitude. It is a lesser achievement, one would suppose,
to create a fine sonnet than a fine epic, and while it is true
that sonnets and epics are not really comparable—neither
is there anything more perfect than perfection—most critics, I think, would still feel that, other things being equal,
the perfect epic (if such a thing is conceivable) would be
the greater achievement of the two.

The Good, the True, and the Beautiful

So we come at last, then, to the naked qualitative judgment, with all the disagreements which this involves, and
all the problems suggested by the age-old criteria of the
Good, the True, and the Beautiful. And, indeed, these three
questions—Is it true? Is it good? Is it beautiful?—have been
applied by critics to the evaluation of literary works since
time immemorial, and only those which have, in varying
degrees, successfully passed these tests have at last gained
acceptance.

The first question is the most comprehensive of the three,
and therefore the most difficult to answer. We have already
seen that this is the question, often slightly transformed by
its passage through a wary or a suspicious mind—"Is it any
good?"—which even the most unsophisticated critics are
likely to ask first of all concerning a work of art. The
question is confusing sometimes because "good" has a moral
as well as an aesthetic bearing—and some aspects of it cannot be considered until we come to the relationship, or lack
of it, between literature and morality—and it is confusing
also because, even in the aesthetic sense, the word "good"
has a kind of blanketing significance. A book is not "good,"
in other words, unless it is also true and beautiful and whatever else a sound work of literature ought to be. If we

cannot, then, discuss goodness in literature by itself, it is also true that we cannot avoid discussing it, whatever worthy or valuable aspects of literature we may chance at the moment to have under consideration.

The Criterion of Truth

But what, now, of truth? Is this a valid criterion? And in what sense does it apply?

We have already suggested that it does *not* mean that art reproduces nature. "Art," says John Livingston Lowes, "demands a medium. That medium is never the same as the thing which it presents. Canvas is not a landscape, stone flesh, the stage reality. Obliterate the difference, and you have actuality, not art." Not even the "candid camera" shot, which is not art but an accident of science, quite reproduces actuality. For one thing, it immobilizes and perpetuates what life knew only in a state of flux, what existed in life merely for a split second on its way to becoming something else. Again, by the mere fact of "framing" his picture, the photographer makes a selection, chooses accent and emphasis, includes and excludes. And frames can be very important, both in art and in life. Does the mirror reflect the room accurately? Not quite. It turns everything around, but that is not all it does:

Why are all reflections lovelier than what we call the reality? [asks George MacDonald, in *Phantastes*]—not so grand or so strong, it may be, but always lovelier? Fair as is the gliding sloop on the shining sea, the wavering, trembling, unresting sail below is fairer still. . . . All mirrors are magic mirrors. The commonest room is a poem when I turn to the glass.

Early readers of fiction did not understand such distinction; consequently Defoe and Mrs. Behn were obliged to pretend that they were writing history. "Since I began this relation, I heard that Prince Tarquin died about three quarters of a year ago." And "I will not be positive whether he said yet forty days or yet a few days." The same thing was true of the early American novelists at the end of the eighteenth century, for, contrary to popular belief at the present time, the Puritans of that day were less concerned over the power of fiction to inflame the imagination—some of their novels were almost as libidinous as our own—than they were about recording or believing something that was not "true." Many of the devices Defoe employed are still being used by our own novelists, but their employment has now become a mere matter of creating verisimilitude, with no intent to deceive.

Much later than this, the naturalistic novelists were sometimes silly enough to talk about their novels being "slices of life." They did not select anything; they just chopped off a hunk of life experience and flung it, raw and bleeding, upon the printed page. Actually, of course, they did nothing of the kind, for the excellent reason that it cannot be done. More recently, "stream-of-consciousness" writers have sometimes entered claims of all-inclusiveness. Edith Wharton said "stream-of-consciousness" was nothing but "slice of life" plus Freudian trimmings. Actually, the naturalists selected their materials just as carefully as the romantic or historical novelist selects his; only they selected them from a different point of view. If you assume that life has no meaning, then that belief becomes the determining factor in your choice and treatment of subject matter, quite as clearly as the opposite assumption may be determinative with another kind of writer. An atheist can be quite as dogmatic as a Christian, and is often much more so.

In a sense, it is even true that there is something more artificial and unreal about an art-form which refuses to recognize the conventions it cannot avoid employing than there is in such novels as those of Anthony Trollope, where the basic conventions of story-telling are accepted as frankly as we accept the limitations of life itself. There has been a great deal of head-shaking over the passage in which Trollope tells the readers of *Barchester Towers* not to worry about which of her unattractive suitors Eleanor Bold is going to marry, for, as a matter of fact, she will accept neither! All the "advanced" critics scream that Trollope is wantonly "destroying the illusion of reality" upon which fiction depends. There can be no question that such aesthetic insouciance *ought* to destroy the illusion of reality in fiction, and if either art or life were as logical as the critics, no doubt it would. Yet as a matter of reading experience, we all know that it does nothing of the kind. Eleanor Bold lives triumphantly, far more triumphantly than many of the people who have their being in novels which are "self-containing entities," and she shares this characteristic with most of the other delightful people in Trollope's book.

Perhaps the fact that art is precommitted by its method to the use of the concrete has made it easier for people to suppose that it must, or should, concern itself with reproducing actualities. It is the philosopher who treats beauty, truth, and goodness in the abstract; the artist can only create a beautiful object, though, to be sure, some artists still manage to suggest that the beautiful object owes its beauty to the fact that it reflects a more moving immaterial beauty behind it. But, as George Edward Woodberry has well said, "the concrete which art creates is not a copy of the concrete of life; it is more than this. The mind takes the particulars of the world of sense into itself, generalizes them, and frames therefrom a new particular, which does not exist in nature; it is, in fact, nature made perfect in an imagined instance, and so presented to the mind's eye, or to the eye of sense." The special delight which art affords is to be found, then, in "that element which artistic imitation adds to actuality." Nor is it only materials which are delightful in themselves that the artist can treat in this way. Dickens's Mrs. Gamp is every drunken nurse who ever existed in England, yet she is none of them. We delight in her society, but we should flee in horror from any one of her "originals." Taine defined art as "nature seen through a temperament," and a French painter once said that he could paint a dozen pictures of the same haystack, each different from all the others, yet all equally "true."

Moving Boston Around

These considerations apply, in a general way, to all literature. There are also, of course, more specific considerations which apply only to certain types. The realistic or naturalistic novel, for example, demands a degree of faithfulness to the conditions which prevailed in a particular place at a particular time which romantic literature and most poetry does not demand. Only the other day, I heard a passage in Whittier's "Snow-Bound" criticized because it seemed to imply that the sound of the sea could be heard at the Whittier homestead in Haverhill, though actually this is probably not the case. Now if "Snow-Bound" had been addressed to a purely local audience, this fact might well have got in the way of the pleasure the reader would otherwise feel in the poem; since this was not intended, and since the poet was not writing a "report" on the life of the Haverhill household, but creating a nostalgic poem, an idyll, in which the life-materials employed had been subjected to the alchemy of memory and the imagination, the criticism seems to me largely beside the point. On the other hand, the author of a realistic novel set in contemporary Boston would be very ill-advised if he should move either the Public Library or Trinity Church from Copley Square over to Scollay Square, even if the exigencies of the narrative were accommodated by such a transference. Nor could the author of a similar novel about Chicago safely put the Civic Opera House on the lake front and the Art Institute on the river.

Yet Sir Walter Scott made changes even more startling than these in *Ivanhoe*—he said frankly that he had confused the manners of two or three centuries—and nobody but a few antiquarians were ever the wiser. Neither, probably, did anybody care when Shakespeare gave Bohemia a seacoast in *The Winter's Tale*. There must have been very few people in Elizabethan London who knew whether Bohemia had a seacoast. But a great many contemporary readers of fiction do know the geography of Boston and Chicago, and a novelist who should wantonly or frivolously juggle with that geography would pay a heavy price. At best, he would find that all the work he had done on the setting of his novel had been thrown away; at the worst, his reader would be so much distressed by the anomalies and absurdities involved that he might well fail to make any vital contact with the book in its other aspects, completely satisfying though these might be. The present writer recalls in this connection an absurd Maurice Evans telecast of *Hamlet*, in a *Prisoner of Zenda* setting, with the actors tricked out in a mad hodge-podge of costumes, ranging all the way from the first Elizabethan Period to the twentieth century! Thanks primarily to Mr. Evans's own eloquence, the play defied its production and survived, but it survived only by a hair and after a hideous struggle against unnecessary handicaps. On the other hand, the 1951 stage production of *Romeo and Juliet*, starring Miss Olivia de Havilland, was gloriously mounted, with exquisitely appropriate Italian Renaissance settings until the Tomb Scene was reached, when the astonished eyes of the spectators encountered a hideous structure which might best be described as standing midway between an eighteenth century "Gothick" ruin and something which, I should think, might have served very appropriately to suggest Grendel's lair in a production of *Beowulf*.

The discussion so far might seem to suggest that it is all a matter of what you can "get away with," and that what you can get away with will be determined only by the ignorance of your readers. Scott's refusal to be faithful to any particular period in *Ivanhoe* did spoil his book for those who knew enough to be aware of it; it certainly prevents *Ivanhoe* from being classified as an historical novel, in the sense in which (to take a recent magnificent example) Miss H. F. M. Prescott's *The Man on a Donkey* (1951) is an historical novel; *Ivanhoe* must take its place, rather, as an historical fantasia. But it is not only a matter of what you can get away with; what you can get away with is more artifice than art.

Primarily your concern as a writer is faithfulness, not to actuality, but to the aesthetic problem which you have set for yourself. If that problem involves describing life in contemporary Boston, then you are obliged, not to put the Boston of actuality on the printed page (for that, as we have already seen, cannot be done), but simply to create the illusion of having done so, by bringing to life, in terms of the medium in which you are working, some kind of equivalent of that.

In order to achieve this, you must avoid anything and everything which will interfere with, or negate, or vitiate your attempt to create such an illusion. Otherwise, you will be standing in your own light, getting in your own way, making it difficult or impossible to achieve the purpose to which you have dedicated yourself. Your obligation, however, is still not to the Boston of fact but to the Boston of your novel, which is a created realm, but a created realm which is subtly dependent upon, and minutely interrelated with, the Boston of fact. Moving the Public Library over to Scollay Square is not objectionable in itself; it merely becomes objectionable in the kind of book you are writing because it interferes with the achievement of your purpose. On the other hand, if you are creating not a realistic novel about Boston but a Boston fantasy, then it might be very amusing to have the Public Library in Scollay Square. It might even be amusing to move the Old Howard burlesque theater to the Public Garden, or to make it a part of either the Ritz-Carlton Hotel or the Arlington Street Church across the street. The "real" Boston will never encounter any of these diverting anomalies, but that is no reason why we should be deprived of them in the world of the imagination.

The Moon Behaves Strangely in "The Eve of St. Agnes"

For a more detailed illustration of all this, let us go to John Keats's poem, "The Eve of St. Agnes." This lavish and beautiful romantic narrative—best of all the literary offspring of *Romeo and Juliet*—tells of one bitter winter night when Porphyro stole his love, Madeline, from the house of her father, his enemy. Here are the three stanzas containing the poet's description of the heroine at prayer, just before she gets into her bed:

Out went the taper as she hurried in;
Its little smoke, in pallid moonshine, died:
She closed the door, she panted, all akin
To spirits of the air, and visions wide:
No uttered syllable, or, woe betide!
But to her heart, her heart was voluble,
Paining with eloquence her balmy side;

As though a tongueless nightingale should swell
Her throat in vain, and die, heart-stifled, in her dell.

A casement high and triple-arched there was,
All garlanded with carven imag'ries
Of fruits, and flowers, and bunches of knot-grass,
And diamonded with panes of quaint device,
Innumerable of stains and splendid dyes,
As are the tiger-moth's deep-damasked wings;
And in the midst, 'mong thousand heraldries,
And twilight saints, and dim emblazonings,
A shielded scutcheon blushed with blood of queens and kings.

Full on this casement shone the wintry moon,
And threw warm gules on Madeline's fair breast,
As down she knelt for heaven's grace and boon;
Rose-bloom fell on her hands, together prest,
And on her silver cross soft amethyst,
And on her hair a glory, like a saint:
She seemed a splendid angel, newly drest,
Save wings, for heaven:—Porphyro grew faint:
She knelt, so pure a thing, so free from mortal taint.

And now, as the puzzle people ask, What is wrong with this picture?

This: That Keats has attributed to moonlight a stronger power than it actually possesses. He has, in fact, caused the moon to behave like the sun. A brilliant sun shining through stained-glass windows would be able to carry color in just the way the poet has described. But moonlight is too pale and wan.

Now is this a fault in the poem? I realize that this is a question upon which there may be some room for legitimate difference of opinion. My own answer is no, and if you will read the whole poem through carefully, I think you will agree with me. I think you will find that, in such

a poem as "The Eve of St. Agnes," it is entirely appropriate
that the moon should shine more brilliantly than it shines
out of any earthly sky.

For this poem is not a picture of life as we know it, but
a romantic glorification of that life. In another poem, Keats
himself has stated the principle. Here he pictures the "Bards
and Passion and of Mirth"

> Seated on Elysian lawns
> Browsed by none but Dian's fawns;
> Underneath large blue-bells tented,
> Where the daisies are rose-scented,
> And the rose herself has got
> Perfume which on earth is not.

That is just the way it is in the world of "St. Agnes."
It is not only the moonlight which has gained in brilliancy.
Love is warmer and more passionate. Lovers are bolder.
Girls are more innocent and more uninhibited. Hatred is
fiercer and more unyielding. Night is darker. Cold is more
piercing and more penetrating. Even food is more delicious
and enticing. The comparatively weak moonlight of our
world would be as much out of place here as the comparatively mild and decorous ardors of our own courtship. The
poet has been faithful not to our world (in which his poem
does not exist) but to his own created world. And this is
all that we can reasonably ask of him.

Moreover, he had the wit to choose a theme which is well
suited to this manner of treatment. That theme is young
love. And young love does transform the world, does cause
the commonest aspects of experience to take on all the
color and glamour of a fairyland in romance, beyond anything else that lies within the range of ordinary men and
women. All the romantic poets have known that. Shakespeare knew it. That is why he put into the mouth of

Romeo and Juliet some of the most wildly extravagant language he ever wrote. Quoted out of context that language is strained and ridiculous. Used as Shakespeare used it, it is exquisitely appropriate. These young people are swept away, carried clear out of themselves by an overwhelming experience. The most extravagant words in the language are weak as a means of expressing what they feel about each other.

But suppose now that we were to encounter some such effect as Keats has created in a very different kind of work. Suppose two young lovers, slum-dwellers, in a realistically described American city. Suppose them to be dirty, dishevelled, ignoble people. Suppose their passion not to be idealized, as in Romeo and Juliet and "The Eve of St. Agnes," but presented unsympathetically, as something about as close to mere animalism as young love can get.

Now suppose them to be passing a deserted city church at night. On an impulse, they try the door, not expecting it to be unlocked. But it is, and they go in. And as the girl passes before a rose window, the moonlight, suddenly flooding the glass, stains her with an unearthly glory, throwing "warm gules" upon her "breast," "rose-bloom on her hands," and "soft amethyst" on the cheap ornaments that she is wearing.

That would be just what happens in Keats's poem. It would certainly be no more untrue to fact here than it is in Keats's poem. Yet the reader would almost certainly refuse to accept it. But he would refuse to accept it not because it was not true to life but because it was not true to art.

His refusal, in fact, would be dictated by the same considerations which compelled acceptance in "The Eve of St. Agnes." This time, the effect would be completely out of harmony with the general character of the work under consideration. Indeed, I fear my story suggests nothing else quite so much as those dreadful films that were made in the early days of Technicolor, films mostly in black-and-white which would suddenly and bewilderingly, as they approached a climax, burst forth into a "Technicolor sequence"!

The present writer has tried to teach "The Eve of St. Agnes" to many classes; having brought them to accept the point of view concerning the moonlight episode which has just been outlined (and this generally entails no great difficulty), he has sometimes proceeded to draw upon the blackboard a rough sketch, showing a man climbing the brow of a hill on a windy day. The man is wearing a long cloak which streams out in the wind behind him. But the branches of the tree at the top of the hill are being blown in the opposite direction.

My students generally refuse to accept this picture, even though they have just accepted "The Eve of St. Agnes." And when I, as an artist, insist that I will not be discriminated against, and that I claim for myself the same privileges they have willingly accorded Keats, somebody nearly always insults me by declaring that he *would* accept my picture if it were as good a picture as "The Eve of St. Agnes" is a poem.

That, of course, is only another way of saying that it is all right provided you can get away with it. And if I have a student of painting in the class, he is very likely to point out just here that the extension of the man's cloak in one direction nicely balances the extension of the tree in the other direction, and that this gain is ample justification for my having disregarded faithfulness to nature.

Now I must admit that personally I can see no reason why an artist should not have the privilege of painting a picture in which winds blow in opposite directions at the same time if that is the kind of picture he wishes to paint. But if he avails himself of that privilege, he must realize what he is getting into. A world in which the wind blows in two directions at the same time would also, I should think, be a world in which a man might walk in two directions at the same time. It would be a world in which the branches of trees would grow down as well as up, and in which faces might be worn on the back of the head as well as on the front. Now you might say that this is the kind of world that Lewis Carroll described in *Through the Look-ing-Glass*. But Lewis Carroll was quite clear that he was describing a dream-world. He did not start out to give us a picture of actuality and then falsify it in some particular because he found it convenient to do this in order to secure some particular effect. In other words, the artist who sets out to paint a hill in fairyland has a different problem from the artist who sets out to paint the hill behind the barn. Most people, I believe, would say that the latter assumes obligations from which the former is absolved. One of these might well be to achieve whatever balance he may need in his composition without violating the laws of the world he has chosen to portray.

One point, however, which my students generally fail to perceive unaided is this: Actually, I did not, in my picture, do what Keats did in "The Eve of St. Agnes." Keats merely heightened or intensified nature. I contradicted her. I di-vided her against herself. Here, again, we find that Keats himself, in another connection, stated the principle for us: "I think poetry should surprise by a fine excess, and not by *singularity*."

"Truth" in Romantic Literature

We do have, then, a certain "truth," a certain faithfulness to the facts of experience, even in a work so romantically conceived, and so cavalier in its treatment of actualities, as "The Eve of St. Agnes." And that kind of truth we do, I believe, have a right to expect even of the romantic school.

Take, for example, *The Pilgrim's Progress*, by John Bunyan. Here is the story of a man who made a journey from the City of Destruction to Paradise. On the way, he had many thrilling adventures: he fell into the Slough of Despond; he was attacked by Apollyon; he sojourned in the prison of Giant Despair. Nobody ever made that journey upon this earth, as Bunyan describes it; the whole book is an extended metaphor, an allegory. And yet, in a far deeper sense, thousands, perhaps millions, of people have made that journey. Everyone who has lived and died a Calvinist made that journey; indeed, some of the implications of the book are so broad that they touch all religiously-minded people, whatever their particular creed may be. Who shall say, then, that *The Pilgrim's Progress* is less "true" than *An American Tragedy*, by Theodore Dreiser?

Take another illustration, this time from the modern drama. Take Sir Arthur Wing Pinero's play, *The Enchanted Cottage*. This work deals with the love-life of a shell-shocked soldier and an ugly woman. Laura Pennington and Oliver Bashforth are not tricked into union through the glamour of romance; theirs is purely a marriage of convenience. Each is alone in the world; neither has anybody else to care for; on purely prudential grounds, they decide to merge their lives. For some time they live restlessly in the Enchanted Cottage, that favorite haunt of dead lovers, haunted by visions of a kind of life which they know they can never attain. Then, one day, Oliver looks at Laura and finds that she is no longer ugly. The thick lips, the heavy nose, the clumsy body are gone; Laura has become radiantly beautiful. At the same time, Laura begins to see

Oliver in a new light. His legs are not twisted any more, and he shows no signs of the strain of his war experience. Both persons are now fit denizens of the Enchanted Cottage.

That, surely, is romanticism, naked and unashamed! Nothing like it has ever happened on earth! But are we sure? What is Pinero saying except that love beautifies the beloved object, that the eyes of love are not the eyes of the world, that the lover sees clearly that which others cannot discern at all? And considered merely on the level of fact, is not this quite as true as this other fact: that somewhere, yesterday, a drunken motorist killed a child?

As a matter of fact, Pinero is using a very old and always popular narrative situation. It was already old when Chaucer used it in "The Wife of Bath's Tale." Mme. Le Prince de Beaumont did wonderful things with it in that most profound and moving of all the French fairy tales, "Beauty and the Beast." In the older forms of the story, we have a human being under the spell of an actual enchantment, from which deliverance can only be achieved through love. Sometimes it is a man who has been transformed and sometimes a woman. Pinero doubled the situation, transforming both the man and the woman, and at the same time he rationalized it and made a parable of it; his title-page carries the subtitle "A Fable in Three Acts." But the essential meaning of the old story has not been altered.

The Criterion of Beauty

So much, then, for Truth. What now of the Beautiful?

The problem might, a priori, seem a very simple one. If the artist would create beauty, what is there to it except that he should admit into his picture only those elements which comprise beauty—whatsoever is pure, lofty, and of good report?

This, in effect, is what many artists have tried to do,

especially during periods when the general literary temper was idealistic, and when even moral "teaching" through literature was likely to consist in holding up an ideal for emulation rather than a horrible example which we must avoid. Thus the famous dramatic critic of the New York *Tribune*, William Winter (1836-1917), uncompromising foe of the modern realistic drama and a great power in his day, wrote of Julia Marlowe's Viola in *Twelfth Night:* "Viola is a perfect ideal of beauty, and such an ideal, suitably presented on the stage, as it was by Miss Marlowe, sinks into the mind, remains in the memory, and beneficently influences the conduct of life."

There is much more to be said for this ideal than is likely to be perceived by the young critic who imagines that both life and literature changed suddenly, about 1925, greatly to the improvement of both, probably because he happened to be born in that year. But there are certainly great difficulties in applying it in an age in which, whether we like it or not, most writers tacitly assume that the materials of their art, however they treat them, must be drawn from actual life.

Furthermore, even the idealists recognize the need of contrasts in art. If there were nothing sour in the world, we should probably have no conception of sweetness. If everything were red, we might well have no color sense at all. And if there were no evil in life, it would certainly be much more difficult to form any vital conception of good. Even in a work like *The Faerie Queene*, idealized virtue is, therefore, likely to be balanced by idealized villainy, just as many sizes larger than life. Good examples of this tendency in modern literature may be found in the novels of E. R. Eddison (1882-1945)—*The Worm Ouroboros, Mistress of Mistresses*, and *A Fish Dinner in Memison*. Eddison, who liked to lay the scenes of his novels in Zimiamvia, probably came closer than any other writer of our time to conducting himself as if the realistic movement had never existed. His affinities were all with Greek epic and Icelandic saga. What the typical modern critic is likely to feel about writers who concern themselves largely with moonlight and roses is that they are guilty of evading life and of using their art as a means of buying exemption from it. There has been so much cheap, dishonest, artificial optimism in popular American literature, and so much shying away from the consideration of real evils, that one can hardly blame those writers who, by way of reaction against this, have gone to the other extreme of bitterness and negation. There have been times, of late years, when the field of imaginative creation has tended to take on the character of a dumping ground. Here sores and deformities have been perpetually on exhibition, with every attractive face as carefully veiled as those of Mohammedan ladies; here dirty linen is aired in public, without the use of either deodorizers or disinfectants; here, as James Lane Allen might have put it, we go about emptying our ashcans over one another's heads.

One may, as I say, understand how this tendency has come about without completely sympathizing with it, or even without feeling that the writers involved have behaved very intelligently. Because one admits the reality of scorpions is one obliged to deny the reality of butterflies? And does the undeniable existence of the Gobi Desert automatically cancel out Lake Geneva? Is a vision of life which limits itself to scorpions and Gobi Deserts necessarily less partial than a view which limits itself to butterflies and Lake Genevas? "I cannot see the effects you speak of in that landscape," said the lady to the great painter. "In fact, I cannot see anything in your picture at all." "I am well aware of that, Madame," was the serene reply, "but don't you wish you could?" After all, the spiritual aspirations of mankind are here; devotion and honesty and self-sacrifice are a part of human experience just as truly as crime and cruelty and stupidity are a part of human experience. It is true that some men spend their lives in an alcoholic fog, but it is also true that there are men who do not spend their lives in an alcoholic fog. It is true that there are mothers who neglect—and even murder—their children. But most mothers still love their children, and care for them with varying degrees of intelligence and devotion.

Another difficulty which I, at least, have, at this point, with most of our "hard-boiled" writers is that they do not seem to me to have achieved even the special advantages which one might expect a "hard-boiled" writer to achieve. In fact, some of them have already taken their places with our most incorrigible sentimentalists. Now it is true that Victorian writers were often very sentimental. But in general they did show some common sense in deciding what they were going to be sentimental about. Dickens, for example, was dreadfully sentimental about Little Nell and Paul Dombey and Tiny Tim. But Dickens was never in any danger of sentimentalizing Daniel Quilp or Uriah Heep. Ernest Hemingway, on the other hand, has sentimentalized the bull-ring, reading lofty moral meanings into all the stinking, bloody killing that goes on there, glorifying the "art" of men who devote their lives to devising rhythmic and colorful means of inflicting hideous tortures and a horrible death upon helpless animals. John Steinbeck can, in effect, shed more tears over the death of a psychopathic idiot who ought never to have been born than Dickens shed over Little Nell, Paul Dombey, and Tiny Tim put together.

Beauty and Terror

Beauty in literature, it is time to remind ourselves, is not necessarily limited or restricted to what we ordinarily think of as beautiful—certainly not "pretty"—things. A physician may speak of a "beautiful operation," having witnessed horrors which would cause many admirers of "hard-boiled" literature to "pass out" alongside any delicate Victorian spinster you might care to name. What was "beautiful" in such an instance was, of course, the operating surgeon's masterly technique, the ease and boldness with which he entered the house of life, the courage and self-mastery with which he conducted himself in areas where one false move, one momentary, nerve-induced disability, might well have cost the patient his life. And there is a moral element, too, in the admiration which such a sight awakens, for here is a man who, in the performance of his professional duty, has risen above ordinary human weaknesses and limitations, and who may even, in the case of the more difficult and experimental types of operation, have dared to attempt the impossible—and bring it off.

Beauty shows in the artist's mastery over recalcitrant materials in literature also, and if the materials themselves are terrible, our sense of admiration for the writer may well be increased. Unity, symmetry, and proportion are nobler and more fundamental elements in beauty than mere charm or decorative quality; "the father of rhythm," says the old sage, "is God." We shall have occasion to consider this matter later in connection with great tragedy; the satisfactions referred to can exist also on a lower level, as in the accomplished tales of Edgar Allan Poe or William Faulkner.

How far the sense of beauty can be divorced from the moral element is a very nice question however. The problem does not arise in connection with the operation, for the surgeon is the very type of the man of good will, daring greatly to heal and to save. But it does arise in other connections. Americans (some of whom, unhappily, were soon to be shown up as no more sensitive in such matters than he) were greatly shocked when the son of Mussolini frankly described how much he had enjoyed bombing Abyssinians from the air. It seems that the shape of the bombs' explosion, as they struck the earth, was very satisfying to his aesthetic sense. Objectively considered, an atomic explosion is probably very beautiful—that magnificently aspiring mushroom growth, opening like a rose. But in view of the menace the atomic bomb has brought to mankind, only a monster or a half-wit could feel free to view the phenomenon from the aesthetician's point of view. Yet the writer himself well remembers a night, early in World War II, when coming suddenly round a bend in the road, in a state on the Pacific Coast, he found spread out before him, some hundreds of feet below, and away on the other side of the river, in illumination of breath-taking beauty, what seemed, from that distance, a veritable glimpse of fairyland. Certainly no stage designer had ever been set free to spend the money necessary to create such a magnificent effect. It was a munitions plant, where men and women were working around the clock to produce the means of destroying life ever more rapidly and efficiently. And I should have remembered that Longfellow had seen this horror at a less advanced stage of development, more than a hundred years before, when he visited an arsenal, and had not only discerned beauty in it but drawn beauty out of it:

> This is the Arsenal. From floor to ceiling,
>   Like a huge organ, rise the burnished arms;
> But from their silent pipes no anthem pealing
>   Startles the villages with strange alarms.
>
> Ah! what a sound will rise, how wild and dreary,
>   When the death-angel touches those swift keys!
> What loud lament and dismal Miserere
>   Will mingle with their awful symphonies!

It is the function of art, as has been observed, to give aesthetic pleasure, and no piece of writing exists as a work of art until it has done this. Longfellow gives such pleasure in "The Arsenal at Springfield" (only the first two stanzas of which have been quoted here), in spite of the fact that a large part of his space is devoted to evoking a vision war's terrors through the ages. The use of the extended figure of speech upon which the poem is based—the implied comparison between the store of munitions piled up in the arsenal and the pipes of a great organ—is a literary device. By using it, the poet impresses the horror of war upon our minds much more powerfully than we should have felt it if we had merely heard somebody say, "Isn't it terrible that all these things should be piled up here for destructive purposes!" Yet the more we feel the horror, the more successful we judge the poem to have been.

Beyond Beauty

The function of art is to create beauty and to give the reader the satisfaction which the contemplation of true beauty, in any form, always evokes. But we do not need Matthew Arnold to remind us that it is also the function of art to achieve an "interpretation of life."

There is a great deal of art which has no function save to bring before us, for our delight, that which it is a pleasure to see or to possess. And the joys which we thus encounter should be received with thankfulness whether it is a pleasant thought which is in question or a pretty girl. But few good critics, I think, would feel that a work of art which does only this could deserve to be placed in absolutely first rank.

What of the works which can be so placed? What of the best of the Greek tragedies? Shakespeare's greatest plays? *The Divine Comedy? The Ring of the Niblungs?* Beauty?

Yes—beauty to burn! But more than beauty. Is there not, beyond the beauty, and through it, and above it, a passionate striving toward the interpretation of life—that life which, though nobody has ever succeeded in defining it— is something of which beauty, marvelous though it is, is only a part?

But let us forget interpretation for the moment and return to beauty. Even here *The Divine Comedy* would be a case in point. Quite without reference to its overwhelming spiritual meaning, *The Divine Comedy* is one of the most sheerly beautiful creations that humanity has achieved. But where in literature will you find more loathsome and distressing images than appear in the first part of *The Divine Comedy?*

Why do we accept them here? Why are they more effective here than in Edgar Lee Masters's *Domesday Book*, for example, or even the stories of Poe and Faulkner which have already been spoken of as triumphs in this kind? Partly, no doubt, because Dante was, as everybody would admit, a greater writer than any of these others. But partly, too, I think, because Dante does not stop where they stop. His vision of life is wider and deeper and more comprehensive and more satisfying: with him, hell is only a prologue to heaven.

For my part, I am quite ready to concede the artist's right to make me suffer. He may break my heart if need be—and if he can. What I do insist upon is that I must not be made to suffer frivolously or perversely; neither do I care to be dragged through seas of muck and filth simply because the author happens to have a taste for that kind of scenery. There is a great difference between submitting yourself to the vision of an artist who has achieved a fair and comprehensive vision of life and going along with the maunderings of a psychopath who is no less a case of arrested development because he happens, in the technical sense, to be able to write.

Theme and Treatment

The artist's purpose—the reader's assessment of his purpose—and the writer's own success in achieving it—the degree to which his work contains the Good, the True, and the Beautiful; thus far we have come. What else should we keep in mind in our evaluation of the quality of literature?

It would seem that, other things being equal, a book with a great theme would stand on a higher level than a book with a small theme. And a great theme is a theme which deals with the essentials of human character and conduct. A great theme is a primal theme, a theme of universal interest, a theme which concerns humanity, not just a little group of men living at a particular time in a particular place.

Here, again, one returns to Shakespeare. Why have Shakespeare's plays lived in the theater while Ben Jonson's, for example, have died? Because Shakespeare was a greater playwright? Technically I am not sure that he was. It is true, of course, that he had more charm. But Jonson himself stated the very best reason when he wrote the line that Sothern and Marlowe used to display like a banner across the top of their curtain: "He was not of an age, but for all time."

You need a dictionary of Elizabethan English—and a good knowledge of Elizabeth's London—to understand *Bartholomew Fair*. But the passionate ambition that surges through Macbeth, the bitter jealousy that consumes Othello —this is not something that you can learn out of books. *King Lear*, perhaps the greatest of Shakespeare's plays, is not Elizabethan at all in the sense in which *Every Man in His Humour* or Chapman's *An Humourous Day's Mirth* is Elizabethan. It is basic, elemental. The characters wander about in a kind of indefinite no-man's-land which must have been almost as much of a foreign country to the Elizabethans as it is to us.

Yet the value of the theme depends absolutely upon the treatment. Better by far a small theme, adequately developed, than a great theme which the writer has "funked." One of the reasons for the failure of much popular literature lies just here: writers will persist in choosing themes which they are not competent to handle. Mother love, for example, is one of the greatest subjects in the world. And nine times out of ten it is handled mawkishly.

In general, writers would seem to stand much less in need of great experiences than of a great attitude toward experience. Human beings have a way of making their experiences—as materials for art, at any rate—just as wide and just as deep as they need to be. Perhaps the truth is that there are no commonplace experiences but only commonplace people. To commonplace people the coming of Christ itself may be commonplace. They are like Mark Sabre's wife in A. S. M. Hutchinson's novel, *If Winter Comes:* "One was born, one lived, one died. What was there odd about it?" On the other hand, everything that happens to the extraordinary person is extraordinary. Thoreau travelled extensively in Concord. Jane Austen's was the limited village experience of an English spinster, yet she became one of the great novelists of the world. Browning was inspired to write his greatest work, *The Ring and the Book,* when he inadvertently came across the records of a sordid, long-forgotten murder trial.

The Importance of Form

Form, too, is important in the creation—and preservation—of literature. It is not enough that you have perceived, or even set down, beauty or truth. The world is crammed with beauty, alongside of, and interpenetrating, all its ugliness. Sometimes it seems as if there were less wisdom, but however that may be, neither you nor I may claim a monopoly of it. If our expression of truth, of beauty, of any other good thing, is to survive, it must be because we have been able to give it an embodiment which, in one way or another, is so attractive in itself that men are not willing to let it go out of their lives.

Form is easy to appreciate in a limited, minutely organized, highly developed type of work like the sonnet; we are less conscious of it in more elaborate, more loosely-organized works. But even here, when the problems of structure and development have not been solved successfully, we are all aware that something is wrong. Is it because the various portions of the work have not been proportionately developed, in their proper relationship with each other? (Henry James harshly declares of his own books that he always has a tendency to make the head and trunk too long and the legs too short!) Or is it because a situation which has been elaborately prepared for fails to come off, as when Scott devotes a large part of the opening chapters of *Guy Mannering* to the tiresome business of the astrologer, who is to have nothing of importance to do with the story? Or is it because a character, perhaps out of regard to the needs of the plot, is made to behave in an utterly unconvincing manner, as when Lucy Gayheart, in Willa Cather's novel of that title, is made to lie to her lover, in a fit of pique, about her relations to another man?

Of course this does not mean that a work in which such a flaw appears must therefore be rejected as worthless. Very few books and very few people possess all the good qualities, and though it is, unfortunately, not possible for a woman to marry one man for his dependability and another for his charm, there is nothing to prevent any of us from reading Emerson for his idealism and Montaigne for his level-headed sense of reality. Scott rarely mastered the problem of structure; he is one of the greatest novelists who ever lived not because of this fact but in spite of it.

Many years ago, I saw a silent film based on Zane Grey's novel, *Wanderer of the Wasteland*. I specify the film because I have not read the book and do not know, therefore, to what extent the author's own work was transferred to the screen. In *Wanderer of the Wasteland* as I saw it, a man spent years in a life of restless roaming because he had accidentally killed another man and feared apprehension by the law. Comes a time when he falls in love with a fine woman, who loves him in return, and to whom he confesses his past. She convinces him that the only honest and practicable thing is to return to the scene of the accident and give himself up. Having done this, he finds not only that the boom town involved and its authorities have entirely disappeared but also that he never did kill the man at all; for all these years, he had been laboring under a misapprehension.

Now it is easy to see how such a situation might be used by a master as an ironic commentary on human life. Guy de Maupassant did something like that in "The Necklace." But it was not so employed here. The happy ending was only an easy way out; it opened up the way for the heroine to tumble into the hero's arms in the last few feet of film.

What, then, did the film *Wanderer of the Wasteland* say about life? If it said anything, it said this: It is only necessary in this world to *want* to do right. You will not actually be called upon to suffer for your ideals or to live up to your convictions. Just see that your heart is right; make a gesture. If you do that, nothing can harm you. Everything will come out the way you want it, even if towns have to be razed from the face of the earth to bring it about.

You cannot say that something like that could not happen. It probably has happened more than once. But the implications of the situation that was presented here are completely false. It all added up to that particular kind of possibility which is so much less true, in art, than any complete impossibility could ever be.

Furthermore, the film lacked unity of tone. What was the use of all the agony if this was to be the outcome? The audience goes away with the uneasy sense of having been tricked. A thoroughly artificial situation has been devised as a means of playing upon our emotions under false pretenses. The result of the whole experience is sheer emotional waste.

If the reader will compare this feeling of emotional letdown with the sense of *katharsis* that may sweep through us at the end of a great Greek tragedy, he will begin to understand the difference between real tragic emotion and this illegitimate, synthetic substitute for it which, unhappily, is the closest approach to it that many readers ever come to know.

To all this, I am immediately constrained to add, however, that what happens at the end of *Wanderer of the Wasteland* is no worse than the ending of many an Elizabethan tragedy, where we find the stage strewn with dead bodies simply because it is the tradition of the tragic drama that people must die. There is a delightful story about a troubled student who, not having read Professor Stoll, still believed Elizabethan drama to be logical, and who, therefore, asked her instructor what a certain Elizabethan tragic character "died of." "He died," was the frivolous, but accurate, reply, "of the fifth act." Well, insofar as any character in a tragedy dies only of the fifth act, a structural weakness in the play is indicated. "Unhappy endings," in other words, are no more "artistic" per se than happy endings.

Which is called for depends entirely upon what has preceded. Both must be prepared for; both must develop logically out of the situation which has been described.

"Fame's Great Antiseptic," Style

Good literature, again, is marked by style. A man's style is simply his way of saying things—the perfect word in the perfect place, Swift calls it—but the whole mystery of literary creation is there. What is a man's personality if not his point of view, his way of looking at things and of expressing himself, an attitude toward experience which is just a little different from that of anybody else on earth? In those who express themselves in literature, this distinctive quality is reflected in style. Hence it comes about that we say the style is the man.

No man's style can be imitated exactly by another man (except on the level of burlesque and parody) because no man is another man. George Eliot and Charles Reade each wrote a great novel about Renaissance Italy, and both worked up an elaborate background in the period. Joseph Shearing and Rachel Field each wrote a novel about the Praslin murder. But *Romola* and *The Cloister and the Hearth* are not at all the same kind of book, nor will *Forget-Me-Not (The Strange Case of Lucile Cléry)* give you the same reading experience as *All This and Heaven Too*. Some people even think Hawthorne treated the Praslin murder obliquely in *The Marble Faun*, and that is altogether different again.

The really fine stylist's mark is upon everything that he has written. Third- or fourth-rate scribblers all write pretty much alike, but an artist does not need to sign his work; it is signed for him automatically in every line. "I have a friend," writes John Livingston Lowes, "a distinguished man of letters, whose expression is so individual that a single line on a post card will unconsciously and infallibly betray his authorship."

. . . Who shall say which style is the best? [asks John Burroughs]. What can be better than the style of Huxley for his purpose,—sentences level and straight like a hurled lance; or than Emerson's for his purpose,—electric sparks, the sudden, unexpected epithet or tense, audacious phrase, that gives the mind a wholesome shock; or than Gibbon's for his purpose,— a style like solid masonry, every sentence cut four square, and his work, as Carlyle said to Emerson, a splendid bridge, connecting the ancient world with the modern; or than De Quincey's for his purpose,—a discursive, round-about style, herding his thoughts as a collie dog herds sheep; or than Arnold's for his academic spirit,—a style like glass; or than Whitman's for his continental spirit,—the processional, panoramic style that gives the sense of mass and multitude? Certain things we may demand of every man's style—that it shall do its work, that it shall touch the quick. To be colorless like Arnold is good, and to have color like Ruskin is good; to be lofty and austere like the old Latin and Greek authors is good, and to be playful and discursive like Dr. Holmes is good; to be condensed and epigrammatic like Bacon pleases, and to be flowing and copious like Macaulay pleases. Within certain limits the manner that is native to the man, the style that is a part of himself, is what wears best. What we do not want in any style is hardness, glitter, tumidity, superfetation, unreality.[4]

I have said that it is impossible for one man to imitate another except on the level of parody or burlesque. Why this should be so is one of the mysteries. Even Henry James was amused by Max Beerbohm's consummate take-off on his later style, "The Mote in the Middle Distance," in *A Christmas Garland*. When Caruso heard Cissie Loftus's imitation of himself, he put his finger on her chest and cried

[4] John Burroughs, "Style and the Man," in *Literary Values and Other Papers* (Houghton Mifflin, 1902). See, also, J. Middleton Murry, *The Problem of Style* (Oxford University Press, 1922).

out in astonishment, "My voice—it's in there!" Yet Miss Loftus was never able to take Caruso's place at the Metropolitan.

It may help us to understand this matter of style more clearly—and it ought certainly to be amusing on its own account—if we look briefly at some good burlesques. Let us turn to John Masefield's lecture on Chaucer. Masefield's basic situation is very simple: "The Rat sat on the Mat" and "The Cat came in." But different poets might treat this situation in completely different styles. Thus:[5]

The Homeric poet might use such an incident to preserve tribal legend:

> The Rat and Cat strode forward, girded with·gleaming bronze
> And when they were near each other, first Rat shouted:
> "Ho, Trojan Cat, now shall my pitiless spear point
> Tear you, and I will take your armour for mine
> And fling your corpse far into eddying Xanthos
> For the little fishes and twirling eels to pluck at."
> So saying he hurled his great long-shadowing spear
> Nor did he miss, but struck on the bossy shield,
> Great, knopp'd with silver, bronze-bound, seven bulls' hides
>   thick,
> Which Ares wrought for Ilos in pleasant Ida
> And Ilos gave it to Phylax who dwell'd in Lycia
> By the black-flowing holy waters of far Kayster.
> But him the horses of God killed in the mountain,
> The golden horses that crop the undying grass
> In the glens where the Nymphs go dancing and singing songs.

Dante, shall we say, might take the tale as an illustration in some part of his system:

> Within that seventh circle of red hell
> There came what seemed a squeak, and looking near,

[5] From *Recent Prose*, by John Masefield. Copyright, 1933, by The Macmillan Company, and used with their permission.

Lo, a black-visaged Cat, exceeding fell,
Who on the shadow of a Rat made cheer.
Then I, to my sweet Guide, said, "Master, tell,
If it be not forbidden, what are these
Shades dim as faces not remembered well?"
Then he to me: "The active influences
Acquire on the heart good power or bad.
This is the end of too much love of cheese."

Or coming nearer home, William Wordsworth might take the tale and mix it with morality and mountains in an address to Samuel Taylor Coleridge:

O Friend, as we descended to our tea,
The mountains spoke to us of these high things
And the red sunset sang: deep thoughts were ours
Of Man and Nature: Man's unconquer'd Will
And Nature: topic vast: poetic theme.
When lo, by Wilkinson's green cabbage-plot
A village Idiot Boy, swinging a Rat
Which my Companion's Cat has lately kill'd,
Brought sudden horror into both our Minds.[5]

Beginning students of Shakespeare are often rather distressed when they discover that the dramatist had the habit of borrowing his plots. They wonder why he did not invent them, and their respect for him as an artist may suffer considerable diminution in consequence. The remedy for this state of mind is very simple: it is only necessary to read a few of Shakespeare's sources or some of the other works in similar stories are related. Here, by way of example, is Shakespeare's beautiful description of the death of Ophelia, as announced by the Queen, in *Hamlet*:

> *Queen.* One woe doth tread upon another's heels
> So fast they follow. Your sister's drown'd, Laertes.
> *Laertes.* Drown'd! O, where?

Queen. There is a willow grows aslant a brook,
That shows his hoar leaves in the glassy stream.
There with fantastic garlands did she come
Of crow-flowers, nettles, daisies, and long purples
That liberal shepherds give a grosser name,
But our cold maids do dead men's fingers call them;
There, on the pendent boughs her coronet weeds
Clamb'ring to hand, an envious sliver broke,
When down the weedy trophies and herself
Fell in the weeping brook. Her clothes spread wide,
And, mermaid-like, a while they bore her up;
Which time she chanted snatches of old tunes,
As one incapable of her own distress,
Or like a creature native and indued
Unto that element. But long it could not be
Till that her garments, heavy with their drink,
Pull'd the poor wretch from her melodious lay
To muddy death.

Laertes. Alas, then, is she drown'd?

Queen. Drown'd, drown'd.

Laertes. Too much of water hast thou, poor Ophelia,
And therefore I forbid my tears. But yet
It is our trick. Nature her custom holds,
Let shame say what it will; when these are gone,
The woman will be out. Adieu, my lord;
I have a speech of fire that fain would blaze,
But that this folly douts it.

Now turn to the same incident in the debased German version of the Hamlet-story, *Fratricide Punished (Der Bestrafte Brudermord)*. Here Ophelia's death is announced as follows:

Queen. Gracious lord and king, I have to announce to you a great calamity!

King. Heaven forbid! What is it?

Queen. Ophelia went up a high hill, and threw herself down, and killed herself.

Leonhardus (= Laertes). Alas! Unfortunate Leonhardus! thou hast lost within a short space of time both a father and a sister! Whither will misfortune lead thee? I could for grief wish myself dead.

Now what are the differences between Shakespeare and this petulant, insensitive drivel? A sufficiently insensitive reader might reply that the difference is merely that in one account Ophelia is drowned while in the other she is killed by a fall from a high place. And, indeed, that is the only important difference there is, except one thing—STYLE!

These illustrations would seem to testify more eloquently to the importance and value of style than a ream of discussion.

The Question Period

That, really, is the end of this particular lecture. But the lecturer can tell by the expression on people's faces that they are expecting a question-and-answer period. And he is more than ordinarily inclined to hold this because he perceives that there are a few places where he would like to clean up after himself.

1. Are any absolute judgments possible in literature? and if not, then isn't one man's opinion just as good as another's?

Absolute judgments in the sense in which the absolute exists in mathematics, no. Literature deals with human beings. Human beings are infinitely complex and variable, and nobody who has any sense would ever claim that he completely understands another. It is doubtful, indeed, that any of us completely understand ourselves. That is why it is that when we come to a really great and many-sided piece of literature like *Hamlet*, no critic can be expected to agree completely with any other critic. For this reason, the final essay on *Hamlet* will never be written, and even you and I may reasonably expect to be able to say something about it which has not been said before, and which other readers may find helpful and enlightening—provided, that is, that we do not go off on some wild tangent, or commit ourselves to some interpretation so patently wrong-headed and unsupported by the text of the play itself, that we shall find ourselves shedding not light but darkness.

Yet we do achieve agreement on many points. *Hamlet* does not mean the same thing to everybody, but everybody whose opinion matters will agree that *Hamlet* is a great play. Presumably there are people who consider Ella Wheeler Wilcox to have been a greater poet then Whitman, or who find Edgar Guest more stimulating than Shelley. But as soon as this point of view has been expressed, we know at once that it would be a waste of time to listen to anything that that man might have to say about literature. Edgar Guest thinks of himself not as a poet but as a newspaperman who writes verses. I once had a friend, a clergyman, who seriously assured me that as a creator of character, Shakespeare had been quite equalled by Harold Bell Wright, who was then at the height of his vogue as a popular novelist. I always took pains thereafter to keep the conversation in the field of religion, where my friend knew what he was talking about.

But competent judges agree about more than the mere presence or absence of quality in literary work. We should all agree, for example, that Shakespeare is more genial, more worldly, more companionable than Dante. "Shakespeare," says John Jay Chapman, "is full of the sun and of the present; Dante of the planets and the starry heavens, of the past and the future. Shakespeare is Day; Dante, Night." We should all agree, I think, that Milton's poetry has a grandeur which is not to be found in the excellent verses of Robert Herrick; that Fielding is more aristocratic than Richardson; that Dickens has more gusto than Thackeray; that D. H. Lawrence was more passionately in earnest than Sir James Barrie; and that there is a devotional spirit in Christina Rossetti which is altogether lacking in Edna St. Vincent Millay. All this still leaves the way open for a great many disagreements concerning these writers, but the disagreements themselves exist in a pattern of agreement. Moreover, not all these disagreements are real. Some are due to semantic confusion, some to prejudice, personal idiosyncrasy, or original sin—just plain "cussedness" on the critic's part. A critic has often attempted to overthrow the conclusions of a predecessor in order to present an interpretation which is entirely reconcilable with these conclusions.

On the other hand, it is certainly not true that because complete agreement cannot be achieved, then one man's opinion is as good as another. The value of an opinion always depends upon the qualifications of the person who holds it—his information and his good judgment. There are some people in the world who do not know enough to have an opinion on any subject, and there is nobody who is so wise that his opinions on every subject are entitled to respect. What fools some great scientists have made of themselves when giving us the benefit of their wisdom on politics or religion! And specialists in other fields have done quite as badly.

When a difference in interpretation appears concerning which expert judgment is necessary, then all the layman can do, in literary criticism as in any other field, is to consult the experts. Now it is quite true that such disagreements cannot be settled by majorities, but it is also true that six sensible, well-informed men are somewhat less likely to go off on the same tangent at the same moment than any one of them.

2. *In speaking of Wordsworth's* Lyrical Ballads, *you pointed out that Wordsworth, in his Preface, has told us what he meant to do in that work. But most authors do not write that kind of a preface. When the author does not tell us, how can we be sure what he means? Does the author himself always know what he means?*

When the author has not declared himself, there is, at least, more room for difference of interpretation. I mean, of course, where obscurity appears, since the most important piece of evidence bearing upon the author's intention is the work itself. But you need not, therefore, despair. In the case of many of the more famous writers, we have biographies, letters, journals, records of conversations, etc., in all of which we may find valuable clues to the author's mind and his intention.

This is the kind of material that scholars work with. That is what literary scholarship means, and that is why a scholarly interpretation is more valuable than mere impressionistic chatter, such as essays on "What ———— Means To Me." This is what George Edward Woodberry meant when he said that the highest form of criticism was aesthetic criticism, "by which I may at last become one with the soul of the artist and see his vision with the meaning and atmosphere it had to himself." But he immediately felt constrained to add that it was only through using the methods of historical scholarship that this vision could be achieved.

Now with many writers not all the evidence is in—or ever will be in—and we should always be ready for new light from any quarter. A true scholar holds all his opinions tentatively, recognizing that they must be subject to revision either as new evidence may be presented or as somebody may be able to show that previously existent evidence has been misinterpreted.

Of late years there has been some controversy about the meaning of Henry James's story, "The Turn of the Screw." Traditionally this has always been interpreted as a ghost story. But a school of critics arose who sought to overthrow this interpretation. It was not subtle enough to please them. The ghosts, they said, existed only in the mind of the narrator, the governess who tells the story. James was, therefore, not writing a ghost story: he was making a study of a psychopathic personality, a woman suffering from sexual starvation.

This view was never very reasonable, and few reasonable people accepted it. But when, in 1947, James's *Notebooks* were published, containing an entry for January 12, 1895, in which the idea developed in "The Turn of the Screw" was described in terms which committed James, at the outset at least, to thinking of his piece as a ghost story, then the case against the Freudian interpretation was certainly strengthened.

If the author is living, he may be consulted upon doubtful points. Teaching Walter de la Mare's story, "The Riddle," I repeatedly encountered a difference of opinion as to the symbolic meaning of the disappearance of the children in the oak chest. Some people thought the incident indicated death; others felt that it might well represent the children's growing up and going out into the world to establish a new life. I put the question to Mr. de la Mare, who replied, "Yes, I did mean to indicate that the children died." So that settled that. But when I went on to ask him whether the Grandmother in the story had been intended as a sinister figure, another point on which differences had appeared, he was less conclusive. The Grandmother, he said, "was not meant to be more sinister than—well, than she appears."

If the author is dead, the recollections of his friends may be of value, though naturally such evidence must be used with caution. A recent "novelized biography" described a love affair between a famous American painter and a great art-collector, both now deceased. But one of the painter's Boston friends has declared that not only did he not have a love affair with the lady in question but heartily disliked her.

When all these sources of information fail us, there will still, in the case of those who have produced any quantity of work, be the testimony of the product as a whole to guide us—what James called the writer's "figure in the carpet." This, of course, does not exist in the case of a new writer. But it would be very difficult to make any intelligent reader of Shakespeare believe that any particular utterance in a particular play must be interpreted as committing the writer to some form of authoritarianism. We know Shakespeare well enough to be sure that whatever else he may have been, he was no authoritarian. He was a free spirit, if any man ever was.

As to whether the author knew what he meant, he must have known at least what was in his conscious mind. It is true that the creative imagination can play strange tricks with a man. He may build better than he knows. ("Did I really write that?" we sometimes ask, coming upon our own forgotten work in later years.) He may, too, under the spell of what we sometimes call "inspiration," reach a plane he never knew he had even aspired to. I do not believe that Shelley was "converted," in the course of writing "Adonais," from the pantheistic to the Christian view of immortality; I believe, rather, that he was driven, towards the end of the poem, to express, or to imply, the Christian view, simply because there is no other view which is emotionally satisfying. The poem is a lament for the dead Keats.

Now when you die, one of two things happens: either you go on living on another plane, or else death is the end of you. There is no use trying to straddle the fence and say, as the pantheist does, that you go on living but do not know that you are alive! If you do not know that you are alive, then for all practical purposes you are dead. And this illustration happens to be a case in point because, though we might have gone astray if we had depended upon the testimony of "Adonais" alone, we are saved from misunderstanding by our general knowledge of Shelley's views and beliefs, as derived from other sources.

I am willing to grant, too, that the author need not always understand all the implications of his work: though he' knows what he *meant*, he may not know everything that the work *means*. I have said that there is nothing in the book that does not come from the man. Perhaps it would be more accurate to say that there is nothing in the book that does not come *through* the man. Harriet Beecher Stowe said that God wrote *Uncle Tom's Cabin*; she only set it down. And even the unmystical, hyper-intellectual George Eliot declared that "in all that she considered her best writing, there was a 'not herself' which took possession of her, and that she felt her own personality to be merely the instrument through which this spirit, as it were, was acting."

But let us leave mysticism out of it. A book is the product of the man who writes it. It is also the product of its age. It is the product of the civilization which produced it because that civilization also produced its author. Simply because what it contains may have become commonplace to the author through long familiarity, or because he moves on a higher level than his readers, or for some other reason, he may fail to assess its full significance or to savor its impact as it strikes them.

Yet it is exactly at this point that extreme caution needs

to be exercised. If you are going beyond the printed page to *interpret* your author, how do you know that you are not reading yourself into him? Oddly enough, the better you know him, the more intimately you have lived with him, the more likely is this danger to engulf you; the more you feel at home with him, the harder will it be for you to tell where he leaves off and you begin.

If the author did not know what he meant, at least there is nobody else who is likely to know better than he did what it was that the author meant. Those who had rather be safe than sorry will always be inclined to stop at the bounds of demonstrable knowledge, and when they pass beyond those bounds, they will say frankly that they do not know what the author meant. These people will never be in any danger of finding current villains in the Book of Daniel. They will also, probably, miss a good deal of fun. To venture in dangerous places, trusting to your own surefootedness and common sense to carry you through where others have perished, is undeniably a perilous business. In this it resembles life itself.

3. You speak very contemptuously of the critics who write essays on "What ———— Means To Me." Do you, then, see no value in impressionistic criticism?

Was it Anatole France who described criticism as "the adventures of the soul among masterpieces"? "Impressionistic criticism" is criticism which is not based upon historical knowledge, or background knowledge of any kind; neither does the author pretend to be expounding the work authoritatively, according to any set of judicially or authoritatively established critical principles. He simply reads the work, responds to it, and passes his "impressions" on to the reader. Sometimes this kind of criticism may itself turn out to be literature. That happened with Lamb and Hazlitt. It may even have happened occasionally with H. L. Mencken, who frankly called his critical essays *Prejudices*.

This does not necessarily mean that when these people wrote good literature, they were also writing good criticism. Indeed, their creative gifts may even have stood in the way of their writing good criticism. It is not the primary function of the critic to give us himself; it is rather his function to give us a clearer and stronger view of the work which he has under consideration. Unless the creative writer-turned-critic possesses a much greater capacity for self-abnegation than we generally attribute to creative writers, he is always going to labor under a great temptation to let the other man's work go hang while he proceeds to embark upon his own. Many of Macaulay's essays begin as book reviews. But the book is likely to serve merely as a point of departure, a peg upon which Macaulay hangs his own independent discussion of the subject, or even of some idea which may merely have been suggested by it.

But this is not to say that there is no value whatever in impressionistic criticism. I should expect a Coleridge, a Lamb, a Hazlitt, a Virginia Woolf to be able to find something in a book which I had not been able to find for myself. I should expect them to be able to say something worth saying about what they had found. Even when I did not agree with them, I should expect to be interested in their point of view. Just as I might be interested in the appearance of a great actress in a role for which she was eminently unfitted—Sarah Bernhardt in *Hamlet*, for example. I should think that must have been pretty bad Shakespeare, but it may well have been very good Bernhardt. If I had been about when Madame Sarah was doing it, I should certainly not have stayed at home.

The value of the impressionistic critic, in short, depends entirely upon the depth and interest of his impressions. He has no authority beyond that which inheres in his own perceptions. But if he is a man of genius, he may still well have something to say that is worth considering, even when he is so absurdly and violently prejudiced as D. H. Lawrence was about Galsworthy, for example.

4. Why is it necessary to read the literature of the past? Do you really believe that it is better than what is being written now? If so, why? And if not, why is it necessary to bother with it?

The literature of the past is not necessarily better than the literature of the present, but it does have one very important advantage over the literature of the present: it has proved it survival value.

Only the best of the literature of the past has survived. Only the wheat has been garnered up; the chaff has been blown away. And the sifting process is still going on: we are not interested in all the classical authors that mediaeval readers were interested in. If a writer has survived, you can be sure that men and women still want to read him. And I do not see how you are going to stop them.

The literature of the present has not, in the nature of the case, yet had an opportunity to prove its survival value. I firmly believe that some of it will. But for the time being, the wheat and the chaff are all mixed up together.

Literature, as we have already learned, is a social art, an exercise in communication. And here again the past has an advantage.

When we read Thomas Mann, we have a sense of fellowship with intelligent, forward-looking twentieth-century readers all over the Western world. And that is much. But when we read Virgil, we commune with all the intelligent readers of the last 2,000 years.

You do not see why that is important? I think it is tremendously important. For this is just the kind of thing that delivers us from the provincialism which seizes upon and imprisons those who have never been made to feel at home in anything except their own country and their own time. And it often seems to me that this provincialism—which is a form of provincialism to which "smart," up-to-date, superficially cultured people are peculiarly susceptible—is the most narrowing form of provincialism there is.

Different ages have their own different ways of being provincial. It has happened before this that a whole generation has missed a very important truth of life, and needlessly impoverished itself in a very vital aspect of human experience.

I think we must grant that, simply by virtue of coming after him, Thomas Mann can give you something that Virgil cannot give. Because he inherited the tradition of European civilization to which Virgil so importantly contributed, Thomas Mann almost certainly has a good deal of Virgil in him. On the other hand, Virgil has no Thomas Mann in him. In this sense, I am even willing to grant that Thomas Mann may be, for you, a more important writer than Virgil.

But that fact could not in itself rob Virgil of his importance. Even if Thomas Mann should finally be judged a greater writer than Virgil—and that is something that cannot be settled for a long time yet—still, nobody seriously doubts that Virgil was a great writer. Neither can Thomas Mann ever make himself the voice of Roman civilization. If you are seriously interested in great literature, you wish to read as many great writers as possible. Why should you deprive yourself of what Virgil (and his age) have to give, simply because it is possible for you to read Thomas Mann? or William Butler Yeats? or T. S. Eliot? or James Joyce?

or whoever happens to embody the current notion of what a great modern writer ought to be?

It has often been said that to learn a new language is to gain a new soul. It is, at any rate, to enlarge your knowledge of humanity. Anybody who has ever really learned a second language, ancient or modern, knows that with the language he learned a good deal about the people who used it. Deliberately restrict your reading to one period or country, and you are arbitrarily cutting off vast possibilities of growth through reading.

Man has always been hemmed in by time and space; space he has, of late years, gone far toward conquering. Time is still a problem. It is true that the late J. W. Dunne, a physicist and mathematician who developed a theory of "serial time" which has had considerable influence upon British fiction, speculated fascinatingly about the possibility of travelling in time. So far as most of us are concerned, however, this has hitherto been most satisfactorily achieved in such books as *The Time Machine*, the work of one of the friends of Dunne's early years, H. G. Wells, than it has in actual experience.[6]

Indeed, books always have been an incomparable time machine, and we are very foolish if we do not take a ride. A great book, the product of a bygone civilization, has a great advantage over Wells's machine: it not only takes you to the place where it was written, but it takes you inside the minds of the people who wrote it. I should much

[6] Dunne published *An Experiment with Time* (Macmillan, 1927); *This Serial Universe* (Macmillan, 1938); *The New Immortality* (Harper, 1939); and *Nothing Dies* (Faber, 1940). For further discussion and bibliographical references, see the present writer's *Cavalcade of the English Novel*, pp. 464-465, and his *Six Novels of the Supernatural* (Viking Portable Library, 1944), pp. 776-778. Philip Van Doren Stern's *Travelers in Time* (Doubleday, 1947) is a delightful collection of stories based essentially on Dunne's ideas, though not, in all cases, necessarily indebted to him directly, with an illuminating introduction.

rather read *The Canterbury Tales* than be set down before Canterbury Cathedral, some morning in the fourteenth century, and be left to explore it with my own poor twentieth-century mind.

That great American architect, the late Ralph Adams Cram, well described some of the advantages of such travelling in time in his eloquent introduction to Henry Adams's great book, *Mont-Saint-Michel and Chartres*, which, though ostensibly a study of Gothic architecture, is actually a distinguished probing of the very soul of medieval civilization:

If it gives new and not always flattering standards for the judgment of contemporary men and things [wrote Ralph Adams Cram], so does it establish new ideals, new goals for attainment. To live for a day in a world that built Chartres Cathedral, even if it makes living in a world that creates the "Black Country" of England or an Iron City in America less a thing of joy and gladness than before, equally opens up the far prospect of another thirteenth century in the times that are to come and urges to ardent action toward its attainment.[7]

Matthew Arnold used to be fond of talking about seeing life *"sub specie aeternatatis."* To view life in the light of eternity is an ambitious program, though I grant that, if you want to do a really thorough and satisfying job, nothing else will suffice. But leaving eternity out of it, how many of us are imprisoned in the year, the month, the week, or even the moment! How many people persuade themselves, when calamity comes upon them, not only that they are desperately unhappy now (which, one might think, would be enough), but that life never was worth living, and never can be worth living again! Probably most suicides could be prevented if the subject could be reached at the

---

[7] Henry Adams, *Mont-Saint-Michel and Chartres* (Houghton Mifflin, 1904). "Editor's Note," by Ralph Adams Cram, pp. vii-viii.

psychological moment and persuaded, not to abandon his intention, but simply to postpone carrying it out for, say, six months. Six months is a very long time to hold fast to despair—or any other overwhelming emotion, as many honeymooners have learned.

I believe firmly that no secular means at our disposal can serve us more effectively in escaping from the kind of provincialism I have been discussing here than our ability to explore past ages through reading the literature of the past. Entirely apart from the question of whether or not it is "better" than our own, that is one reason why I think it very important to read such literature.

5. What, if any, is the relationship between literature and morality? Does good literature have to be morally sound?

That, my friend, is a part of the next lecture. And your having asked the question at this point, seems to furnish a good occasion to conclude this one, which, I am sure you will agree, has already run quite beyond all reasonable bounds.

CHAPTER FOUR

The Book and the World

~~~~~~

Two Worlds

The drama—or so Henry James declared incidentally, in one of his Prefaces—is a very tight literary form. "We are shut up wholly to cross-relations, relations all within the action itself; no part of which is related to anything but some other part—save of course by the relation of the total to life."

"The relation of the total to life" is a very suggestive phrase. James here raises a fundamental question, and the considerations involved do not apply to the drama alone.

He reminds us that literature does not create its own frame of reference. It is not, save, in a limited way, a self-containing entity. On the contrary, it represents one plane or aspect of a larger human activity. The world of the printed page exists in, stands over against, a much larger world.

What is the relationship between these two worlds?

Literature and Morality

It is idle to reply that there is no such relationship. This reply has been made from time to time, but even those who make it can hardly intend it to be taken quite literally. Often their statement has no more significance than that of a protest against those who are unable to distinguish between an aesthetic experience and other types of experience, or who refuse to admit or to recognize the legitimacy and dignity of the aesthetic experience itself. As such, it may well be wholesome and necessary. Actually, however, we all know that the relationship—a very complicated and many-sided relationship—does exist.

More than a generation ago, when the shadow of Woodrow Wilson filled the land, there was much talk in the United States about "idealism." And persons unsympathetic toward the policies or the personality of the President were often heard to declare that "Idealism has no place in business or in politics."

Insofar as they meant that success in business or in politics is impossible for impractical men, or for men who do not know how to achieve a meeting of minds with those who must work with them, these persons may well have been right. Some would even argue that the melancholy end of Wilson's own career proved that they were right. Taken literally, however, the statement would have a much more sinister meaning. Taken literally, it would mean that idealism has no real place in life. It is all well enough for dreamers to flatter themselves, or to amuse themselves, by playing with ideals, but you must not expect anybody to take ideals seriously, or to attempt to apply them, or to permit his conduct to be activated by them in the business of living.

Such an "idealism" would soon wither away and die for lack of nourishment. And I fear that an art similarly detached from life would encounter the same fate.

This seems particularly true of the art of literature, which, as we have already seen, is not quite like any other art. Perhaps there are no moral implications in a landscape or in a geometrical design, though not all critics would be willing to grant even that. A design involves, for example, the principle of order, and it would be argued in some quarters that order is itself profoundly meaningful and therefore moral. But nobody would claim that the landscape painter, or the mosaic worker, uses human conduct and human emotion as the very stuff of his art, as the novelist and the playwright do. Neither, of course, does the musician. What Aristotle called "imitation" is a smaller element in music than it is in any other art, with the possible exception of abstract painting. The musician does not reproduce the world. On the contrary, he creates a new one:

> That out of three sounds, he frame, not a fourth sound,
>   but a star,

as Browning's Abt Vogler puts it. To which Walter de la Mare rightly adds,

> When music sounds, gone is the earth I know.

It is for this reason that music is generally regarded as the most creative of all the arts.

But literature is different, and it is different first and foremost because human behavior cannot be described except by reference to an explicit or implicit moral code. Thus Joseph Conrad, opposing overt didacticism in fiction, immediately adds that "every subject in the region of intellect and emotion must have a morality of its own if it is treated at all sincerely; and even the most artful writer will give himself (and his morality) away in about every third sentence."

Moral Referents

This is as true of the nursery tale as it is of the parable, of the melodramatic "thriller" as of the psychological novel. How can you interest yourself vitally in Jack's adventures

in Beanstalk Country unless you feel that stolen goods
should be restored and restitution made for injuries sustained? But these are "moral" attitudes, based upon moral
assumptions. Leave out the element of the monster's riches
having been stolen from Jack's father, and the whole ethical standing-ground of the tale would be importantly
modified, though, to be sure, we might still admire the
young hero for his courage in attacking against enormous
odds (which admiration would, in itself, be a moral attitude). The yarn itself might be as well told even if the
Giant were not a robber, and its appeal to the imagination
might be quite as great, but the nature of the appeal to the
reader would, nevertheless, be modified. The story would
automatically move closer in its appeal to the history of that
other Jack, Jack the Giant-Killer, whose adventures, for
all their exciting quality, do fail to satisfy many readers
on the moral side.

As for melodrama, it has always been on the side of the
angels; indeed, a visit to an old-time melodrama theater (if
we could only find one!), would be one of the most reassuring excursions that could be undertaken by anyone oppressed by doubts concerning the fundamental "rightness"
of human nature. How we hissed the villain! How we
cheered the impossibly perfect hero! How naïvely we accepted the angelic nature of the heroine! Did any popular
dramatist ever try to enlist the sympathies of an audience
on the side of evil? And what would have happened to him
and his play if he had done so?

Our "thrillers" and detective stories are, in some aspects,
the successors of the old melodramas; like them, they have
often been attacked for their sensationalism and preoccupation with violence. In individual cases, this attack has sometimes been justified, but in the larger aspects it falls to the
ground. The writer of "murder stories" would be the last

man among us who could wish to question the sacredness of human life. Once that is gone, his job will be gone along with it. His choice of murder as his particular theme, his realization that upon this foundation alone can a mystery story of ultimate intensity be built, is a perfectly sincere, though oblique, tribute to the sincerity of his faith in the basic postulate of Christian civilization. It is not the writer of detective stories who is in danger at this point. The danger comes rather from the broad-minded, wide-visioned soul who gravely inquires how, in the face of contemporary mass murders, you can expect him to become greatly concerned over the fate of one victim and an imagined victim at that! It is he, not the devotee of detective stories who has been hardened by the horrors of our time, for he confesses, in the very form of the question he asks, that only "real" horrors still retain their power to move him. Worse than that, retail murder itself has grown tame; he has moved over into the wholesale branch of the business.[1]

None of this means that the writer must necessarily hold his morality consciously in mind at all times; the more firmly and unquestioningly he possesses it, the less will he find it necessary to do this. It is sick people, not well people, who think about their health; the accomplished virtuoso does not place the metronome on the piano at the beginning of the concert. Oddly enough, men think more about morality in troubled or transitional times, when there is no widely or generally accepted code, than they do under more settled conditions: thus, the libertarian novelists of today are far more obsessed with moral questions than Jane Austen or Sir Walter Scott. And if the Victorians, too, sometimes seem obsessed in a different way, the reason is,

[1] For a fuller discussion of this matter, see the writer's introduction to his anthology, *Murder by Gaslight*, a collection of Victorian "thrillers," published by Prentice-Hall in 1949.

clearly, that they were already beginning to feel a little unsure of themselves. This is why Virginia Woolf looked back enviously to Scott, who, unlike herself and her contemporaries, had a code which he held without question, and which he so completely assumed his readers to hold without question, that he never even found it necessary to stop to ask himself whether they did or not. This set him free to assume his ethical standing-ground and then disregard it; he was not, like modern novelists, obliged to start from scratch in every book he wrote. The foundations were laid already, and he had the opportunity, denied to them, of going on to erect his superstructure.[2]

Two Kinds of Writer

Considered from this point of view, the writers of the world can be divided into two classes: those who are satisfied with art in itself—and, by implication, themselves satisfied to be artists—and those others who have the feeling, more or less clearly defined, that art must be used as a means of approach to something beyond itself. For those who speak the English language, Chaucer and Shakespeare are the great patron saints of the first group, and of all who write without a sense of "mission" to urge them on, content to use the manifold resources of their art to glorify and to illuminate the manifold, enthralling aspects of human experience in their exhaustless and never-failing variety. The second group is handicapped by the presence of that vast horde of disreputable camp-followers, the avowedly didactic writers, all as diligent to discover the "moral" of everything as the Duchess of *Alice in Wonderland*. Most of these writers are not artists at all, but merely pedagogues.

[2] See Virginia Woolf's essays on "Modern Fiction" and "How It Strikes a Contemporary," in *The Common Reader* (Harcourt, Brace, 1925).

It is the "lesson" upon which their attention is centered, and the aesthetic element in their work, if it exists at all, has been applied like a veneer, or like the sugar coating on a bad-tasting pill.

But we cannot dismiss all those in the second group so cavalierly as this. There are very great writers among them. Dante, for one, who wrote one of the three or four greatest poems in the world to dramatize the theology of St. Thomas Aquinas, and to expound the conditions under which human beings can save their souls. Milton, for another, who created *Paradise Lost* to

> assert Eternal Providence,
> And justify the ways of God to men.

The young Milton was almost as much interested in music as he was in poetry; with his temperament and convictions, it was inevitable that he should finally devote himself to the latter, for you cannot "justify" in music, you cannot argue or reason or convince. Finally, in our own time, we have had, on a less lofty level, but to the profit and delectation of us all, the late Bernard Shaw, who, never remiss in frankness, informed us bluntly that for art's sake alone he would not have faced the labor of writing a single sentence.

Modern Didacticism

Shaw's presence may help us to mark the transition from one kind of didactic writer to another, for it is often far too carelessly assumed that all didactic writers are concerned to defend a conventional religion or morality. As a matter of fact, of course, an attack may be quite as didactic as a defense, and there is a great deal of religious literature that is not didactic at all. The hymn is not, for the most part; it merely expresses, for their own encouragement, the religious aspirations and convictions of the group. The religious lyric, as exemplified outstandingly by George Herbert, is no more didactic than the secular love lyrics, and of course mystics in general have always been notably disinclined toward propaganda.

It has sometimes been urged, with considerable reasonableness, that, in their attitude toward art, the economic radicals are the real Puritans of our time. Always strongly inclined to extend Matthew Arnold's notion that conduct is three-fourths of life another twenty-five per cent and make it all embracing, the Puritans were inclined to feel that art, like everything else which belonged to this world, was of no value for its own sake; if it could be justified at all, it must be upon the ground that it contributed in a subordinate way to moral uplift and spiritual welfare. It was, in other words, a means to an end. The god of the Marxians differs from the Puritan God in that he is in this world and not above it, but he is no less totalitarian in his outlook. Consequently we were hearing a good deal, a few years ago, about "proletarian" novels, and a number of bright young men were lined up to evaluate all fiction on the basis of whether or not it enlisted the author in the "class conflict," and not only that but enlisted him on the right side, that is to say the left side! But this worked out much less happily for the proletarians than it did for the Puritans: the proletarian *Pilgrim's Progress* and *Paradise Lost* are still unwritten. Except for a few very fine Russian films, their product in general has not been impressive. And even here, Sergei Eisenstein, the genius of the Russian film, found himself at last completely out of sympathy with the conditions under which a Soviet artist is expected to create.[3] Meanwhile the general run of proletarian literature has turned out such a dismal business from anybody's point of view that we all seem now to have reached a tacit agree-

[3] See Marie Seton's biography, *Sergei Eisenstein* (A. A. Wyn, 1952).

ment that the less we say about the whole matter, the better it will be for all of us.

Didactic and Creative

But what shall be said of didactic literature in general? Whatever the shortcomings of such novels as *Uncle Tom's Cabin, Quo Vadis?, Ben-Hur,* and *The Robe* may be, it would be ridiculous to pretend that they would be better books than they are if the didactic element were taken out of them. If the didactic element were taken out of them, the vitality of the book would go with it. If the didactic impulse had been lacking, the book would never have come into being at all. In these instances, it was the didactic urge which inspired the creative urge.

A priori, then, there is no reason whatever why the didactic urge and the creative urge should not occasionally coincide. There is certainly no reason why the creative and the religious urge should not coincide. This has happened again and again, and it has produced much fine literature. But it must always be remembered that a book cannot be a fine religious novel, or for that matter a fine any-other-kind-of novel, without first being a fine novel. It must have been written by a fine writer. There is no substitute for that. We cannot accept good intentions as a surrogate for a well-told story. We cannot permit a devotional spirit to take the place of the ability to create believable characters. We cannot even assume that a man is going to be able to write good religious literature simply because he is a deeply and sincerely religious man. Even if he is a writer, his religion may express itself in other ways. Oliver Wendell Holmes was, I think, a sincerely religious man, but his muse turned more naturally to *vers de société* than it did to hymns. And when the didactic or religious element and the creative element do not coincide, when the one is, as it were, superimposed upon the other, either because there is something in the writer himself which tells him he "ought" to do it, or because the "demands of the market" seem to make it necessary, then the results can be pretty distressing for everybody concerned, and most of all, I fear, for those who really care for the expression of moral or religious reality in literature.

Closing the Gulf

Yet though there may be a great gulf fixed between the Shakespeare-type of writer and the Dante-type, the gulf is not so deep or wide as it is often thought to be. The tremendous advantage on the side of the Shakespeare-group is that they always know what literature is, what the aesthetic experience is. They know the difference between literature and non-literature, and they are never in danger of substituting one for the other. But the Dante-people have their natural advantage too. If the followers of Shakespeare are sometimes in danger of forgetting that "you can't write writing," it is the special virtue of the Dante group that they never fail to keep this in mind. They always know exactly what they believe, and their convictions give them a hold on reality which their fellow-writers often have to struggle much harder to possess themselves of. Furthermore, they believe supremely in the importance of what they are doing, and to believe this, even for the wrong reasons, is to take a very long step toward making the reader believe also.

Nor, for all the differences between their respective attitudes toward their art, is the Dante-writer's method of creation anything like so different from the Shakespeare-writers as one might have supposed it would be. Shaw called Bunyan, Blake, Hogarth, and Turner the four Englishmen above all others "whose peculiar sense of the world

I recognize as more or less akin to my own." There was more here than admiration for didacticism. Moreover, Shaw admired Mozart and Dickens and Shakespeare himself, and though his theories about art caused him to express a special admiration for the "problem comedies" with which Shakespeare came closest to his own type of play, and to call *Little Dorrit*, admiringly, "a more seditious book than *Das Kapital*," it is clear enough that some of the elements in Dickens which enthralled him most were those farthest removed from the Victorian novelist's tendencies toward propaganda. Moreover, Shaw had mastered journalism and the soap-box forum long before he turned to playwriting. There must have been something in him which the soap box could not satisfy; otherwise, why should he undertake the not inconsiderable labor of mastering the playwright's craft? Milton, too, won European fame as a pamphleteer before he wrote *Paradise Lost*. To write one of his pamphlets in defense of Cromwell's government, which, as he conceived it, was destined to bring heaven to earth, he sacrificed his eyesight. Yet he himself said that he wrote all his prose works with his left hand! Evidently if you are born to be an artist, nothing else will do for you, whatever you may "believe" about the value of other activities.

In addition to all this, there are a great many borderline cases—writers who cannot be classified in either one camp or the other but who keep a foot in each. Both Tennyson and Longfellow are among these. Read Tennyson's definition of poet's function in "The Poet," and you may feel that he made no distinction between poet and prophet. His discourse is all of the ethical aspects of the poet's mission. Of strictly aesthetic concerns he says nothing. Yet nobody could claim that he neglected this aspect in his own poetic practice. As for Longfellow, there is a widespread impression in many quarters that he was characteristically a writer of rimed moralities and exhortations, like those contained in "A Psalm of Life," but this impression survives in defiance of the facts of the case.

The Writer's Intention

In itself art is neither moral nor immoral; its moral effect depends entirely upon the use made of it, and this is determined by the character and purpose of the individual artist. Longfellow was not a better artist because he was a good man, nor Oscar Wilde because he was not a good man. But since it is not the aesthetic man alone who reads a book but the whole man, not much decadent or corrupt literature has permanently established itself on a high level in the world's hierarchy of fine art. Naturally one is not concerned here with the incidental indecencies which appear in such writers as Chaucer, Fielding, and Shakespeare. Depending upon the critic's individual point of view, such things are either lamentable flecks of earth in the writer's product, or else a welcome testimony to his virility, but no sane person would argue that their presence corrupts the product as a whole. And one must also, I think, agree with Bliss Perry that "The more stress is laid on technique the less important does the question of morality become. . . ." But Perry is equally right when he continues: "we may say that the moral element enters into every art in proportion as that art touches human life and character." The author selects, presents, and interprets his material according to his own sense of values—and if the reader feels that the picture is seriously out of focus, then no grace of style or charm of expression will suffice to overcome this handicap.

Naturally this does not mean that the reader must "agree" in every aspect with the author's world view, nor even with all the articles in his moral code. If this were true, no Christian could read any classical literature with satisfaction, not, for that matter, the literature of the Old Testament. And, by the same token, the modern Jewish reader would be cut off from understanding and appreciating the literature of the whole Christian world. One need not accept Lucretius' philosophy to feel the greatness of his spirit; neither are Thomas Hardy's admirers, in any sense, limited to those who find themselves in intellectual agreement with his sombre views. "Religion is such a great thing," says Lavinia, in Shaw's *Androcles and the Lion*, "that when I meet really religious people we are friends at once, no matter what name we give to the divine will that made us and moves us." The statement is true of religion, but it is true of other things as well.

In general, men have loved their great artists and admired them and looked up to them. You do not admire a man merely because he is skilled in the use of words; "the gift of the gab" is, in itself, a contemptuous term. Even in the theater, which often places a high premium on the meretricious, the artist who does nothing more than excite the nerves of his audience does not generally last long. The kind of popularity that is worth having comes rather to those who, be their talents large or small, do, in some way, express the hopes or the aspirations of mankind. That, to take two recent instances, was the kind of popularity long enjoyed by Mary Pickford and by John McCormack, and we may easily see, by reference to such persons as Eddie Cantor and Gracie Fields, that it can be an important factor even in the career of a frankly "popular" entertainer. "For after all," wrote Howard Pyle, "a man is not an artist by virtue of clever technique or brilliant methods; he is fundamentally an artist in the degree that he is able to sense and appreciate the significance of life that surrounds him, and to express that significance to the minds of others."

Great artists are not plaster saints, free of the errors,

faults, and weaknesses of humanity; neither are they, as a class, more notably successful than other people in living consistently upon the level of their highest aspirations. Plaster saints, indeed, do not often turn to artistic expression; they are too much inclined to approach life negatively, not positively. "Is not character always in some way negative?" asks Paul Elmer More, in his essay on Charles Eliot Norton. "Is it not of its very essence to act as a check upon the impulsive temperament and even upon the ranging enthusiasms of the soul?" If this is an adequate definition of character—and I do not believe that it is—then the important thing is not what you do but what you don't do. Nevertheless, I think it must be granted that it is both the artist's temptation and his glory to respond more eagerly than other men to all the varied stimuli of life; it is always his natural tendency to ask first of a proferred stimulus not whether it is "good" but whether it is "strong."

Three marginal questions often trouble readers in connection with this matter of literature and morality, and it is to these that we must now turn.

Why Do Evil Men Write Good Books?

I am not sure that they do. I am not sure, that is to say, that it was the "evil" in the man that produced the literature that was "good." Human character cannot be presented in terms of black-and-white, and few of us know enough about anybody else to justify us in passing a definitive judgment upon him.

When a man falls into a spectacular scandal, as Byron did, or Wilde, it becomes very difficult to avoid thinking of him as a "bad" man, and it is generally on such occasions that people begin to ask how a bad man can produce good literature. Sometimes we choose the other horn of the dilemma and decide that the man's work is not good, though we have been reading it until now with delight, and apparently without contamination. Sufficiently stupid people may even, at this juncture, begin to urge that books should be burned or films banned; I do not know just why, unless perhaps it seems desirable to them that the offender should be cut off from wholesome activity altogether and shut up with his wickedness!

It has often been said of Byron that the faults of his poetry are the faults of his life, which was what his fellow-poet, John Drinkwater, had in mind when he remarked that the particular kind of discipline which means chastity was out of Byron's range both as an artist and as a man. On the other hand, we must remember that as no man is wholly bad, so, also, no artist has ever succeeded in getting the whole of his experience into a work of art: as Lord David Cecil never tires of reminding us, a writer's creative range is that part of his experience which can be fertilized by his imagination. When this range is comparatively narrow, as it is with some writers, a man may well be able to create almost wholly in terms of some area of his experience which is largely unaffected by the errors of his life. Wilde's fairy tales are certainly "pure," and so, in general, is the work of the Elizabethan, Robert Greene, who led a depraved life. Conversely, many artists who have been reproached for the immorality of their work, have led exemplary lives. So Robert Herrick declared of himself:

> To his Book's end this last line he'd have plac't,
> Jocund his Muse was; but his life was chast.

In another area, I am told that the distinguished English actress, Dame Sybil Thorndike, who is a woman of uncommonly lofty spirit, once declared that during the two years when she was appearing in particularly harrowing roles, she enjoyed exceptionally sound and refreshing sleep.

Her explanation of the paradox was simple: "I got it off my chest."

Rascals in Literature

Again we are asked why it is, if literature is in alliance with morality, that the scoundrels and rascals are so often much more interesting than the good people. I do not believe myself that this is literally true, either in literature or in life. Is Hitler really more interesting than Lincoln? Are Gandhi and Albert Schweitzer and Jane Addams dull people? Is there no thrill for us in the heroic virtue of Saint Francis of Assisi and Saint Joan of Arc?

It is true, of course, that Shakespeare created one of his most fascinating characters out of the rascal Falstaff, but we are not precisely bored by Hamlet and Othello, who are good characters, nor yet by the bewildering richness and variety of Shakespeare's virtuous and enchanting heroines. Indeed, a novel or a play populated wholly or largely by unsympathetic characters generally fails to interest the reader very deeply, for it offers him no center of spiritual rest; neither do the characters seem to possess enough emotional importance to make it worth while for him to try to get deeply interested in their fortunes. In many works of the imagination, the people whom we dislike or disapprove of owe such power as they possess over our imaginations to the fact that they constitute a menace to some "good" character in whom we are interested. It was on these grounds that Dickens objected to Wilkie Collins's dramatization of his own novel, *Armadale:* "you could only," he told his friend, "carry those situations *by the help of interest in some innocent person whom they placed in peril, and that person a young woman.*"

When we are bored by "good" people, either in literature or in life, the reason is generally not that they are good but that they are dull, or that they are good in a dull way. Negative, timid goodness, with no quality of adventure or aspiration in it, and no challenge about it, could not well be expected to be interesting. And that kind of goodness is unfortunately much more common than the heroic variety. But badness can be very dull, too, as May Sinclair has shown us in one of the most terrible ghost stories ever written, "Where Their Fire Is Not Quenched." There is no fire and brimstone in Miss Sinclair's hell: her sinners are simply condemned to go on forever committing the same old sin over and over in the same old way!

The Norm and Its Variations

But there is another element which enters here, and which does complicate the problem for those who would interest their readers in "good" characters. Incidentally, it leaves those who make evil their special stock in trade open to the accusation of having chosen the easiest way.

It is always easier to vivify eccentricity than the norm; this is true of physical and moral eccentricity alike. How, for example, would you describe a perfectly beautiful woman,

> The very pattern girl of girls,

who sets the standards by which others must be judged, and who herself constitutes that standard? Is her nose long or short? Does she have a high or a low forehead? Are her eyes far apart or close together? Obviously none of these questions can be answered, for everything about her is just right!

Homer faced this problem in the *Iliad*, where Helen is perfect beauty. He solved it triumphantly by never describing her directly but simply giving us the effect her beauty has upon others, notably upon the old men of Troy, as she passes out through the city gates. Had the beauty of Helen been praised by the Greeks, we might have discounted what was said, for they were her own people. Had she been praised by young Trojans, we might still have supposed them to be led astray by the green judgment—and appetites—of youth. But when the old men of Troy, who are past the age for love, and who might be supposed to have been prejudiced against Helen by the calamity she had brought upon them, when these are overwhelmed by her, then the poet has done his utmost to establish Helen as a very beautiful woman.

Everything individual is, in a sense, a departure from the standard, the norm; everything human exists in terms of a divergence from pattern. Personality itself involves limitation, for if you are this, then obviously you cannot be that. The farther you go from center, the easier it will be to individualize your character. And does not "He's a character" itself equal, in popular speech, "He's an odd one"? This has long been recognized in acting; that was why Shaw defined a character actor as an actor who can't act. He doesn't need to; his make-up, his dialect, and all the other aids that the performer of "straight" roles has to get along without, do it for him. One reason we know that Jane Austen was such a great novelist is that she kept her eccentrics where they belong—in her supporting casts. Her heroines are all normal English girls, with "none of the attractiveness of excess." They belong, too, to the same social group; there were very few handles she could grab hold of to differentiate one from another. But she did not need them. Elizabeth Bennet, Emma Woodhouse, Anne Elliot, and the rest—they all live, each with her own particular life, and no reader has ever been in any danger of confusing one with another. "A woman of moral depravity," said Julia Marlowe, "offers the modern playwright greater scope than a good woman because her life is full of incidents which are dramatic. But it takes a greater artist to make a good woman interesting than to make a base woman sympathetic and thrilling."

The Abnormal in Literature

The third question which is often asked—Why are contemporary writers so much preoccupied with the unwholesome and the abnormal?—is much more difficult than the other two. Some answers have already been suggested. If it is sensationalism that you are after, the evil has its obvious advantages, and if the writer himself is abnormal, or confused in his sense of values, then it is inevitable that these things should have a special attraction for him. The turmoil and confusion of our times have upset standards also. Art is not life, but it does take its materials from life, and if the age is monstrous and violent, it is foolish to expect that its literature will be wise and gentle.

The investigation, for scientific purposes, and under laboratory conditions, of some aspects of behavior which our ancestors were satisfied to shudder over without understanding has supplied new materials—and sometimes even new techniques—for the creative writer. And precisely because the Victorians did not talk about such things at all, we sometimes find ourselves talking about them too freely and too loudly.

This was what Ellen Glasgow had in mind when, towards the close of her life, she complained of those young writers who could find no better use for the freedom which she and her generation had won for them than to shout dirty words in the streets. She was too wise a woman not to know that this was inevitable, but it did not annoy her less on that account.

There is no law against being as much annoyed as we

like about such matters, but we shall be very unwise if we allow our annoyance to warp either our sympathies or our understanding. It is not only biologically that there is much waste in the processes of creation, and if a writer has really made up his mind to be slag, there is not much the rest of us can do except to help him wash himself away as quickly as possible. But we shall only make fools of ourselves if we allow these things to embitter us to such an extent that we find ourselves in the position of the newspaper editor who told a friend of mine that he could not possibly expect his book to be successful because "only dirty books sell nowadays."

What Makes a Book Immoral?

The truth is that most "dirty books" do not sell, and that among those which do, a good many are not "dirty books" at all but only seem to be. It is often hard for the inexperienced reader to remember that a book is not necessarily immoral because it deals with immoral people or describes immoral conduct. If that criterion were to be applied, the Bible itself would be a "dirty" book. The writer's purpose is the test, the sense of values which his work communicates, and the interpretation he offers of the relationship between good and evil.

Neither can the morality of a work of art be estimated solely on the basis of the writer's manners or his vocabulary. A careless and partial reader of the writings of William Faulkner might well believe and declare this writer to be a half-mad degenerate, but this view could not survive a careful and understanding perusal of the body of Faulkner's work. Similar assertions might be made concerning the writings of John Steinbeck. And however seriously one may disagree with Ernest Hemingway's morality, a phenomenal amount of dullness would be required of a reader who should fail to perceive his burning interest in, and constant preoccupation with, moral problems.

Perhaps it is easier to understand these things in connection with once controversial works of the past which have established themselves than it is with reference to those whose ultimate fate is still in doubt, and which themselves still serve as storm centers in current controversies. The really meretricious works sink in time under their own weight and are forgotten, and the works of quality cease to shock. Is anybody shocked today by Dreiser's *Sister Carrie* or the *Sons and Lovers* of D. H. Lawrence?

A less illustrious example may perhaps make all this clearer. In 1909 David Belasco produced in New York a drama by Eugene Walter called *The Easiest Way: An American Play Concerning a Particular Phase of New York Life*. The central character, Laura Murdock, who was touchingly portrayed by Frances Starr, was a young woman who maintained a somewhat precarious foothold in the theater through her personal relationship with a wealthy but corrupt man. When Laura falls in love and leaves Brockton, he starves her into submission. Through a combination of unfortunate circumstances and her own weakness of character, she loses, in the course of the play, both her lover and her protector. The final curtain leaves her confronting complete degradation. The easiest way has led straight to hell.

It would be difficult to exaggerate the consternation which this play awakened. The New York Evening *World* called it "an evening of good acting and bad morals." Boston banned it altogether. As late as 1913, William Winter devoted ten sumptuous pages of *The Wallet of Time* to an impassioned denunciation of its depravities.

Yet though the situations presented in *The Easiest Way* are almost consistently offensive—only one minor character is a decent person—the play is almost oppressively moral. An important document, despite its own technical short-comings, in the history of American theater realism, it is also one of the strongest sermons ever preached on the text, "The soul that sinneth, it shall die." The world of *The Easiest Way* is a moral world, and every violation of decency and righteousness carries its own penalty with it. It may offend your taste, but if it affects your morals at all, it will affect them for good. By 1921, Professor Thomas H. Dickinson found it safe to include it in the Second Series of his *Chief Contemporary Dramatists*, an anthology intended primarily for college use.

This is my judgment of a particular play; it is not intended as a blanket endorsement of the "horrible example" method teaching. Pope's lines,

> Vice is a monster of so frightful mien,
> As to be hated, needs but to be seen;
> Yet seen too oft, familiar with her face,
> We first endure, then pity, then embrace,

are not altogether complimentary to humanity, but he would be a brave man who should assert categorically that there is no truth in them. Winter himself was quite right when he declared, in another connection, that a play may be immoral not because of what it *teaches* but because of what it *shows*. Each case must be judged upon its own merits, and it would be foolish to expect all judges to agree.

Temporary and Permanent Values

This question of the moral implications of literature, which has been our primary concern thus far in this chapter, indicates perhaps the most important aspect in which we confront the question of the impingement of the world upon the book. It is not the only one, however. Political prejudices and party principles have played their part, too, in the judgments that have been passed upon books, and it is not often that those who write for the needs of the moment find, with the passing of time—and the crisis which exists in time—that they have served the ages too. Nor is it often that posterity sees a conflict between either men or nations in terms of the simple black-and-white antithesis which the men whom it involved conceived it to be. Even *Uncle Tom's Cabin* is only a partial exception to the rule that partisan works do not survive the age which produces them, for Mrs. Stowe used slavery as an approach to more permanent human interests and problems. She denounced slavery, to be sure, but she had no "policy" toward it: indeed, at the outset, she intended her book as a pacificator. It lived because its vitality transcended the political crisis which produced it and which was exacerbated by it.

Reference has already been made in these pages to Milton's prose works. Milton laid aside the poetic ambitions of his youth to serve Cromwell's government, and his decision very nearly robbed the world of *Paradise Lost*. It would certainly have done so, had Charles II's government been less merciful than it was or Milton himself a less phenomenally strong man. Even so, there is no telling how much it did cost us; if it had not been for his Commonwealth years, Milton might well have found time to write the King Arthur epic he always wanted to write, a work which, one would think, might have meant a great deal in the life of the English people.

It is impossible not to respect Milton for the decision he made; it is also impossible not to question his good judgment. If he had been a wiser man, if he had known the world better, he would not have placed such an absurdly exaggerated estimate upon the importance of a change of government, for he would have known that men cannot be regenerated by political action. Goethe took the other road, when he lived through the Napoleonic wars and more or less ignored them, recognizing frankly that many men could fight Napoleon, but that he had a special work to do, which, were he to leave it undone, must be lost to the world forever. There is a coldness, as well as a wisdom, in such a decision by which most human beings cannot avoid being repelled. Intellectually, however, there can be no doubt that Goethe was right.

Let me repeat: The best claim literature has upon our gratitude is the enrichment of life which it brings us, the enlargement of sympathy and comprehension which we experience through our imaginative entrance, by way of literature, into other lives. An aesthetic experience is worth while for its own sake. There is no need to apologize for it, or to ask that it should camouflage itself as something else. It is not the function of art to solve the problem of over-population, to destroy war, or to save our souls. It is its function to create beauty and to give aesthetic pleasure. And if it fails to do this, it will not solve the problem of overpopulation, or destroy war, or save our souls. It will simply not exist. And we shall all be the poorer for its absence.

To quote Henry James once more: "The content and the 'importance' of a work of art are . . . wholly dependent on its *being one:* outside of which all prate of its representative character, its meaning and its bearing, its morality and humanity are an impudent thing."

Literature and Leisure

Once this has been clearly understood, however, there is no reason why we should be too "precious" about it. Because the aesthetic man is also the moral man and the political man and a good many other men besides—and because all these men are the same man—literature, which is an art, does still serve many social ends, and it may not be out of place to look briefly at a few of these here.

I should say, first of all, that an interest in literature—or in any art—leads to a wise and fruitful use of leisure. I have already pointed out the glaring inadequacy of any educational program which should provide only for what a man is to do in his working time. Great social problems generally arise out of what men do in their leisure time. The devil still finds work for idle hands to do—unless God and the aspiring human spirit put more enthralling work into them first. If you would learn the truth about a people you must study not only how they work but especially how they play.

The improper use of leisure is the source of much of our crime and more of our vice today. Now, cultured people are quite as human as others, and quite as liable to human weakness and temptation. But they are interested in other things. Literature is inexhaustible. Any aesthetic interest is inexhaustible. Those who give such things an important place in their lives have much less time than others to get into mischief.

Of course, such an argument cannot be pressed too far. I have opposed in this book all those who would encourage religion and morality and social consciousness to trespass on the preserves of art. By the same token, I resist the tendency of art to trespass upon these other preserves. I do not believe that religion can take the place of art; neither (despite all Matthew Arnold's theorizing on the subject), do I believe that art can ever take the place of religion. Culture alone will not solve the problem of human life. As a surrogate for the Holy Spirit, a hobby will not do!

Literature as a Refuge

In the second place, I believe that literature provides an incomparable and, in the present stage of human development, a vitally necessary refuge, or, if you like, means of escape, from life. I know that "escapism" is at present a fighting word. Many critics never utter it without an accent of contempt. I have already made it clear that I have no sympathy with those who use books like narcotics, or cling stubbornly to a type of mental pabulum which, in the course of nature, they ought long since to have outgrown. But this is not the basic question. In the larger aspects, all art is "escapism"! We use it because it gives us something we need, something we cannot get in any other way.[4] But this matter has perhaps already been sufficiently considered elsewhere.

In addition to this, "escapist" art has special functions to particular groups and at particular times. What about the sick, the shut-in, the bereaved? Do you want them to escape into the magic world of Dumas, Sabatini, or Mary Johnston? Or would you rather have them hang themselves? Well, we are all sick, shut-in, or bereaved at some period of our lives, and we all feel the need, at times of retiring temporarily from the fray.

> . . . he who fights and runs away
> May live to fight another day.

Woodrow Wilson paid public tribute to the values he derived during these "blessed intervals" from the reading of detective stories. Otis Skinner, too, has testified upon this point:

The fate of the travelling actor . . . is that he is sent away from home for many golden days. . . . There are long railway

---

[4] See Willa Cather's letter to Michael Williams on "Escapism," reprinted in *Willa Cather on Writing* (Knopf, 1949).

trips to negotiate, cities filled with uninteresting people to visit, hours of tedium and waiting to endure, food prepared by cooks who are not cooks to devour. His world is cabined, cribbed, confined, and his days are filled with irritation.

If he is not a bridge fan or devoted to golf, solitaire, or tiddle-dy-winks, his existence is an arid waste unless he rings up his curtain on the life that lies between the covers of books.

The wise use of such "blessed interludes" or the refusal to use them wisely may often make the difference between being able to carry the burden and fainting under it.

Literature and Understanding

Finally, I do not see how it can be denied that literature and the arts—and the devotion of human beings to literature and the arts—makes for harmony and understanding among men. It breaks down the walls of prejudice and becomes a powerful factor toward the establishment of a world community. It is their feeling for English literature, their appreciation of the soul of the English people as expressed in their literature, rather than their admiration for the policies of the British government, which enables most Americans to sympathize more readily with Great Britain than they do with other foreign countries. But the true lover of art feeds his soul upon the beauty of all lands and peoples. He reads *King Lear* and *Les Misérables* and *The Divine Comedy* and *War and Peace* and *The Tale of Genji*. He listens to the music of Purcell and Debussy and Wagner and Verdi and Rimsky-Korsakoff. Is he not in the best, in the only true sense, a citizen of the world?

In Charles Edward Russell's *Julia Marlowe: Her Life and Art* there is an interesting account of how the great Shakespearean actress and her equally distinguished actor-husband, E. H. Sothern, many years ago consciously rebuked race prejudice by going to the Paul Dunbar High School, in Washington, D. C., to talk and read for the pupils. It was the first time famous white persons had ever done such a thing, and the result, as Russell describes it, seems to have been profound. As one of the teachers wrote Miss Marlowe afterwards:

I may not be a judge of artistic greatness but surely only greatness of soul could have revealed to us, as you and Mr. Sothern did, the oneness of humanity at its depths. In some marvelous way your presence with us in that high school auditorium has given us a new revelation of the brotherhood of all men and has gone far to stifle the bitterness of spirit fostered by the peculiar injustice we suffer.[5]

Yet it ought not to have seemed strange to anybody that Sothern and Marlowe felt as they did about race prejudice. For they had devoted their lives to the study and interpretation of Shakespeare, the poet who, above all others, furnishes the best antidote to prejudice, who sees and judges human beings as human beings, and never permits them to be swallowed up, or to merge their individuality, in a group. If anybody was shocked by what Sothern and Marlowe did that day in Washington, then what they were really asking of them was that they should fail to understand their own job.

This is an excellent illustration of the spirit that we need to solve the "race problem," or any comparable problem, in America. Where we have that spirit, we do not need legislation. Where it is lacking, legislation may well do more harm than good. It was no accident that Emerson and Thoreau, who have been accepted by the whole world as the outstanding representatives and embodiments of the New England spirit, should have been the very men who contemplated the invasion of New England by the Irish immigrants with perfect sympathy and equanimity.

[5] Charles Edward Russell, *Julia Marlowe: Her Life and Art* (Appleton, 1926), pp. 518-520.

CHAPTER FIVE

Tell Me a Story

~~~~~~

Definitions

We have completed our consideration of the qualities and characteristics of literature in general; we must now turn to the defining of various kinds of literature. And it seems fitting to begin with narrative, for this is probably where the reader's own interest in literature began.

The race has loved "stories" as far back as racial memory goes. Thackeray conjures up a glamorous picture of "a score of white-bearded, white-robed warriors, or grave seniors of the city, seated at the gate of Jaffa or Beyrout, and listening to the story-teller reciting his marvels out of *Antar* or the *Arabian Nights*." In this respect, as in others, the individual relives the history of the race, and "Tell me a story" is, if not one of the earliest, at least a very early sentence which the lips of childhood learn to frame. Many "stories" have already been referred to in these pages, for in the first unspecialized portion of this book the author has naturally taken his illustrations wherever he found them. But we have not hitherto been concerned with fiction for its own sake.

One or two definitions seem necessary at the outset. Our nomenclature in this field is ludicrously inadequate; it is a wonder that we are able to discuss the problem of fiction as intelligently as we do. "Story" itself is only a shortened form of "history." Because they wanted to convey the idea that they had turned away from the romances toward a picture of actual life, some of the great eighteenth-century novelists actually called their books "histories"—*The History of Tom Jones, A Foundling*, etc.—but if there is anything that a fictional narrative is not, it is history. "Novel" itself is almost a silly term, for it means merely "something new," and the connotations of "fiction" itself, as implying falseness, are certainly unfortunate when we remember that we are concerned with an art which prides itself upon its ability to present a truthful picture of life.

Fiction—prose fiction—as the term is used today, means, in common parlance, the short story and the novel; and publishers' and booksellers' announcements often list these works as "Fiction" and everything else as "Nonfiction." Since this classification throws narrative poems and all plays into the nonfiction class, it is obviously quite illogical, whatever practical advantages it may have. Surely a story is a story, whether it be told in prose or verse, whether it be divided into scenes or chapters. Indeed, the mere fact that we speak of "prose fiction" shows that there is fiction in the world which is not written in prose. The *Iliad* and *Odyssey*, *The Canterbury Tales*, the English and Scottish popular ballads, the *Orlando Furioso*, *The Faerie Queene*, *Tales of a Wayside Inn*, and *John Brown's Body*—here are varied examples of fiction in verse—several of them older than any novel as we now understand that term.[1]

[1] The most useful general studies of prose fiction, for beginners at least, are still Bliss Perry, *A Study of Prose Fiction* (Houghton Mifflin, 1902, 1920), and Clayton Hamilton, *The Art of Fiction* (Doubleday, 1939). There is a brief analysis in Fred B. Millett, *Reading Fiction* (Harper, 1950). For the history of the novel in England and in America, the reader is referred to the present writer's *Cavalcade of the English Novel* and *Cavalcade of the American Novel* (Holt, 1943, 1952). Some illustrations from these books have been used in the present chapter. This material is copyrighted, 1943, 1952, by Henry Holt and Company, Inc.

The Elements of Fiction: The Tale

Let us begin, then, as simply as possible, with one of the best and simplest and most familiar stories in the world, a story which the reader will have been asked to consider many times from the point of view of its religious values, and let us look at it as a piece of narrative art. This is the so-called Story of the Prodigal Son, as told by Jesus, in the fifteenth chapter of the Gospel according to St. Luke. I am using the "Authorized," or "King James," translation, but I have disregarded the "verses," and arranged the story in paragraphs, with modern punctuation.

A certain man had two sons.

And the younger of them said to his father, "Father, give me the portion of goods that falleth to me." And he divided unto them his living.

And not many days after, the younger son gathered all together, and took his journey into a far country, and there wasted his substance with riotous living.

And when he had spent all, there arose a mighty famine in the land; and he began to be in want. And he went and joined himself to a citizen of that country; and he sent him into his fields to feed swine. And he would fain have filled his belly with the husks that the swine did eat: and no man gave unto him.

And when he came to himself, he said, "How many hired servants of my father's have bread enough and to spare, and I perish with hunger! I will arise and go to my father, and will say unto him, 'Father, I have sinned against heaven, and before thee, and am no more worthy to be called thy son; make me as one of thy hired servants.' "

And he arose, and came to his father.

But when he was yet a great way off, his father saw him, and had compassion, and ran, and fell on his neck, and kissed him.

And the son said unto him, "Father, I have sinned against heaven, and in thy sight, and am no more worthy to be called thy son."

But the father said to his servants, "Bring forth the best robe, and put it on him; and put a ring on his hand, and shoes on his feet. And bring hither the fatted calf, and kill it; and let us eat, and be merry. For this my son was dead, and is alive again; he was lost, and is found." And they began to be merry.

Now his elder son was in the field: and as he came and drew nigh to the house, he heard music and dancing. And he called one of the servants, and asked what these things meant.

And he said unto him, "Thy brother is come; and thy father hath killed the fatted calf, because he hath received him safe and sound."

And he was angry, and would not go in: therefore came his father out, and intreated him.

And he, answering, said to his father, "Lo, these many years do I serve thee; neither transgressed I at any time thy commandment; and yet thou never gavest me a kid, that I might make merry with my friends. But as soon as this thy son was come, which hath devoured thy living with harlots, thou hast killed for him the fatted calf."

And he said unto him, "Son, thou art ever with me, and all that I have is thine. It was meet that we should make merry and be glad, for this, thy brother, was dead and is alive again, and was lost and is found."

Now, what have we here?

Well, we have a "story."

But what does that mean?

It means that something happens.

But nothing can happen unless there is somebody for it to happen to. So something happens to somebody.

But this somebody—or these somebodies—is/are not floating unattached in general space. They are living somewhere, under certain conditions.

Something happens, then. Something happens to somebody, under certain conditions. But that is not all. The something that happens causes something else to happen.

The people in the story do not stay the way they were in the beginning. Somebody does something that causes trouble. In this way, a problem is created which has to be worked out. As the story goes on, this trouble gets worse and worse. But at last there is a change, or a turnabout, and then the people in the story begin to solve their problem and make things right again. And, finally, when this has been achieved, the story comes to an end.

There are people, then, in the story. There are three of them: a father and his two sons. The people in a story are called the "characters." In this story, they are introduced in the very first sentence, before anything at all has happened. What happens in a story is called the "plot."

In a way, there are more than three characters. There are the wanton companions of the prodigal in the far country. There is the "citizen" of that country who gives him employment when he is down and out. There are the members of the father's household staff—servants and even musicians. But these are all background characters, not actually presented in the story; we do not see them or hear them speak. To be sure, one servant is allowed to speak once to the elder brother. But his is purely a utility function in the story, and he does not really come to life.

At the beginning, the father and his two sons are living together. We are not told where they live. We are not told anything about how they live. In other words, the "setting" of the story is not specifically described. But from what we observe, we infer that the household is a substantial one— with servants, abundant provisions, and the kind of comfort that money can buy. The elder son, too, is in "the field" when his brother comes home. From this we understand that farming is being carried on.

Things begin to happen in the story when the younger son demands his inheritance. This request—and the father's compliance with it—starts the story going. Without it there would have been no story.

When the younger son leaves home, the scene of the story shifts from the father's household to its second setting—the far country. The reader—the reader's imagination—goes with the prodigal, instead of staying at home, with the father and the elder son.

In the far country, the younger son lives happily, though disgracefully, until his money is gone. He has already suffered a spiritual fall; his material fall comes later, when he begins to be in want.

His miserable condition, at this point, is not caused only by his own extravagance: there is a famine in the country. The famine is more background-action than setting: it is something that happens. And though it does not happen to the prodigal directly, the hunger which he feels as a result of it does.

The Author's Standing Ground

Modern novelists sometimes carelessly assume that they were the first to introduce the economic factor into fiction, or to display what is called "social consciousness" in their consideration of the characters' problems. Yet here, in this ancient tale, both are involved.

But they are handled very differently from the way a modern naturalistic novelist would handle them. The author of our story assumes the freedom of the will: the prodigal arrests his downward progress by "coming to himself." A pessimistic naturalist who believed that social and economic forces were basically determinative in life, and that the freedom of the will is an illusion, could never have permitted that.

Our young man slides rapidly downhill until he reaches the bottom. It is at this point that he suffers a change of heart and turns away not only from his degradation but from what brought him to it. "I will arise and go to my father."

In religious terms—which are here relevant, since this is a religious story—this is the young man's "conversion," or the point at which he turns from evil to good, and moves toward identifying his will with the will of his father. Technically considered, this is the "climax" of the story; having reached the highest point of complication, the situation now begins to unravel itself.

There follows the prodigal's return to his father and his acceptance by him, which last, the father being what he is, entails no particular difficulty. Had the father been a different kind of man, there would have been barriers to surmount at this point, or he might have refused reconciliation altogether. And that, to use Kipling's expression, would have been "another story," and a very different one, with the climax, very likely, still to come.

But never mind the story Jesus did not tell: let us return to the story in hand! It is clear that this story has fulfilled the Aristotelian formula: it has a beginning, a middle, and an end. The action begins, it develops to its highest point of complication, and at last it is resolved.

At the end of the story, the prodigal has solved his problem as a physical and spiritual being alike. Because he has returned to his father's house, his physical needs are provided for, and he is no longer under the necessity of filling his belly with the husks that the swine did eat. But because he has learned his lesson, because he has turned away from evil, his spiritual needs have been provided for also. He has saved his soul alive, and he is at peace.

All this sounds as if the story came to an end with the prodigal's return to his father. And so it does insofar as it is the prodigal's story. The entrance of the elder son, his

154 • TELL ME A STORY

objection to his father's conduct, his complaint and his father's reply—all this represents the introduction of a new interest. Whether this is to be regarded as an epilogue or anticlimax—technically an imperfection in the story—need not be considered at this point. But it is not difficult to see why Jesus included it.

"Meaning" and Technique

We began by thinking of a story as something that happens, and we immediately perceived that nothing could happen unless it happened to somebody, in some place; thus the three elements in fiction—the plot, the characters, and the setting—were at once inextricably bound together. But by this time we have also perceived two other things.

The first of these is that it is quite inadequate to think of a plot as merely consisting of things happening. The things that happen must stand in a causal relationship to each other. An element of pattern or continuity is involved. Through the action, some theme is being worked out.

In the course of one day, a busy man might well participate in as many activities as are recorded in this story. But they would not add up to a plot because they would not be related to each other.

The second thing we have learned—or ought to have learned—is that though we have divided the story into plot, characters, and setting, there is something else in it which does not come under any of these headings. I speak now of the "values" of the story, of what it "means."

The story with which we are here concerned is, as we have been hearing all our lives, a "parable," and *Webster's New Collegiate Dictionary* says that a parable is "a short fictitious narrative from which a moral or spiritual truth is drawn." (Caution: Not all stories with "morals" are parables!)

Now, what "moral or spiritual truth" is here involved? The story, as has already been stated, comes from the fifteenth chapter of St. Luke. Let us look at it in its setting; let us turn back to the beginning of that chapter:

Then drew near unto him [i.e., Jesus] all the publicans and sinners, for to hear him. And the Pharisees and scribes murmured, saying, "This man receiveth sinners, and eateth with them."
And he spake this parable to them, saying:

But he does not proceed at once to the story of the Prodigal Son. He leads up to it with two other parables. The first is the parable of the Lost Sheep, and the second is the parable of the Lost Coin.

The point of the first is that any sensible shepherd, having lost a sheep, would go off into the wilderness to search for it, even though he might have ninety-nine other sheep that had not strayed at all, and that, having found it, he would bring it home rejoicing and invite his friends and neighbors to rejoice with him. And the point of the parable of the Lost Coin is that a woman who had lost a piece of silver would sweep and search through her house diligently until she had found it again, though nine other pieces of silver were safe in her possession, and that having recovered it, she would behave very much like the shepherd who had found his sheep. From here Jesus goes on to the story we already know.

Neither of the first two stories is as interesting as the story of the Prodigal Son. And Jesus follows each with an explicit statement of his "point": "I say unto you that . . . joy shall be in heaven over one sinner that repenteth, more than over ninety-and-nine just persons which need no repentance." And again: "Likewise I say unto you, there is joy in the presence of the angels of God over one sinner that repenteth." But no such moral is explained at the end of our story. Jesus is much more the artist here, in the culminating parable, and much more disposed to permit the tale to speak for itself.

And what does it say? What does it say in the light of the audience to which it was addressed?

Jesus, we perceive, is defending himself against the accusation of the Pharisees. And he is defending his friends (the publicans and sinners who came to hear him), also. He is stating implicitly what he elsewhere makes explicit, that he has come "to seek and to save that which is lost."

It is their hostility to Him, not His hostility to them, that keeps sinners away from God; as soon as they "come to themselves," God receives them gladly, and with rejoicing. God is the Good Shepherd. God is the Faithful Housewife. God is the Good Father who sees his wicked, but now penitent, child returning and runs to welcome him while he is yet afar off.

But God has other children too, not like the publicans and sinners, not like the prodigal son in the story, but like the scribes and Pharisees, who are (as we now see clearly), represented by the other son in the story. They do not run off to the far country and waste their substance with riotous living. But they must not carelessly assume that, for that reason, all is necessarily harmonious between themselves and God.

There are other sins besides gluttony and harlotry and wine-bibbing. There is the sin of pride. There is the sin of self-righteousness. There is the sin of hardness of heart.

And so the task of the father in the story is not done when he has reconciled his younger son to himself. He must reconcile the elder son, the "good" brother, also. Toward him he shows the same patience, the same understanding and tolerance, that he has already manifested toward the prodigal.

But Jesus does not tell us whether or not the father's touching appeal to his elder son succeeded. At the time he told the story, Jesus was clearly more inclined to be optimistic about publicans and sinners than about Pharisees. The publicans and sinners in his audience did not, at the moment, need to be stirred up. They had already come to themselves; otherwise they would not be there. They needed reassurance, needed to know that God was a forgiving and a loving God. That reassurance the story is designed to give them. But the Pharisees? They *do* need stirring up! For them the story *is* an appeal to conscience! It can have no ending save that which they themselves supply.

Thus all the features of this story—the plot, the characters, the setting, even the structure (including the double climax and the indeterminate ending)—have been dictated by the narrator's purpose. The story has, of course, no title in the New Testament, and it may be that we are wrong to call it, as we always do, "The Story of the Prodigal Son." Is not the theme announced in the opening verse: "A certain man had two sons"? The story deals with both of them. The story concerns God's dealings with all His children, or, at any rate, with two distinct types among them. Why, then, is it always called "The Story of the Prodigal Son"? Well, the prodigal is much the more picturesque fellow of the two, and even the more "sympathetic." Prodigals usually are sympathetic if you do not have to live with them. Moreover, his story is more fully developed than his brother's. Nor is this the first time that a prodigal nosed out a Pharisee!

If it has accomplished nothing else, the foregoing analysis will at least have shown that even a very brief and simple story involves a much larger number of elements than we might have expected to find in it. Therefore, if we would really understand such a story, we must pay considerable attention to that "dry" and frightening business, "technique." And if this must be said of a parable, what shall we say of the vastly more elaborate kind of story that we get in a long novel?

The Elements of Fiction: The Novel

There are many kinds of novel, and I cannot analyze them all here. Indeed, I cannot analyze even one in its entirety. But I shall offer a partial analysis of Jane Austen's *Pride and Prejudice*, particularly from the point of view of the organization of its plot. I have chosen this particular novel both because it is as likely to be familiar to my readers as any that I might select, and also because its organization is both "natural" and beautifully symmetrical.

Naturally, it is not possible here, as in the case of the parable, to place all the material under the reader's eyes; the best I can do is to offer a summary:

When Mrs. Bennet, mother of five daughters, hears that the neighboring house of Netherfield Park, has been taken by a London bachelor named Mr. Bingley, her hopes for her girls are at once aroused, though she gets no encouragement in her plans from her somewhat sardonic husband. The Bennet girls soon meet Mr. Bingley and his sisters at a ball, and the mother seems justified, for he is at once drawn to the oldest among them, Jane; at the same time the pride and hauteur of his friend, Mr. Darcy, arouse the dislike of the second daughter, Elizabeth. Bingley's sisters, too, seem friendly toward Jane, though not to Elizabeth, for Miss Caroline Bingley is greatly interested in Mr. Darcy, and she shows considerable uneasiness over the interest Darcy seems to manifest in Elizabeth herself, when she comes to Netherfield Park, to care for Jane, who has been taken ill during a visit there.

Shortly afterwards, a toadying, time-serving, and self-important clergyman, Mr. Collins, a distant relative of the Bennets, whose patroness is Darcy's proud, ignorant, and fantastically bad-mannered aunt, Lady Catherine de Bourgh, proposes marriage to Elizabeth, and is rejected, after which he turns to her friend, Charlotte Lucas, who promptly accepts him. About the same time, the frivolous younger Bennet girls, Lydia and Kitty, become greatly interested in Mr. Wickham, a flashy young army officer, who is stationed nearby. Wickham tells Elizabeth that Darcy cheated him out of his inheritance, and she believes him. This, of course, deepens her dislike of Darcy. When, shortly afterwards, the Bingleys suddenly leave Netherfield Park without explanations, Elizabeth is convinced that Darcy is at the bottom of it. After a Christmas visit to the Bennets, Mrs. Bennet's sensible sister, Mrs. Gardiner, takes Jane to London with her for a visit.

Elizabeth is herself invited to visit the Collinses in Kent, which invitation she accepts. During her visit, they are entertained by Lady Catherine de Bourgh, whom Elizabeth at once intensely dislikes, and for whom she proves a match. Darcy comes to visit his aunt, and one day he greatly startles Elizabeth by appearing at the parsonage to propose marriage to her. She gives him a decided refusal. When he presses her for a reason, she cites his unfriendliness toward her sister and his mistreatment of Wickham. He does not argue the matter with her, but he writes her a long letter, in which he meets both charges frankly. This letter opens Elizabeth's eyes to Wickham's thoroughly unprincipled character. As to the other matter, Darcy does not deny that he urged Bingley not to marry Jane, but he does convince her that he was honest and unmalicious in his opposition to what he regarded as an unsuitable match for both parties.

After Elizabeth's return home, Lydia is permitted, over Elizabeth's protests, to accept an invitation from a young officer's wife; shortly thereafter, Elizabeth herself departs for a tour of Derbyshire with the Gardiners. During this period, she again, unexpectedly and embarrassedly, encounters Darcy, who proves extremely agreeable. But her pleasure is cut short by the receipt of a letter informing her that Lydia has eloped with Wickham. In her distress, she communicates the news to Darcy, before leaving hastily for home. Wickham agrees to marry Lydia, and when the silly girl arrives home with her husband, she is as frivolous and shameless as ever. Incidentally, she remarks that Darcy was present at her wedding.

Bingley now returns to Netherfield Park, with Darcy as a guest. The romance between Jane and Bingley is renewed, and an engagement results. Shortly afterwards, Lady Catherine calls, having heard rumours of her nephew's interest in Elizabeth; she wants Elizabeth to promise not to marry him. In one of the most spirited encounters in fiction, Elizabeth puts Lady Catherine in her place, and declares that she will be guided entirely by her own wishes and not by Lady Catherine's. The indignant old woman is foolish enough to repeat the substance of this conversation to Darcy, who at once renews his proposal to Elizabeth, and is accepted.

"Yes," the reader may say, "I see the naturalness, all right. But where is the symmetry?" Let us see.

The Whole and Its Parts

The theme of *Pride and Prejudice* is mating, matchmaking; and the plot is made up of four romances. These are, in order of importance: Elizabeth and Darcy; Jane and Bingley; Lydia and Wickham; Charlotte Lucas and Mr. Collins. The book opens with Mrs. Bennet's interest in the new inhabitants of Netherfield Park, it being "a truth universally acknowledged that a man in possession of a good fortune must be in want of a wife," and it closes with the gratitude of Elizabeth and Darcy toward the Gardiners, "who, by bringing her into Derbyshire, had been the means of uniting them."

But how do we know that the Bennet-Darcy romance is the main interest? By at least three circumstances: (1) It gets more space than any of the others; (2) Elizabeth's is much the fullest portrait in the book—and Darcy's, correspondingly, the most elaborate male portrait; (3) Elizabeth's affair becomes the determining factor in all three of the others. Had she not rejected Mr. Collins, he would never have turned to Charlotte Lucas. Had she not been loved by Darcy, Lydia's escapade would have ended in shame, not marriage. Had she not renewed her acquaintance with Mr. Darcy in Derbyshire, and come to admire and at last to love him there, the misunderstandings which barred the way to the fulfilment of Jane's desires could never have been removed.

The preëminence of the Bennet-Darcy affair appears again under another type of analysis.

Viewed chronologically, the book divides itself into six "acts," or blocks of action:

The first (Chapters I-XII), centers around Jane and Mr. Bingley, opening with the coming of the Bingleys to Netherfield Park and closing with the return of Jane and Elizabeth to Longbourn, following Jane's illness in the house of her friends. This illness, a great source of joy to Mr. Bennet, gives a fine opportunity for Jane and Bingley to know each other better and to fall in love. In this same section, Darcy's pride erects a barrier between him and Elizabeth, but his interest in her begins to develop. The interest manifested by Lydia and Kitty in the soldiers at Meryton prepares us for Lydia's later escapade, though Wickham himself has not yet appeared. Thus the Bennet-Darcy romance begins uncertainly, and as quite subordinate in interest to the romance between Jane and Bingley.

The next "act" (Chapters XIII-XXV), is concerned mainly with the affairs of Mr. Collins. It also introduces Wickham. Elizabeth's passing interest in Wickham deepens her dislike for Darcy. About the time Miss Lucas accepts Mr. Collins, the Bingleys depart for London, Miss Bingley hinting that her brother is to wed Miss Darcy. The entirely subordinate interest of the Lucas-Collins romance is consummated in this section, but Jane and Bingley suffer a serious setback, and at the end Darcy seems further than ever from Elizabeth's favor.

In the third section (Chapters XXVI-XL), the Bennet-Darcy romance becomes dominant, as it thereafter remains. Elizabeth receives and repudiates Darcy's proposals, charging him with unpardonable conduct and serious faults of character. His haughty but convincing defense, though apparently closing the door upon any further intercourse between them, actually opens her mind to his worth, thus preparing for his later success. Jane is in London, with no hope of a renewal of Mr. Bingley's attentions in sight. The Collinses have provided the background against which the Bennet-Darcy interest has become dominant.

Section Four (Chapters XLI-XLV), is a very brief section in which the development of the foregoing interests is continued. Elizabeth, in Derbyshire with the Gardiners, again meets Mr. Darcy, who rises steadily in her esteem.

In Section Five (Chapters XLVI-LIII), Lydia's elopement apparently dashes Elizabeth's hopes. But it really offers Darcy a splendid chance not only to raise himself in Elizabeth's esteem but also to show the reader the fundamental fineness of his character. It is, of course, through his friendly intercession and generosity that Lydia is saved from disgrace, though Elizabeth does not know this at the time.

The last section (Chapters LIV-LXI), which effects a clear understanding between Elizabeth and Darcy and between Jane and Bingley, also brings us to the culmination of both romances in the quiet charm of Longbourn. Not even the smug satisfaction of the fatuous Mrs. Bennet is allowed seriously to disturb either Darcy's contentment or the reader's.

Pride and Prejudice shows how a gifted novelist uses the materials of life. As we read, all seems casual and convincing; even the confusions and complexities of life are there. But all this has been passed through the alembic of the writer's mind and given forth again in new forms which have been created by that mind. Actually, the result is not "natural" at all; it only seems so. It is not a candid camera shot; it is a work of art.

The Plot

The importance of the plot in a novel could hardly be better suggested than in such an analysis as we have made. Is the plot, then, the most important element in a work of fiction? more important, say, than the characters or the setting?

The very question will offend those who stand ever on guard to remind us that a work of art is a unit (which it is), or an "organism," as they sometimes call it (which it certainly is not). Even Henry James, whom we shall be obliged to cite presently in another connection, asks, "What is character but the determination of incident? What is incident but the illustration of character?" On the other hand, Aristotle's analysis of Greek tragedy left him with the feeling that the plot *is* the most important element and that the characters must be subordinated to it.

This seems a little startling to most modern readers of fiction, for the whole psychological trend of modern literature is against it. The work of Chekhov and of Katherine Mansfield, for example—to mention only two of the most distinguished writers in this kind—is far removed from what Poe or Guy de Maupassant or O. Henry thought of as the short story. Often in the work of such writers, the plot drops out altogether. These "stories" are hardly even episodes or anecdotes. They offer reflections of some aspect of experience or express a mood. Not even the drama has been completely unaffected by these tendencies. Shaw said of Ibsen that for the rising action-climax-unravelment of the older drama, he had substituted rising action-climax-talk about it.

Where Shall the Writer Begin?

But to return to James. In the famous Preface to *The Portrait of a Lady*, in the "New York Edition" of his works,[2] James referred approvingly to Turgenev's idea that the author ought to begin with his characters, seeing them "as *disponibles*," as "subject to the chances and complications of existence," and going on from there "to find for them the right relations." Robert Louis Stevenson, who shared James's intense interest in fiction as an art, though he was likely to prefer a rather different kind of subject-matter, was less dogmatic about it: he was willing to have the writer begin with plot, characters, or setting! "You may take a plot and fit characters to it, or you may take a character and choose incidents and situations to develop it, or lastly you may take a certain atmosphere and get action and persons to express and realize it." He added that he himself had begun with his setting in *The Merry Men*.

Now it is easy to see what James was after. As we have already seen, nothing can happen unless it happens to somebody, but it is also true that the accent of interest may fall either (a) upon what happens, or (b) upon the person it happens to. Where the emphasis is placed will in turn depend (a) upon the author's gifts and limitations, and (b) upon his intention. In Shakespeare's *The Comedy of Errors*, where the whole plot turns upon the amusing confusions which result when one person is mistaken for another, the

[2] James's "New York" Prefaces have now been reprinted in *The Art of Fiction*, by Henry James, edited by R. P. Blackmur (Scribners, 1934).

unbelievability of the situation must have been accentuated precisely according to the degree in which the playwright should have individualized his characters. In the Story of the Prodigal Son, which concerns God's dealings with *humanity*, the application would have been needlessly narrowed, and the artist's purpose defeated, if the characters had been given individual names, or their story localized any more than was necessary to make it believable.

Nothing can happen, then, unless it happens to somebody, but that somebody may be a fully rounded individual, or he may be a lay figure, a cipher, a tailor's dummy, a blank check. There are many melodramas, many detective stories and other "thrillers," whose heroes and heroines might well be interchanged and nobody would ever be the wiser; the author supplies the reader a kind of stock character, and the reader may, if he likes, put himself in the place of the hero, and his "best girl," or his favorite film actress, in that of the heroine. This is sometimes true even in literature which, in other aspects, may be of high quality; it is true of many mediaeval romances and, so far as the hero and heroine are concerned, of some of the novels of Sir Walter Scott. And these are all works in which a strong premium is placed upon action. If, however, you are going to emphasize not what happens but what causes it to happen, then the personalities of the actors will become very important. And this, naturally, brings us back to where we began; it brings us back to James. Begin with your story, choose your characters merely to tell your story, and it would seem that you have greatly increased the danger of their behaving out of character in order to get the story told. Begin with them, and confine the plot to what they have to do to express themselves, and the danger of violating their integrity seems much slighter.

Now these are no idle questions that we have been asking here; neither are they questions of no interest to the layman or the general reader. For if the writer begins with his characters, then the reader is likely to get one kind of novel, and if he begins with the plot, then the reader is likely to get something very different. For many years now, as I have already said, dominant tendencies in fiction have been in the direction of the "psychological" novel, and people who could not sympathize with this have been obliged to confine themselves largely to historical novels and detective stories.

Why Plot Is Important

But there have been protests. As far back as 1923, the distinguished British critic, J. Middleton Murry, who, as the husband of Katherine Mansfield, was certainly not unfamiliar with, or unmindful of, the merits of psychological fiction, published a significant article on "The Break-Up of the Novel." [3] Murry pleaded for plot, for story, on the ground that art is necessarily concrete. Give all your attention to characterization, test your novelists, as Lord David Cecil says they should be tested, by their ability to create living characters, and by that alone, and you may have distinguished psychography, but you will not have fiction. In fiction, spiritual realities must be externalized; you can resolve your conflicts and realize your characters only through plot.

Recently the distinguished Irish novelist and story-writer, Elizabeth Bowen, herself often classified with the psychological writers, has been talking very much like this. In a lecture at Boston University in the spring of 1953, Miss Bowen indicated clearly that she thought "stream-of-consciousness" fiction played out. She declined to say whether

[3] J. Middleton Murry, "The Break-Up of the Novel," *Yale Review*, XII (1923), 288-304.

plot was more important than characters, but she did say that her own plots always came to her first. In her extremely suggestive "Notes on Writing a Novel," [4] however, she goes farther than this:

What about the idea that the function of action is to *express* the characters? This is wrong. The characters are there to provide the action. Each character is created, and must only be so created, as to give his or her action (or rather, contributory part in the novel's action) verisimilitude.

In talking with Miss Bowen after her lecture, I told her that her statement had surprised me as coming from her kind of writer. "I should have expected it," I said, "from Daphne du Maurier, but not from you." She laughed, and we went on to agree that though James may have *said* that the novelist *should* begin with the characters, the testimony of his own *Notebooks*, in which the origin of so many of his works is recorded, shows that, as a matter of fact, he himself often did begin with the vision of a situation, or of a character in a situation. When he did begin with the character, the character was not floating unattached in general space. He was doing something, or something was being done to him, or he was caught up in some kind of activity. Miss Bowen said she did not see how fiction could be created in any other way.

No doubt, writers differ greatly, in this matter as in others, and it is interesting to compare Miss Bowen's testimony with that of some other important women writers of the twentieth century. Elsie Singmaster seems quite in harmony with her when she writes:

In the beginning my characters have a somewhat shadowy personality, suggested by an acquaintance or some of the traits of an acquaintance, or perhaps by someone seen only for a few

[4] See Elizabeth Bowen, *Collected Impressions* (Knopf, 1950).

moments. They may have their origin in the exigencies of the plot in which they are to figure. As the story develops they develop with it, until they become rounded beings. If they are suggested by a living person, they are very apt to cease to resemble him or her and become entirely different.

Edith Wharton apparently could do it either way: "In my own case, a situation sometimes occurs to me first, and sometimes a single figure suddenly walks into my mind." Ellen Glasgow has recorded how Roy, of *In This Our Life*, came into her consciousness crying, "I want something to hold by. I want something good." It then became her task to find "something good" for her, or to record her search for it.

This process necessarily involves a good deal of selection and rejection. "Action," says Miss Bowen, "is the simplification (for story purposes) of complexity." Quite. The potentialities of actual human conduct are manifold, and the same is true of the more completely realized characters of fiction. Hamlet would have been a different man if his father had not been murdered, and Becky Sharp thought she could be a good woman on five thousand pounds a year. In "Roads of Destiny" O. Henry tries to tell what would have happened if his hero had found it possible to take not merely one fork in the road but all of them.

The Order of Events

Before we turn from plot to characters, it might be well to speak briefly of the order of events in fiction. In both the works we have analyzed, this is the straight, simple, chronological order. But this method, though usual, is not universally employed.

Horace wanted the epic poet to begin in the midst of the action (*in medias res*), and then loop back until he brought the reader up to the point at which, as motion-picture goers would say, he "came in." George Eliot secures a very vivid and character-revealing effect when she begins *Daniel Deronda* with a scene taken out of its chronological order, so that we may be introduced to Gwendolen Harleth at the gaming-table.

The extremely complex and wide-ranging story which is Emily Brontë's in *Wuthering Heights* begins in the middle. Mr. Lockwood encounters Heathcliff and the second Cathy at first hand, and his interest in them is aroused by the strange things that happen when a sudden snowstorm makes it necessary for him to spend the night at their dwelling. After his return to Thrushcross Grange, where he is staying, his housekeeper, old Ellen Dean, tells him of the first Cathy and her strange love for Heathcliff, bringing him, as it were, "up to date." What occurs from here on he gives us, partly through Ellen's further narration, and partly as he himself observed it.

Some writers have a general fondness for disturbing chronology. Joseph Conrad is one of these. In *The Secret Agent*, the bomb outrage is reported on p. 70 of the trade edition. Then Conrad digs back into its antecedents, and we do not hear of it again until we reach p. 190. Moreover, it is not until p. 210 that Winnie learns that her brother was killed by it. In *Under Western Eyes*, the events of Part I are continued not in Part II but in Part IV. If *Chance* were to be rearranged chronologically, p. 273 would have to be printed after Chapter I. The apparently trifling incident of the dog's disloyalty to Flora Barral, on p. 43 of this same novel, is brought up again on p. 202, and now shown to have exercised an almost determinative influence upon the plot.

Is this "good" narrative technique or "bad" narrative technique? In itself it is neither; everything depends upon how the author uses it and what effects he is trying to secure. In the case of *Wuthering Heights*, I think all sensitive readers would agree that Emily Brontë could have told her strange story with equal effectiveness in no other way. But in Conrad's case, the choice of method is sometimes determined less by the materials themselves than by the author's temperament. Conrad, consequently, will always be read more enthusiastically by those who enjoy having a share in the task of telling a story, through piecing it together from scattered hints here and there, than by those who would rather cuddle down snugly in the author's lap and simply absorb what he has to tell.

The Characters

We come now to the characters, and this is the great mystery. How is a human being made to live upon the printed page? Nobody knows. How, for that matter, is biological life created? Copulation, conception, gestation, parturition—these are the steps in the process, but only the first is under the control of the persons concerned. Conception may or may not follow: if it does not, there will be no life, and nothing that any human being can do will produce it. So it is also in fiction. Every means hereinafter described may be conscientiously employed. The creation of character may—or may not—be the result.

The means, at least, can be described. And the means which the novelist has at his disposal are varied and abundant.

1. He can describe his characters. The older novelists often did this formally and in detail, including a minute notation of costume, when the character is first introduced —or sometimes reintroduced. There are many examples in Scott: see his descriptions of the Templar and of Isaac of York in the fourth and fifth chapters of *Ivanhoe*, and the

much more elaborate portrait of Mary Queen of Scots in Chapter XXI of *The Abbot*. Dickens often uses this technique also:

> She was a fat old woman, this Mrs. Gamp, with a husky voice and a moist eye, which she had a remarkable power of turning up, and only showing the white of it. Having very little neck, it cost her some trouble to look over herself, if one may say so, at those to whom she talked. She wore a very rusty black gown, rather the worse for snuff, and a shawl and bonnet to correspond. . . . The face of Mrs. Gamp—the nose in particular—was somewhat red and swollen, and it was difficult to enjoy her society without becoming conscious of a smell of spirits. . . .
> —*Martin Chuzzlewit*

> [Uncle Pumblechook was] a large hard-breathing middle-aged slow man, with a mouth like a fish, dull staring eyes, and sandy hair standing upright on his head, so that he looked as if he had just been all but choked, and had that moment come to. . . .
> —*Great Expectations*

But Dickens has a tendency to be more "modern," i.e., more selective or impressionistic, in his descriptions than Scott. He does not try to tell everything. He knows that it would stop the story if he were to try to tell everything, and the reader would not remember it anyway. Perhaps even the author might not remember it, since there is a passage in *Ivanhoe* where Scott has the Templar, whom he had previously described as bareheaded, remove his bonnet. Dickens shows a tendency to help the reader remember by choosing, by centering attention upon, some vivid detail, or by dramatizing the character and allowing us to see him in action.

Modern novelists generally prefer to have their characters emerge gradually: we are told enough at the outset to rouse our curiosity but not enough to satisfy it. We may never learn that the heroine has beautiful eyes until some other character notices it, when she has occasion to raise them to him appealingly in some crisis of the story.

Henry James gives us no formal description of Isabel Archer when she first (Chapter III) appears in *The Portrait of a Lady*. Mr. Touchett tells her that she is beautiful, but he does not specify in what way. She talks, mostly about inconsequentialities. She sits down and folds her hands "upon her black dress; her head was erect, her eyes lighted, her flexible figure turned itself this way and that." We are left, for the time being, to make what we can of these things.

2. The author can analyze his characters directly. George Eliot was very fond of doing this:

It was a characteristic fact in Tito's experience at this crisis that no direct measure for ridding himself of Baldassare ever occurred to him. All other possibilities passed through his mind, even to his own flight from Florence; but he never thought of any scheme for removing his enemy. His dread generated no active malignity, and he would have been glad not to give pain to any mortal. He had simply chosen to make life easy to himself—to carry his human lot, if possible, in such a way that it should pinch nowhere; and the choice had, at various times, landed him in unexpected positions. The question now was, not whether he should divide the common pressure of destiny with his suffering fellow men; it was whether all the resources of lying would save him from being crushed by the consequences of that habitual choice.

—*Romola*

And Thomas Hardy describes Eustacia Vye as follows:

Eustacia Vye was the raw material of a divinity. On Olympus she would have done well with a little preparation. She had the passions and instincts which make a model goddess, that is, those which make not quite a model woman. Had it been possible for the earth and mankind to be entirely in her grasp for a while, had she handled the distaff, the spindle, and the shears at her own free will, few in the world would have noticed the change of government. There would have been the same inequality of lot, the same heaping up of favours here, of contumely there, the same generosity before justice, the same perpetual dilemmas, the same captious alternation of caresses and blows that we endure now.

—The Return of the Native

But it is not always done so formally as that. Trollope is short, sharp, quick, and decisive when he calls Lily Dale "a French prig." When he thrusts himself into *Barchester Towers* to tell the reader, "I never could endure to shake hands with Mr. Slope," he seems naïve, but the effect is deadly. The reader knows that Trollope is real; if Trollope held Mr. Slope's hand, must not it be real too, and the man to whom it belongs with it? Arnold Bennett achieves something like this, though quite without malice, in *The Old Wives' Tale:* "I have often laughed at Samuel Povey, but I liked and respected him."

3. The author may create his characters in terms of what other characters say and feel about them. Willa Cather's heroine in *My Ántonia* is a Czech immigrant girl in pioneer Nebraska whose family lacks even the bare necessities of life. But to the author she is a glamorous figure, "a rich mine of life, like the founders of early races." To show us such a character from her own point of view would, obviously, be to miss everything significant about her; to give her to us as the author sees her might be quite unconvincing. Willa Cather, accordingly, lets her reader see Ántonia through the eyes of Jim Burden, a boy of about her own age, who was not in love with her, but whose imagination her primitive, earthy integrity enthralled. Even at the end of the book, when he sees her again after a long interval,

"a battered woman now, not a lovely girl . . . she still had that something which fires the imagination, could still stop one's breath for a moment by a look or gesture that somehow revealed the meaning in common things."

In another novel, *A Lost Lady*, Willa Cather had, in one respect, a more difficult problem, for Marian Forrester's is another kind of glamour, and it must survive her moral degradation. To Niel Herbert, who has boyishly idealized her, she brings bitter disillusionment; through her he learns that

> Lilies that fester smell far worse than weeds.

But he does not permit this to destroy his affection for her. At the very end of the novel, Niel and another of Mrs. Forrester's admirers are discussing her last days:

"So we may feel sure that she was well cared for, to the very end," said Niel. "Thank God for that!"

"I knew you'd feel that way," said Ed Elliott, as a warm wave of feeling passed over his face. "I did!"

But before he can decide to trust one character's interpretation of another, the reader must, of course, make up his mind what he believes about the character who is making the report. Sometimes the reporter is frankly what drama critics call a "chorus character"; it is clear that he speaks for the author and in his behalf; some authors even have a stock type of chorus character which they use in book after book. In the quotation just made from *A Lost Lady*, Willa Cather reinforces Niel Herbert's feeling for Mrs. Forrester by checking it against Ed Elliott's. In Walter de la Mare's *Memoirs of a Midget*, the reader learns from his own observation of Fanny Bowater that she is a malevolent creature; when she enthralls the curate, Mr. Crimble, who kills himself over his passion for her, we discover that she is also a fascinating one. Still, Mr. Crimble is a man, under the spell of sexual passion, which is notoriously deceptive, and, as the event proves, he is something of a fool. De la Mare takes a very long step toward convincing the reader that Fanny really does have glamour, and greatly increases the complexity of her character, by causing his narrator, Miss M., who is neither a man nor a fool, to be enthralled by her also.

Some characters, like Thackeray's Beatrix Esmond, have the gift of analyzing themselves for the reader's enlightenment. If we are to take such material at face value, it must be reinforced by our own observation of the character and by what others believe about her, or else we must have been convinced that the character concerned is exceptionally clear-sighted. Beatrix Esmond is just this, but it is her tragedy that she lacks the will to use her knowledge, either for her own benefit or that of others. On the other hand, Meredith's Sir Willoughby Patterne in *The Egoist* is gradually unmasked, in the course of the novel, as everything he does not believe himself to be.

Sometimes, too, it suits an author's purpose never to let the reader see a character as he is, or even as he appears to himself, but only as he appears to others. Galsworthy uses this method with Irene in *The Man of Property;* we see her only through Forsyte eyes, as a "concretion of disturbing Beauty impinging upon a possessive world." In *The Arrow of Gold*, Conrad lets us see Rita only as M. George saw her; the objection sometimes heard that she is not "convincing" shows, therefore, that the reader has not grasped the author's intention in creating her. We are under no obligation to agree with M. George.

4. Finally, the author of a work of fiction may create his characters as a dramatist creates them, in terms of what they themselves do and say.

The first aspect requires little discussion. A work of fiction is a story, and unless a character is revealed through action, he will never be revealed at all. Or at least, he will never be revealed as a character of fiction. He will not live in the book in which he has his being. We may understand him intellectually, as we understand an historical character, but we shall not realize him in the much more vital way in which we are given the privilege of realizing a character in a work of art.

Furthermore, when the actions of a character conflict with what we have learned about him from other sources, we shall regard his actions as determinative. When Emerson made his famous remark about "what you are" sounding so loudly in his ears that he could not hear "what you say," he was thinking about "real" people, not characters in fiction. But the statement applies to fictional characters also. Mr. Pecksniff (*Martin Chuzzlewit*) professes great benevolence, Uriah Heep (*David Copperfield*), vast humility. But the behavior of both shows that their true characters are not only different from but diametrically opposed to the masks which they wear before the world, and the reader judges them by what they do.

What the characters say is more difficult to talk about, for the important thing is neither the judgments they express nor the information they give us but something much more subtle than that. It is in dialogue passages that the novel comes closest to the drama; indeed, James distinguished sharply between "picture" and "scene." Edith Wharton tended to rely upon narrative ("picture") for the substance of her story, finding it more varied and supple, less wasteful and roundabout, more "orchestral" than the more sharply limited drama. Elizabeth Bowen says that dialogue "requires more art than does any other constituent of the novel" because it "must appear realistic without being so."

It must be "pointed, intentional, relevant. It must crystal-
lize situation. It must express character. It must advance
plot." Moreover, it is itself action. "What is being said is
the effect of something that has happened; at the same time,
what is being said *is in itself something happening,* which
will in turn, leave its effect." "Did you think what I said
was offensive?" we are sometimes asked by somebody at
whose remark a third person has taken offense. And sometimes we are regretfully obliged to reply, "It wasn't what
you said. It was the way you said it."

So it is, too, in fiction. And by "the way you said it,"
one does not here mean any of the more obvious things: "I
ain't" and "you was" to indicate an uneducated man, or
"I'm after tellin' you" for an Irishman. One need not deny
that subtle and powerful effects may be secured by such
means. How much would *Huckleberry Finn* have lost if
Mark Twain had not written the story in Huck's own
backwoods vernacular! But what we have in mind here is
something larger.

"Every human being who possesses anything approaching personality," writes John Livingston Lowes, "has his
own unique rhythms, tone, inflections, build of sentences."
He is speaking of Chaucer, the earliest English writer who
ever learned how to invent a distinctive, individual turn of
speech for each fully realized character, so that they "talked
themselves alive," as it were, and we came to know them as
we know the people we live with, and by something which,
by permissible analogy, we may call the sound of the voice.
"Wholly apart from subject matter," says Lowes, "you
could not mistake a passage from the Pardoner's Prologue
. . . for one of [the Wife of Bath's]." And it is true, and
in this aspect Chaucer has never been surpassed. But he has
been equalled—by Shakespeare, by Scott, by Dickens, by
Walter de la Mare, and a number more.

It may seem odd that among those who come first to mind, only one should be a dramatist, for this is the dramatist's particular gift, and living characters can rarely be created in the drama without it. One of E. E. Stoll's great contributions to Shakespeare criticism has been his demonstration of the way in which Hamlet, Othello, Macbeth, Cleopatra, and the rest are made to live by their choice of words and the rhythm of their speech, each with his own peculiar "music"; here, and not in formal logic, as Stoll rightly insists, does their integrity as characterizations lie. What tragic heroine but Cleopatra could cry to the asp as she applies it to her breast in suicide:

> Poor venomous fool,
> Be angry and dispatch. O, couldst thou speak,
> That I might hear thee call great Caesar ass
> Unpolicied,

and then, a moment later, to her maid Charmian, flooding even her vulgarity with the bitter splendor of her imagination:

> Peace, peace!
> Dost thou not see my baby at my breast,
> That sucks the nurse asleep?

But even Shakespeare is no greater in this aspect than Scott, nor can I hope to improve upon the well-selected examples of his power that Lord David Cecil has given us in his exciting centenary essay[5]—(but I can quote only fragments of his citations here):

Meg Merrilies, in *Guy Mannering:* "Do you see that blackit and broken end of a sheeling? There my kettle boiled for forty years; there I bore twelve buirdly sons and daughters. Where are they now? where are the leaves that were on that auld ash

[5] Lord David Cecil, *Sir Walter Scott* (Constable, 1932).

tree at Martinmas! The west wind has made it bare; and I'm stripped too. Do you see that saugh tree? it's but a blackened rotten stump now. I've sate under it mony a bonnie summer afternoon, when it hung its gay garlands ower the poppling water. I've sat there, and I've held you on my knee, Harry Bertram, and sung ye sangs of the auld barons and their bloody wars. It will ne'er be green again, and Meg Merrilies will never sing sangs mair, be they blythe or sad. But ye'll no forget her, and ye'll gar big up the auld wa's for her sake? And let somebody live there that's ower gude to fear them of another warld. For if ever the dead came back amang the living, I'll be seen in this glen mony a night after these crazed banes are in the mould."

Habakkuk Mucklewrath, in *Old Mortality:* "Who talks of signs and wonders? Am I not Habakkuk Mucklewrath, whose name is changed to Magor-Missabib, because I am made a terror unto myself and unto all that are around me? I heard it. When did I hear it? Was it not in the Tower of the Bass, that overhangeth the wide wild sea? And it howled in the winds, and it roared in the billows, and it screamed, and it whistled, and it clanged, with the screams and the clang and the whistle of the sea-birds, as they floated, and flew, and dropped, and dived, on the bosom of the waters. I saw it. Where did I see it? Was it from the high peaks of Dumbarton, when I looked westward upon the fertile land, and northward on the wild Highland hills; when the clouds gathered and the tempest came, and the lightnings of heaven flashed in sheets as wide as the banners of an host? What did I see? Dead corpses and wounded horses, the rushing together of battle, and garments rolled in blood. What heard I? The voice that cried, 'Slay, slay, smite, slay utterly, let not your eye have pity! slay utterly, old and young, the maiden, the child, and the woman whose head is grey. Defile the house and fill the courts with the slain!' "

Jeanie Deans, in *The Heart of Midlothian:* "I would hae gaen to the end of the earth to save the life of John Porteous, or any other unhappy man in his condition; but I might lawfully doubt how far I am called upon to be the avenger of his blood, though it may become the civil magistrate to do so. He is dead and gane to his place, and they that have slain him must answer for their ain act. But my sister—my puir sister Effie, still lives, though her days and hours are numbered! She lives, and a word of the King's mouth might restore her to a broken-hearted auld man, that never, in his daily and nightly exercise, forgot to pray that his Majesty might be blessed with a long and prosperous reign, and that his throne, and the throne of his posterity, might be established in righteousness. O, madam, if ever ye kenn'd what it was to sorrow for and with a sinning and a suffering creature, whose mind is sae tossed that she can be neither ca'd fit to live or die, have some compassion on our misery! Save an honest house from dishonour, and an unhappy girl, not eighteen years of age, from an early and dreadful death! Alas, it is not when we sleep soft and wake merrily ourselves, that we think on other people's sufferings. Our hearts are waxed light within us then, and we are for righting our ain wrangs and fighting our ain battles. But when the hour of trouble comes to the mind or to the body—and seldom may it visit your Leddyship—and when the hour of death comes, that comes to high and low—lang and late may it be yours—O, my Leddy, then it isna what we hae dune for oursells, but what we hae dune for others, that we think on maist pleasantly. And the thoughts that ye hae intervened to spare the puir thing's life will be sweeter in that hour, come when it may, than if a word of your mouth could hang the haill Porteous mob at the tail of ae tow."

Elspeth of the Craigburnfoot, in *The Antiquary:* "If I hae sinned, hae I not suffered? Hae I had a day's peace or an hour's rest since these lang wet locks of hair first lay upon my pillow at Craigburnfoot? Has not my house been burned, wi' my bairn in the cradle? Have not my boats been wrecked, when a' others weathered the gale? Have not a' that were near and dear to me dree'd penance for my sin? Has not the fire had its share o' them, the winds had their part, the sea had her part? And oh!

that the earth would take her part that's been lang, lang weary-ing to be joined to it!"

The Setting

There are not many novels—and these are all modern—in which the Setting is anything like so important as either Plot or Characters. Nevertheless, setting can be used in a number of different ways, and these need to be understood and defined.

Surveying the changes that have taken place in the use of this element during the history of fiction, Clayton Hamilton comments on some interesting parallels between literature and painting. He points out that in the earliest pictures there is no background whatever. "The figures in Pompeian frescoes are limned upon a blank bright wall, most frequently deep red in color." Cimabue, "the father of Italian painting," does not do quite that, but he does present his figures "against a background devoid of distance and perspective and detail; and even in the work of his greater and more natural pupil, Giotto, the element of background remains comparatively insignificant."

Early tellers of tales may go almost, though not quite, so far as the creators of the Pompeian frescoes. People do not live against a blank bright wall. But so long as only the basic, universal elements of human experience are involved in your tale, there can be no particular point in telling just where they lived. The people who listened to the parables of Jesus knew—and could have conceived of—no different kind of milieu than that in which they themselves lived; from their own clear, but limited, experience, they automatically supplied backgrounds. Jesus did not, therefore, need to have his "properties" laid out beforehand, in full view of the audience, like the stage manager of a realistic play. He handled them more like a conjurer: when he needed a property, he reached forth and drew it out of the air. It was only when there was something in the story itself that called for a specific setting that he felt it necessary to supply one. Probably his listeners knew that the road between Jerusalem and Jericho was infested with robbers, or at least the attack by which the poor traveller in the story of the Good Samaritan was brought to his parlous pass was readily conceivable there.

Lord David Cecil may exaggerate somewhat when he says that the novelists of the eighteenth century presented character "as a detached phenomenon, owing nothing to its surroundings." He is clearing the way for his contrasting description of Scott's characters as "always envisaged . . . in relation to . . . [their] historic past: . . . shaped and controlled by those vaster, more impersonal forces of historic condition and trend which had shaped and colored the community" to which they belonged:

Parson Adams, Doctor Primrose, Uncle Toby, are presented to us as cut flowers, their outlines sharp, their colors vivid against the white, brightly-lit walls of the botanist's laboratory. We are told nothing of their natural background, the garden where they grew, the weather in which they blossomed; their historic and religious and social environment, and how it made them what they were. Parson Adams is a clergyman and an Englishman; but these facts tell us nothing significant about him. For the aspects of his character with which Fielding is concerned are not those which he has acquired from the world he has lived in, but the individual idiosyncrasies which differentiate him from it. He could be turned into a Catholic Irish priest and we should still recognize him.

Bliss Perry seems fundamentally in harmony with this view when he declares that "ordinarily, even in Fielding's novels, it rains only to delay the coach, and not to affect or symbolize the sentiments of the passengers."

Decorative and Symbolic Settings

When setting does begin to be used more elaborately in fiction, it often comes in as merely decorative material, with no vital relationship to either the characters or the foreground action, as in so many Italian paintings the Holy Family is shown surrounded by Italian scenery and activities, the first of which must have been as strange to these Palestinian exiles as the second would have been incomprehensible. Most readers will agree with Clayton Hamilton that the backgrounds in the *Orlando Furioso* and *The Faerie Queene* are decorative in the main, but there may be some doubt about the great portrait by Leonardo da Vinci which Hamilton uses as his most elaborate illustration: "There is no real reason, with reference to life itself, why the 'Mona Lisa' . . . should smile inscrutably upon us before a background of jagged rocks and cloudy sky. . . ." Perhaps not, and then again, perhaps. Who is brave enough to aver that he understands that most enigmatical of ladies, or the painter's intent in creating her? If he thought of her as anything like so sinister as many modern viewers find her, then the background may well have been intended to convey a subtle suggestion of her mood.

At any rate, setting may be used as I suggest in literature, and very effectively too, and this not only in the obvious and crudest way which Ruskin described as "the pathetic fallacy," as when the weather weeps in sympathy because the hero has either broken his heart or stubbed his toe. On the basis of a different conception of the relationship between man and the universe, cruel contrasts may be used in this connection, and the room in which the despairing hero has just destroyed himself may be suddenly flooded with golden sunshine.

Hawthorne does something better than this when, in *The Scarlet Letter*, he permits the Reverend Mr. Dimmesdale to project the tortures of his own guilty conscience back upon nature itself, seeing the disturbances in the sky in the form of a great letter "A" for Adultery. King Lear finds his own despair both reflected in and reinforced by the storm on the heath—the world without sharing the convulsions of the world within—so that his own passion grows before the spectator's eyes until it takes on cosmic proportions.

In Marjorie Bowen's novels, the dominant emotion of a scene, and sometimes of a whole book, takes on concretion in some material object, which broods over the locale and becomes, as it were, the sanctuary of its malevolent god. In a famous passage in Charlotte Brontë's *Jane Eyre*, the troubled heroine sees a lightning-blasted tree as an expression of her own anguish of spirit:

It was not without a certain wild pleasure I ran before the wind delivering my trouble of mind to the measureless air-torrent thundering through space. Descending the laurel-walk, I faced the wreck of the chestnut-tree; it stood up, black and riven: the trunk, split down the centre, gasped ghastly. The cloven halves were not broken from each other, for the firm base and strong roots kept them unsundered below; though community of vitality was destroyed—the sap could flow no more: their great boughs on each side were dead, and next year's tempests would be sure to fell one or both to earth: as yet, however, they might be said to form one tree—a ruin; but an entire ruin.

"You did right to hold fast to each other," I said: as if the monster-splinters were living things, and could hear me. "I think, scathed as you look, and charred and scorched, there must be a little sense of life in you yet; rising out of that adhesion of the faithful, honest roots: you will never have green leaves more—never more see birds making nests and singing idyls in your boughs; the time of pleasure and love is over with you; but you are not desolate: each of you has a comrade to sympathize with him in his decay." As I looked at them, the moon appeared momentarily in that part of the sky which filled their fissure; her disk was blood-red and half overcast; she seemed to throw on me one bewildered, dreary glance, and buried herself again instantly in the deep drift of cloud. The wind fell, for a second, round Thornfield; but far away over wood and water, poured a wild, melancholy wail: it was sad to listen to, and I ran off again.

Setting as an Influence on Characters and Action

Thomas Hardy, however, uses nature somewhat more intimately than that. In his pages, it does more than symbolize the moods of his characters: often it determines them, and their actions besides. "On these lonely hills and dales," he tells us of Tess of the D'Urbervilles, "her quiescent glide was of a piece with the element she moved in. Her flexuous and stealthy figure became an integral part of the scene." In Chapter II of *The Return of the Native*, a woman's figure rises "from the semi-globular mound like a spike from a helmet." It was "so much like an organic part of the entire motionless structure that to see it move would have impressed the mind as a strange phenomenon." Yet it did move, "descended on the right side of the barrow, with the glide of a water-drop down a bud. . . ."

It would be very unsuitable to indicate such a close relationship as this between nature and most of the characters of modern fiction, but those who dwell on Egdon Heath are a special case. Hardy devotes the whole first chapter of *The Return of the Native* to the Heath: "A Face On Which Time Makes But Little Impression." The reader is introduced to the Heath before he meets any of the characters, before, too, he has any idea what the plot is to be about. It has sometimes been said that the Heath is the hero of the book. The Heath determines the action; it decides the fate of the characters. Those who make terms with the Heath live; those who cannot adjust themselves to it, it destroys.

This is no isolated instance in fiction. If Conrad did not mean the storm to dominate *Typhoon*, then he named his story very carelessly, and George R. Stewart's *Storm* and *Fire* have gone beyond Conrad in this regard. The "local color" writers of the nineteenth century did not all use nature in the Hardy manner, but they were very conscious of the influence of environment upon their characters, none of whom would have been believable in any other milieu. A few examples among many would be the work of Mrs. Stowe, Sarah Orne Jewett, Mary E. Wilkins Freeman, and Alice Brown in New England; of Augustus Longstreet and Joel Chandler Harris (the Uncle Remus tales) in the deep South; Bret Harte's stories of California mining camps during the Gold Rush and George W. Cable's pictures of Creole civilization in Louisiana; Edward Eggleston's stories of early Indiana and Charles Egbert Craddock's explorations of the Cumberland mountains. John Fox, Jr. (*The Little Shepherd of Kingdom Come*, *The Trail of the Lonesome Pine*, etc.) made a formula out of the contrast between Cumberland pioneers and the aristocrats of the Bluegrass.

As a group, the "local color" writers are now often regarded as having shot their bolt, nor is the term "regionalism," which came into vogue at a later date, now heard so often as it was a few years ago. Yet local settings have been, and are, important in the work of many more recent, and some more distinguished, writers than most of those I have named above. Neither Willa Cather nor Thomas Wolfe nor John Steinbeck could be called a regionalist in the sense that their literary stock-in-trade is the exploitation of local idiosyncrasy, but certainly their work strongly reflects, and shows the influence of, their early environment. Neither is the regionalist approach confined to those who live in out-of-the-way places. We speak of Victor Hugo's Paris, Dickens's London, and even of O. Henry's New York, "Bagdad-on-the-Subway," in the brownstone epoch, which is already becoming a legendary period.

Urban, Historical and Sociological Backgrounds

This last point may serve to remind us that when we talk about "setting" and "background" in fiction, we do not always have nature in mind. If Egdon Heath is the dominating influence in *The Return of the Native*, Victor Hugo's *Notre-Dame de Paris* is dominated by the cathedral, and Bulwer-Lytton's *The Last Days of Pompeii* by Mount Vesuvius. I assert no complete parallelism between these books. Thus, in *The Last Days of Pompeii*, Mount Vesuvius erupts, which is an *event*, and at this point a part of the *action* of the book. But at least the comparisons may indicate that what seem like very "modern" developments have often been foreshadowed in earlier works.

Great historic movements are importantly determinative in many novels: the Civil War in *The Long Roll* and *Cease Firing*, by Mary Johnston, and in *The Wave*, by Evelyn Scott; World War I in such varied fictions as *Three Soldiers*, by John Dos Passos, *The Four Horsemen of the Apocalypse*, by Vicente Blasco-Ibáñez, and *A Farewell to Arms*, by Ernest Hemingway; World War II in too many novels to enumerate.

Again, there are so many books which make important use of industrial or occupational backgrounds that one critic has remarked that, for the modern novelist, social forces seem to have taken over the destinal attributes which the Greeks reserved to the gods. Zola used a mining background in *Germinal*; in *The Octopus*, by his American admirer, Frank Norris, the title indicates the Southern Pacific Railroad, through whose greed and exploitation the characters are controlled and finally destroyed. Albert Halper began with a regional novel, *Union Square*, but in both his second novel and his third—*The Foundry* and *The Chute*—the occupational interest was paramount.

Right and Wrong Uses of Backgrounds

The regionalists share one danger with the sociologists— that of developing backgrounds out of proportion to their importance in the book as a whole. And the sociologists share another danger with a group with which it would shock many of them to be compared—the pious, didactic writers. For if it is not the function of fiction to improve our morals or to save our souls, then it is not the function of fiction to reform the economic system either, nor yet to bring us information about folkways. If you are going to argue that Lloyd Douglas debases fiction by forcing his tales out of a normal and convincing course of development (if that is the way his books impress you) because it seems more important to him to teach his readers how to be good Christians than it does to create a perfect work of art, then you are going to have to condemn your sociological novelist also when he does the same thing in the interest of saving society.

Insofar as *The Grapes of Wrath* was read for its sociological interest, it no more encouraged the development of the art of fiction than *Uncle Tom's Cabin* did insofar as it was read as anti-slavery propaganda, nor *In His Steps* insofar as it was read as a religious tract. Nor do our book-review journals encourage the development of the art of fiction when they give p. 1 to a novel which has "news interest" and relegate to p. 27 the novel which is merely a perfect work of art. Yet both *Uncle Tom's Cabin* and *The*

Grapes of Wrath are, with very different reservations, good novels, and if *In His Steps* is a bad one, the reason is not that Charles M. Sheldon was a religious man but simply that he was not a novelist.

Aesthetically, it matters not one whit where the novelist finds his material; what matters is how he uses it. It does not matter whether his industrial background, if he has one, is as richly described as Arnold Bennett's in *Clayhanger* or left to the imagination altogether, like that of Henry James in *The Ambassadors*. What does matter is whether or not he needs it, and whether, if he does need it, he has been able to transmute it into the stuff of fiction. George Eliot was quite correct when she said that the backgrounds of *Romola* were no more elaborately indicated than those of *Adam Bede* or *The Mill on the Floss*, but she forgot that she had been able to vitalize and assimilate the materials she grew up with much more successfully than she had been able to do this with the information she had dug out of books in the Magliabecchian Library. "Scene," to quote Elizabeth Bowen's pregnant article once more, "is only justified in the novel where it can be shown, or at least felt, to act upon action or character. In fact, where it has dramatic use."

Methods of Telling the Story: Omniscience

I have said nothing so far of the way in which the tale is told. The most "natural" way, it must seem to most of us, since we have been familiar with it from our nursery days, is to tell the story in the third person, from the point of view of the omniscient author, who knows all, sees all, understands all—and tells all besides. The omniscient author assumes a complete knowledge of the deeds and thoughts and motives of all his characters and shifts from one to another as occasion demands:

So the children were left alone in the forest, and Gretel, who was afraid, wept bitterly. Her brother Haensel tried to keep up a brave front—he even whistled softly—so as not to increase her fears, but inside he was as terrified as she was. It was different with the father and the wicked stepmother, as they tramped off through the woods in another direction, for the man sighed and groaned continually, but the only outward sign that the woman's conscience troubled her was her muttering now and then, under her breath, "It was the only thing we could do. There was no sense in all four of us starving." Haensel picked some berries and gave them to Gretel to eat. They were not very good, but to please him she tried to choke them down, for she knew how hard he was trying to help her, and his brave front did not deceive her at all. "Here, Gretel, take, eat; we don't know how far we may have to walk before we find some place to spend the night, and you must keep up your strength." He looked so anxious that she even managed to smile at him. And, far off, the Old Witch chuckled softly to herself in her Gingerbread House, where she had everything ready. The children were too far away for her to be able to see them, but she knew by her evil arts that every step brought them closer. As she looked up, she saw her huge, old black cat by the side of the hearth, beside her broom. He was sitting up very straight, with his tail curled around him; it seemed to her that he was bigger than ever. His green eyes shimmered in the firelight. Like her, he seemed to be waiting for something; once, she almost thought she saw him smile.

The obvious advantage of this method is that the author is never under any necessity to account for the sources of his information. Once grant the basic assumption of God-like omniscience and all else follows.

The Autobiographical Method

The omniscient method is disliked by many modern writers, but it shows no signs of losing its hold. It is still, by all odds, the most widely used method of telling a story.

Indeed, the modern reader is so thoroughly accustomed to it that he finds it rather hard to believe that it was avoided by both the great eighteenth-century pioneer novelists, Daniel Defoe and Samuel Richardson. Robinson Crusoe, Moll Flanders, the Cavalier, and all the rest of Defoe's protagonists give us autobiographical narratives in the first person. Richardson rifled the postbag. In his first novel, *Pamela*, there are only thirty-two letters, and the heroine herself writes twenty-eight of them. Then communication is cut off, and she continues the story in her journal. In *Clarissa Harlowe*, on the other hand, the development is much more complicated. Here we have 547 letters, most of which pass between Clarissa and Miss Howe or between the villain-hero Lovelace and his confidant, John Belford, but nearly all the numerous characters take pen in hand at some time. Footnotes furnish corrections and cross-references; occasionally they summarize and offer supplementary information.

There were sound practical reasons why the early eighteenth-century writers should avoid omniscience, why they should have left it to the author of *Tom Jones*, Henry Fielding, to emerge as the first novelist unashamed, who dared himself to assume control of his material, interpreting and commenting upon it whenever he chose, and boldly staking his claim to attention upon his art and not upon the pretense that he was not an artist but a reporter, as his predecessors had done. For though they had never, in this connection, heard the word, art was precisely what eighteenth-century readers were afraid of. They had not learned to distinguish between fact and truth. So Defoe, who was a practical journalist before he was a novelist, pretends that he is producing a factual record, and he makes such a good job of it that when the satirical Jonathan Swift applies Defoe's method of minute circumstantiality to fairy-tale material in *Gulliver's Travels*, an Irish bishop denounces the book for its "inaccuracies," and one reader is greatly disappointed because he cannot find Lilliput on the map.

Straightforward autobiographical narrative of the Defoe variety has obvious advantages. It is simple; it is clear; the source of the narrator's information is clearly accounted for. Mark Twain's mother once overheard two men in a train arguing about where her son was born. She turned about and told them. "I ought to know," she said. "I'm his mother. I was there." We are always disposed to lend more credence to a man who tells us what he himself did and thought than to one who merely reports concerning another man: this is one of the basic principles of testimony. There is, too, an obvious gain in vividness.

It happened one day about noon [so Robinson Crusoe tells us, in one of the tensest passages in his story], going towards my boat, I was exceedingly surprised with the print of a man's naked foot on the shore, which was very plain to be seen in the sand: I stood like one thunderstruck, or as if I had seen an apparition; I listened, I looked round me, I could hear nothing nor see any thing, I went up to a rising ground to look farther, I went up the shore and down the shore, but it was all one, I could see no other impression but that one, I went to it again to see if there were any more, and to observe if it might not be my fancy; but there was no room for that, for there was exactly the very print of a foot, toes, heel, and every part of a foot; how it came thither, I knew not, nor could in the least imagine. But after innumerable fluttering thoughts, like a man perfectly confused and out of myself, I came home to my fortification, not feeling, as we say, the ground I went on, but terrified to the last degree, looking behind me at every two or three steps, mistaking every bush and tree, and fancying every stump at a distance to be a man; nor is it possible to describe how many various shapes affrighted imagination represented things to me in, how many wild ideas were found every moment in my fancy, and what strange unaccountable whimsies came into my thoughts by the way.

When I came to my castle, for so I think I called it ever after this, I fled into it like one pursued; whether I went over by the ladder, as first contrived, or went in at the hole in the rock, which I called a door, I cannot remember; no, nor could I remember the next morning, for never frighted hare fled to cover, or fox to earth, with more terror of mind than I to this retreat.

Now try rewriting that second paragraph in the third person, from the point of view of the omniscient author, and see how much you lose:

When he came to his castle, for so he called it ever after this, he fled into it like one pursued; whether he went over by the ladder as first contrived, or went in at the hole in the rock, which he called a door, he was never able to remember; no, not even the next morning, for never frighted hare fled to cover, or fox to earth, with more terror of mind than he to this retreat.

But the method works much better for a story like *Robinson Crusoe*, in which we have only one real character, and nothing occurs in which he is not the central participant, than it does in the full-fledged novel, with an organized plot and a variety of characters. For it gives all the advantages of highlighting to the central figure, with the inevitable concomitant disadvantage of leaving all the others in shadow. We see the other characters only as the narrator sees them, and unless he himself is omniscient in understanding, then the reader will never see them as they are, or as the author sees them. Suspense is difficult also; however tight the "spot" in which the hero finds himself, the reader will not worry about his survival, for the mere fact that he is telling the story is the best evidence we could ask for on that point. And suppose it is necessary to include incidents in which the narrator did not participate, or of which the plot of the story may even demand that he should be ignorant? Will you drag in a new narrator at this point? This is what Stevenson does in *Treasure Island*, when Dr. Livesey temporarily replaces Jim Hawkins, and again in *The Master of Ballantrae*, when Mackellar supplements his own recollections with long quotations from the memoirs of the Chevalier Burke. The device is not quite free of awkwardness in either case.

The Epistolary Method

The general advantages of first-person narrative carry over with a difference into the epistolary novel. The impression of immediacy is much greater, however, for now the story is told not in leisurely retrospect, with all dangers safely past, but in the fullness of the tick, with the narrator still firmly in the grip of whatever emotion may have been inspired, and knowing no more than the reader knows of what the next moment will bring forth. This is to come very close to the experience of living, and in a great epistolary novel like *Clarissa*, the suspense can, therefore, be very great.

The great disadvantage of the epistolary method is the enormous strain it places upon credulity. One must assume all the principals to be indefatigable letter-writers, each with an eager confidant, waiting as breathlessly for news as the reader himself. Pamela writes six long letters on her wedding day. Moreover, if the book is to hold its grip upon the imagination, everybody must write as brilliantly as fluently, yet nobody can use the same style as anybody else. To all this must be added the obvious consideration that the epistolary method inhibits the continuity and rapid progression which some readers value most in narrative. It makes, indeed, for a narrative in terms of mosaic work.

"Point of View"

Since Henry James, many novelists have preferred to limit themselves to the "point of view" either of some one particular character in a novel or to a group of characters whose eyes and whose minds are employed successively. In the imposing of a voluntary limitation, this method resembles the old-fashioned autobiographical narrative, but it differs from it in using the third person, not the first; neither is the reflecting consciousness necessarily that of the central figure. Instead, James himself preferred to think of him as "some more or less detached, some not strictly involved, though thoroughly interested and intelligent, witness or reporter, some person who contributes to the case mainly a certain amount of criticism and interpretation of it."

The tendency toward "point of view" begins early in James's work, long before he had completely formulated his theories concerning it. The story of *Roderick Hudson* comes to us essentially as Rowland Mallett sees it, that of *The American* from the point of view of Christopher Newman. In *What Maisie Knew* and *The Ambassadors*, single reflectors are employed—*Maisie* is a particularly interesting tour-de-force because it involves the picture of a corrupt society as seen through the eyes of a child—but there are several reflectors in *The Wings of the Dove*, and *The Golden Bowl* is told from the husband's point of view in Part I and from that of the wife in Part II.

Some of these reflectors are principal actors rather than detached observers, but James never permits himself the loose fluidity of the old biographical novel. When the method is working well, we get a double drama: the happenings themselves and the observer's reaction to them. James is often reproached for lack of action, but in this sense his novels are all action. Through limiting himself and his reader to the range of the reflecting consciousness, he achieves an intensely dynamic quality and a high degree of intimacy. The omniscient author knows everything in advance. Not so the Jamesian narrator. Like Ralph, in *The Sense of the Past*, James's reader "must grow many of his perceptions and possibilities from moment to moment as they . . . [are] wanted." Thus James makes his novel a self-containing entity, not, like the conventional novel, something manipulated from the outside; hence, too, as L. N. Richardson has remarked, "the reader's attention remains always within the pages."

"Stream-of-Consciousness"

James's methods have been, in a measure, extended by the authors of the so-called "stream-of-consciousness" novels, who have not only limited themselves religiously to a single point of view but have also, in some cases, attempted a dataistic record of what passes through the mind. James would not himself have approved of these writers: for one thing, they are too close to life to achieve the form or pattern which he valued in fiction; for another, insofar as they follow Joyce, they concern themselves with the region of the subconscious, in which he, as an artist, felt little interest. Dorothy M. Richardson has written thirteen novels—or one novel in thirteen parts—*Pilgrimage*, in which nothing appears that has not been filtered through the mind of her single heroine, Miriam Henderson. Here is the famous description of the *Haarwaschen* in the German school, from the first of the series, *Pointed Roofs:*

Miriam's outraged head hung over the steaming basin—her hair spread round it like a tent frilling out over the table.

For a moment she thought that the nausea which had seized her as she surrendered would, the next instant, make flight imperative. Then her amazed ears caught the sharp bumping of an eggshell against the rim of the basin, followed by a further brisk crackling just above her. She shuddered from head to foot as the egg descended with a cold slither upon her incredulous skull. Tears came to her eyes as she gave beneath the onslaught of two hugely enveloping, vigorously drubbing hands— "sh—ham—poo" gasped her mind.

But we get farther into the realm of the mind in another passage in the same novel, where Miriam lies in her bed in Germany and conjures up "a vision of the back of the books in the book-case in the dining-room at home." I quote only the first section of it:

Iliad and *Odyssey* . . . people going over the sea in boats and someone doing embroidery . . . that little picture of Hector and Andromache in the corner of a page . . . he in armour . . . she, in a trailing dress, holding up a baby. Both, silly. . . . She wished she had read more carefully. She could not remember anything in Lecky or Darwin that would tell her what to do . . . *Hudibras* . . . *The Atomic Theory* . . . *Ballads and Poems*, D. G. Rossetti . . . Kinglake's *Crimea* . . . Palgrave's *Arabia* . . . Crimea . . . *The Crimea* . . . Florence Nightingale; a picture somewhere; a refined face, with cap and strings. . . . She must have smiled. . . . Motley's *Rise of* . . . *Rise of* . . . Motley's *Rise of the Dutch Republic* and the *Chronicles of the Schönberg-Cotta Family*. She held to the memory of these two books. Something was coming from them to her. She handled the shiny brown gold-toothed back of Motley's *Rise* and felt the hard graining of the red-bound *Chronicles*. . . . There were green trees outside in the moonlight . . . in Luther's Germany . . . trees and fields and German towns and then Holland.[6]

Theory and Practice

Not many writers have been as rigid about method as Dorothy Richardson. And the reader should by this time understand that it is always easier to differentiate between

[6] From *Pilgrimage* (*Pointed Roofs*, Chapter XII) by Dorothy Richardson. Reprinted by permission of Alfred A. Knopf, Inc., publishers.

methods in a theoretical discussion than it is in practice. Sometimes, to be sure, an author will begin with the "wrong" method and be compelled to make a change. Thus James Branch Cabell began writing his fantasy about the man who discovered that his father was a devil in the first person, but it would not "go," and he was compelled to change to the third, even though this involved junking his original title, *I Go To My Father*, and calling his book instead *The Devil's Own Dear Son*. Many stories, however, manage to get themselves told without the author ever having deliberately made up his mind in advance which method he is going to employ. He tells the story as it comes to him, in the way that seems most natural, and the method somehow takes care of itself.

Turn back to my version of a portion of the Haensel and Gretel story on p. 190. I offered it there as an example of the method of the omniscient author, and so, viewed as a whole, it is. But I did not tell the whole truth about it at that point, because I was deliberately setting a trap for you; I wanted to see whether you would notice what I refrained from pointing out.

The fact is that though the author has entered into the consciousness of Haensel, Gretel, and the Witch, he has only *observed* the father, the stepmother, and the Witch's cat, and the last of these has even been observed at one remove.

Concerning the father, the author merely reports that he "sighed and groaned continually"; from this the reader is left to infer that he is very unhappy about having left the children in the forest. In the case of the woman, we hear the two sentences which she speaks, and this time the author interprets for us in advance: this was "the only outward sign that the woman's conscience troubled her." As for the Witch's cat, not only does the author refuse to enter into his consciousness, but he even refuses to let us look at him directly; we see him only as the Witch saw him. She observed him; the author observes her. It was to her that the cat seemed "bigger than ever," and "seemed to be waiting for something"; "once she," not *quite* but *almost*, "thought she saw him smile."

Consciously or unconsciously, the author must decide, in every instance and in every sentence, whether extension or limitation of knowledge will serve his purpose best. In the Sherlock Holmes stories, Dr. Watson's obtuseness—often just half a step ahead of the reader's own—adds to our appreciation of the detective's perspicacity. Perhaps, also, it subtly flatters our ego, and causes us to feel less stupid than we should otherwise feel. *The Moonstone* and *The Woman in White*, both by Wilkie Collins, are still probably the best mystery stories ever written: each comprises a series of narratives or documents, and the whole truth is not in any one of these but in the combination of them all. In Joseph Hergesheimer's *Java Head*, each chapter is written from the point of view of a different character, quite successfully up to the last chapter, where the author tries, climactically, to enter into the consciousness of Gerrit Ammidon's Manchu wife, and to view the situation through her eyes. Only a Chinese novelist could have hoped for success here; Taou Yuen should have been left the mystery to the end that she had been from the beginning.

Sometimes an author, though present on the scene, rigorously refrains from commenting upon or interpreting his material; he gives the reader the facts and leaves the interpretation to him; Willa Cather used to talk about having things and people tell their story merely "by juxtaposition." What the reader perceives thus has a quality of the inevitable about it: it is so not because anybody has told him it is so but because that is the way things are. But many situations are too complicated to be set forth in this way. And though this sounds very "modern," the difference between it and what the older novelists used to do is, after all, a difference in degree rather than in kind. If you had talked to Jane Austen about "juxtaposition" and "point of view" you might have puzzled her, yet her knowledge of her range was absolute, and nobody will ever find out whether it was deliberately or by instinct that she never described a scene in which no member of her own sex was present, and in encounters between a man and a woman always viewed the scene through the woman's eyes.

Novel and Short Story

For some time we have been speaking of the novel: it now becomes necessary to return for the moment to the short story. Not all the brief narratives in the world can be called short stories in the technical sense of the term. Some are only anecdotes; some, on the other hand, like most of the tales in Boccaccio's *Decameron* are *novella*, or little novels; the stuff of a long novel is there in embryo, but it has not been developed.

It was Edgar Allan Poe who formulated the most widely influential theory of what a short story ought to be.[7] The prose tale was his favorite form of fiction. He did not deny the possibility of the novel; he said many good things about Dickens, Bulwer, and Scott, but he seems to have felt that the novel's virtues were of a milder variety than those of the tale. The intrusion upon the mind of other interests in the intervals between sessions of reading seemed to him well nigh ruinous to unity of impression and intensity of effect. Poe did not believe readers capable of preserving the intensity of response which poetry demands for more than a

[7] See Poe's paper on "Hawthorne's *Tales*," in Volume VII of the Stedman-Woodberry Edition of Poe (Scribners).

half-hour to an hour, but he was willing to permit the "short prose narrative" to run as long as two hours. Yet if the story were to be successful, the author must achieve an absolute unity of effect. "If his very initial sentence tend not to the outbringing of this effect, then he has failed in his first step. In the whole composition there should be no word written, of which the tendency, direct or indirect, is not to the one pre-established design."

Poe had great influence on the nineteenth- and early twentieth-century short story both in English and in French, and Brander Matthews, who accepted his ideas, once proposed spelling "short-story" with a hyphen, in order to distinguish the bonafide, certified product from the narrative which merely happened to be short. "A short-story deals with a single character, a single event, a single emotion, or the series of emotions called forth by a single situation."

These views are still widely held; on this basis, the essential difference between a short story and a novel would be that while the short story deals with a single situation, the novel concerns itself with a chain of circumstances. Unity is not lacking in the novel, but it is certainly a much looser unity than Poe was interested in. On this basis, some novels—Robert Nathan's, for example—might well be shorter than some short stories, i.e., some by Henry James. James had no standard length for his fictions; his idea was always to allow the theme such development as it might require. But he was not naturally inclined toward brevity, and he once got a whole volume of stories out of an attempt to produce one 5,000-word tale for *Harper's Magazine!* Some of James's shorter fictions might well come under the head of what the French call the *nouvelle*, which runs beyond the single situation yet lacks the scope and magnitude of the novel. I have already remarked that Katherine

Mansfield's stories do not conform to the Poe definition; neither, I fear, does the kind of story that is favored today by the editors of *The New Yorker*. We may refuse to call such productions short stories if we like, but in that case we shall have to call them something else. And we do not change the nature of things by changing their names.

Novel and Romance

For that matter, there is no universally-accepted definition of a novel. William Lyon Phelps's "a good story well told" is obviously at once too all-inclusive and too loosely defined. What about a bad story well told? Or a good story badly told? Or a bad story badly told? And what about those good stories well told which are not novels but some other type of fiction?

Yet this is no more foolish than many overexact definitions which end by applying to the particular type of fiction which the definer favors and excluding everything else. Take, for example, the many attempts that have been made to differentiate between the novel and the romance. Scott himself once proposed to define romance as "a fictitious narrative in prose or verse, the interest of which turns upon marvelous or uncommon incidents" and novel as "a fictitious narrative, differing from the romance because the events are accommodated to the ordinary train of human events and the modern state of society." Hawthorne, too, had something of this character in mind when he decided that *The House of the Seven Gables* was a romance and not a novel.

For my own part, if a critic wished thus to distinguish, restricting the term novel to works which attempt a serious picture of life and conduct on a believable, everyday level, I do not know how I could prove that he was "wrong." But I do think he should be warned that he is going to run into numerous problems of classification. What, for example, is he going to do with Scott himself? I should be chary of accepting a definition of "novel" which would rule out many of his works, even though he himself might be willing to accept it. What about James Branch Cabell and his chronicles of Poictesme, the most elaborate novel-series in American literature? What of a score of historical novelists? There are comparatively few long works which exist exclusively in either the realistic or the romantic mood. If there is realism in Scott, then there is, by the same token, romance in Zola and in Frank Norris. Romance is the vivifying element in a work of fiction and realism the verifying element. First-rate fiction generally includes both. I do not, therefore, grant that a novel *must* be realistic, any more than I am willing to grant that a short story *must* be romantic, though that too has been urged. I would not myself deny the term "novel" to any developed prose fiction of reasonable length which includes plot, character, and setting, and achieves a reasonable degree of unity. I shall, therefore, continue to speak of "realistic novels" and "romantic novels" and endeavor to distinguish between them.

The Historical Novel

But the realism-romance antithesis is not the only problem of classification that causes difficulty. What about the "stream-of-consciousness" novel? Insofar as it lacks plot, it might seem to fail to meet even the very elastic definition of the novel I have just tried to frame. Yet I am willing myself to accept it as a kind of novel. I am even willing to allow those who insist that it is not to quarrel among themselves as to what, in that case, it shall be called!

Then there have always been those who, to perpetrate something of an Irish bull, have insisted that an historical novel is not a novel. Historical novels may be either realistic or romantic in mood, but the romantic approach is the more popular, for the simple reason that very few people know enough about the past to be able to describe it realistically.

The present great vogue of historical fiction began in the 'thirties with *Anthony Adverse* and *Gone With the Wind*. At their best, our recent historical fictions have been better than the turn-of-the-century books, which seem to have been stimulated by the nationalism fostered by the Spanish-American War. In the face of war and depression, Americans turned to the past to try to find a key to the present. Novelists have led us back to the Rock Whence We Were Hewn, that we might reaffirm our allegiance to the ideals on which this nation was founded.

Concurrently, however, there has also developed a more meretricious kind of historical novel, a kind of literary equivalent of the worst and most tasteless variety of Technicolor "movies"—superficial, violent, sensational, and above all very highly sexed. Two women—Kathleen Winsor (*Forever Amber*) and Rosamond Marshall—are generally cited as the outstanding exemplars of this tendency.

In view of this circumstance, it has been very interesting, these last few years, to watch the emergence of another type of historical novel, making no compromise with public taste: conscientious reconstructions of the past by gifted historians who are also incorruptible artists, novelists who take both themselves and their art with intense seriousness. Thus England has sent us *The Golden Warrior*, by Hope Muntz; *The Golden Hand*, by Edith Simon; and *The Man on a Donkey*, by H. F. M. Prescott, this last, to my way of thinking, the greatest British novel in a generation. A recent (1952) American book worthy to stand beside these is Gladys Schmitt's story of Christians in third-century Rome, *Confessors of the Name*. In view of the credit which has been given to women writers for debauching the historical novel, it is worth noting that every one of these books was written by a woman also.[8]

Problems in Historical Fiction

Dialogue is a particularly difficult problem in historical fiction. If you allow your characters to speak as we speak today, you will create the effect of having installed telephones in Rome, and if you go out for a Wardour-Street "Godwottery," they sound utterly unnatural. Compromise seems inevitable here; perhaps the least unsatisfactory is that which merely seeks to achieve a certain effect of distance by omitting distinctively modern idiom and striving for a somewhat more formal type of utterance than would be expected of a novelist writing about his contemporaries.

The problem is even more difficult when the people in the book are supposed to be speaking a foreign language. Some authors try to remind the reader of this by the occasional use of foreign words and phrases, a most unfortunate device, since it can only emphasize the inappropriateness of the English by contrast. In *For Whom the Bell Tolls* (which is hardly a historical novel), Ernest Hemingway attempted in some passages an English transliteration of Spanish idiom; the result, naturally, was no language at all.

The ideal historical novelist would be a writer of great gifts who should know the period of which he writes, and feel as much at home in it as another kind of novelist knows the world in which he lives. This ideal will not often be achieved, but to say that a form of art is difficult is not to brand it as illegitimate. Neither will I deny the novelist who writes about the past the privilege of going in for romance

[8] This and the two preceding paragraphs have been reprinted from my article, "The Historical Novel—Past and Present," *Chicago Sunday Tribune Magazine of Books*, December 7, 1952. Copyright, 1952, by the Tribune Company.

206 • TELL ME A STORY

and fantasy, any more than I am disposed to deny such privileges to him who writes about the present. Those who attempt such denials are, in my view, simply declaring war upon the human imagination, and that war, like material war between nations in an atomic age, is the kind of war that cannot be won.

Sir Walter Besant once advised the young lady writer of fiction who had been "brought up in a quiet country village" to "avoid descriptions of garrison life," but Henry James rightly protested against such an unwarrantably arbitrary dictum. "The young lady . . . has only to be a damsel upon whom nothing is lost to make it quite unfair . . . to declare to her that she shall have nothing to say about the military. Greater miracles have been seen at that, imagination assisting, she should speak the truth about some of these gentlemen."

Besant did not live long enough to read Marjorie Bowen's first novel, *The Viper of Milan*, when it was published in 1906, and I do not know whether James ever read it or not. Mark Twain did, and delighted in it. Marjorie Bowen might be described as the young lady who did not follow Besant's advice. When her book appeared, her astonished family warned her that she would probably never be able to do anything like it again. They could not have been more wrong. Between 1906 and her death in 1952, she did it some 150 times, under a variety of pseudonyms,[9] producing, among other things, the widest and most varied array of historical novels of any writer of her time.

Turgenev called Dostoevsky an amateur because he could

---

[9] Most importantly, in addition to Marjorie Bowen, George R. Preedy and Joseph Shearing. She was known to the census-taker as Gabrielle Margaret Vere Campbell Long. See her autobiography, *The Debate Continues, Being the Autobiography of Marjorie Bowen*, by Margaret Campbell (Heinemann, 1939), and the present writer's review-article, "The Extraordinary Mrs. Long," *New York Times Book Review*, May 2, 1943.

not objectify his literary processes. Writers often begin with autobiographical materials, but it is a great handicap not to be able to go beyond them. Those who are confined, as artists, to dramatizing what they have lived may produce work of high quality, but they are seldom prolific. On the other hand, the novelist who, like Trollope, can make fiction out of what he has observed, or out of what he reads, as Marjorie Bowen did, may reasonably expect to find his productive ability limited only by the limitations of his physical strength.

Some Special Types of Fiction

Nothing has been said in this chapter of such special types of fiction as the detective story, the ghost story, and science fiction. The first of these has been developed into the largest, and technically the most expert, of our fictional subdivisions; despite the dominantly realistic tendencies of our literature, we are producing more ghost stories than any preceding generation, and among them some of the best; as for science fiction, it has mushroomed so enormously during recent years that, forgetting Bulwer-Lytton and Jules Verne, we are often tempted to consider it our own particular baby. It is not my baby, and I can say little about it here, but the reader who wishes an introduction to it will find abundant material in Donald A. Wollheim's collection, *The Portable Novels of Science*, in the Viking Portable Library, and in a number of anthologies edited by August Derleth.[10]

The detective story, or murder mystery, has now carried expertness in plot-development to the highest point of excellence it has ever achieved in fiction, though I think

[10] *Strange Ports of Call* (1948); *The Other Side of the Moon* (1949); *Beyond Time and Space* (1950); *Far Boundaries* (1951); *Outer Reaches* (1951); *Beachheads in Space* (1952), all published by Pellegrini and Cudahy, which has now been absorbed by Farrar, Straus, and Young.

Katharine Fullerton Gerould wrong when she calls it "purely intellectual." ("The true detective story is as impersonal as Euclid; it has nothing to do with morality or sentiment.") I cannot claim to love the detective story as Mrs. Gerould loved it—or as Vincent Starrett loves it—but I must rise at this point to protect it against her, for she seems to me to degrade it to a lower plane than, at its best, it inhabits. It should also be noted that the line of demarcation between mystery stories and standard fiction is not absolute: Dorothy Sayers and Michael Innes are not the only practitioners who have reached out to draw a good deal of the novel of character into it.[11]

The ghost story, of course, has a far longer and more distinguished literary ancestry, and it is more deeply rooted in the spiritual life of the race. "There is something ghostly in all great art," said Lafcadio Hearn, "whether of music, sculpture, or architecture. It touches something within us that relates to infinity." There have been some interesting discussions of late years as to whether or not the writer of ghost stories should believe in the supernatural. One excellent British writer, A. E. Coppard, assures us that he does not. Walter de la Mare and Arthur Machen, on the other hand, are believers or drawn profoundly toward belief. There is no more reason why it should be necessary to believe in ghosts before writing a technically expert ghost story than there is why it should be necessary to believe in fairies before writing a technically expert fairy story. But one would expect the believer to produce the more vital story of the two.[12]

[11] For a delightful and comprehensive history of the detective story, see Howard Haycraft, *Murder for Pleasure* (Appleton-Century, 1941).

[12] A recent full and ambitious study is Peter Penzoldt, *The Supernatural in Fiction* (British Book Centre, 1953). Collections of ghost stories are legion: see the present writer's *Six Novels of the Supernatural* (Viking Portable Library, 1944), and *The Fireside Book of Ghost Stories* (1947—now published by Grosset and Dunlap).

This is all that can be said here of these special types of story, so fascinating to so many readers of our time. All, of course, are perfectly legitimate types of artistic expression; indeed, I can think of no kind of story which is not. It is not very important whether the writer gets his materials from experience or from observation or from hearsay or from reading. In *Lord Jim*, Conrad uses all these sources. What matters is what he has to say and how well he says it. And the wonderful thing is that he should be able to do it at all, that mankind should have so readily and so cheaply available this exhaustless source of profit and delight—"a tale that keepeth children from play and old men from the chimney corner."

CHAPTER SIX

Theater and Drama

Drama and Fiction

The drama is like prose fiction in that it tells a story, involving the three elements of plot, character, and setting, and requiring the organization of its materials into a beginning, a middle, and an end; but it differs from prose fiction in that it is not absorbed by the individual reader from arbitrary symbols upon the printed page but is acted upon some kind of stage by human beings who are called actors. The individual reader, in other words, is replaced by a collective audience, and the audience does not read the author's words but hears them as they are spoken by the actors. Neither does it visualize the settings in its imagination from a verbal description of them, as the reader of a novel does. Instead, it looks upon them with its physical eyes, after they have been given a material embodiment by the designer and the stage carpenter.[1]

---

[1] *The Oxford Companion to the Theatre*, edited by Phyllis Hartnoll (Oxford University Press, 1951) is a fascinating reference book. A fine, useful book on the technique of the drama is *Invitation to the Theater*, by Frank Hurburt O'Hara and Margueritte Harmon Bro (Harper, 1951). This book has been useful to the present writer, especially in connection with definitions. For world theater, see John Gassner, *Masters of the Drama* (Random House, 1940). Allardyce Nicoll has written many books about British drama: cf. his *British Drama* (Crowell, 1925). For American drama, see Arthur Hobson Quinn, *A History of the American Drama*

This means that the drama is at once a much simpler and a much more complicated form than prose fiction.

It is more complicated because it denies the author direct access to his public. Read *Vanity Fair* and your mind's eye sees Becky Sharp as Thackeray described her. But go to see Maxwell Anderson's *Mary of Scotland* and your physical eyes do not see Maxwell Anderson's Mary at all. Instead they see Helen Hayes.

Loss and Gain

This may be either an advantage or a disadvantage. We are not primarily concerned here with whether the drama is more or less effective than the novel; we are simply concerned to define the differences between them. In general, the advantages of intensity are with the drama. No other form of art exerts, at its best, so powerful, so irresistible, a spell. But the advantages of subtlety are all with the novel. Simply because of its powerful visual appeal, combined with its inability to exhibit the character from the inside, the drama is always tempted to stress the external, the sensational, the "theatrical." "Fiction," says Bernard de-Voto, "holds the interior world in fee simple."

It has been pointed out elsewhere in this book that in the matter of communication between author and reader, there is loss at both ends. Presumably Thackeray did not completely express his conception of Becky Sharp. Presumably the reader did not grasp everything that Thackeray expressed. But see what happens in the case of the play:

---

from the Beginning to the Civil War, Second Edition, and *A History of the American Drama from the Civil War to the Present Day* (Appleton-Century-Crofts, 1943 and 1936); see, also, Glenn Hughes, *A History of the American Theatre* (Samuel French, 1951). A recent, stimulating book about current trends in world theater, is Eric Bentley, *In Search of Theater* (Knopf, 1953).

Presumably Maxwell Anderson did not completely express his conception of Mary of Scotland. Presumably Miss Hayes (and her director) did not grasp everything which he expressed. Presumably Miss Hayes was not able to express everything she had grasped. And presumably the audience did not understand everything that she expressed![2]

This sounds very discouraging—does it not? But let us go on. This is not the whole story.

The Personality of the Actor

How much of Thackeray's (expressed) Becky Sharp the reader of *Vanity Fair* grasps will vary greatly from one reader to another. The intelligent and experienced reader of fiction will get most of it. The stupid reader will lose a great deal—in some cases, almost everything. But one might expect so fine an actress as Miss Helen Hayes to be a very skilful reader—of plays at any rate: the element of loss in her reading of *Mary of Scotland* would, therefore, probably be slight. Furthermore, as we have already observed, most people get much more vivid impressions of what they see than of what they only read about. On this basis alone, a good actor may well give back with one hand more than he has taken away with the other.

But there is more to it than that. The actor is himself an artist, and being an artist, he adds something to the author's work. The actor—and the singer—differ from all other artists in that they themselves—their bodies and souls—are the media in which they work, the instruments upon which they play. To bring a character to life on the stage, an actor

[2] Some of these steps drop out when an actor appears in a play written by himself, or in some such entertainment as Cornelia Otis Skinner's *Paris '90*. On the other hand, consider the number of intermediaries involved between the original author and the audience for a dramatized novel, like Langdon Mitchell's *Becky Sharp*, based on Thackeray's *Vanity Fair*.

must either enrich the creature that the playwright has created with elements drawn from his own personality, or else he must frankly substitute himself for it. There is no other way. No good actor would regard the latter alternative as legitimate procedure, at any rate in the case of a play for which he had any respect. Yet complete "faithfulness" to the author exists only in theory.

Take the mere matter of physical appearance alone. Some playwrights describe in detail just what they want a character to look like; others do very little of this. But except in character roles, where an elaborate make-up may be employed, the vision in the author's mind is rarely seen on the stage except in those instances where a play has been written with a particular player in mind. Miss Hayes, for example, did not find it possible to increase her own diminutive stature to Mary Stuart's own six feet in order to play Mary of Scotland. When Miss Jean Simmons played her heart-breaking Ophelia in the Olivier film, she covered her own dark hair with a blonde wig well suited to a Danish girl, but Julia Marlowe resolutely refused to do this. She couldn't, she said, look like a Dane if she tried, and she wouldn't try. Instead, she would concentrate upon feeling what Ophelia felt, doing what she did, being what she was. If this could be achieved, she believed that the image in the mind of the audience would take care of itself.

Sometimes an actor realizes a character more fully than the author did and builds him up into something far more considerable than the author conceived. Joseph Jefferson did that with Rip Van Winkle, and E. A. Sothern with Lord Dundreary. Nor did Laurette Taylor get, by any means, all the raffish, wistful poetry of her performance in *The Glass Menagerie* from Tennessee Williams's script. In such instances, the actor becomes a virtual collaborator. Who among those who saw Jeanne Eagels in *Rain* or Mary

Garden as Mélisande can ever really accept anybody else in these roles?

Actors have given memorable performances, too, in unsatisfactory plays. Clare Boothe's drama about the martyrdom of St. Maria Goretti, *Child of the Morning*, was not considered worth taking into New York, but nobody who was lucky enough to witness Margaret O'Brien's overwhelming performance in it, when it was shown briefly in the fall of 1951, in Boston and in Springfield, Massachusetts, will ever forget that he was present at the beginning of a great stage career.

The actor is, of course, not the only intermediary between the author and the audience; he is merely the only one of whom the average audience is importantly aware because he alone is seen. In its most elaborate form, the drama represents a combination of all the arts: poetry, pageantry, elocution, music, dancing, painting—the list might easily be extended. It is the only form of literature which makes a visual appeal. Its inclination toward brevity, too, helps it to achieve the forcefulness which comes through concentration.

Methods of Characterization

The playwright's methods of characterization are less varied than the novelist's. He cannot give us his own direct impressions of a character at all. In fact, he can do only three things: He can permit other people to talk about a character. He can make him talk himself. And he can make him do something.

The comments of other characters, to guide the reader's judgment, can be very effective. Almost half of *Tartuffe* is over before Molière permits the name character to enter; during all this time, the other characters are engaged principally in talking about him, to prepare the reader for his entrance. One of the reasons why we know that Shakespeare intended Shylock to be regarded as a villain, in spite of the sympathy which modern audiences often feel for him, is that he caused all the characters of the play whom we are obviously intended to respect to condemn him.

The Shakespearean drama employs soliloquy as a conventional device for informing the audience what is in the character's mind. This has fallen out of favor with modern playwrights, who are less formal and less rhetorical in their technique than Shakespeare was. The "aside"—words whispered *sotto voce,* loudly enough to be heard in the last row of the gallery but conventionally inaudible to all the other characters on the stage—survived into the twentieth century but is now gone.

Yet all such devices are subject to modern refurbishings. In his *Hamlet* film, Olivier took advantage of the resources of modern sound and camera technique to keep Hamlet's lips still while the audience heard the soliloquies, thus effectively suggesting that the words were merely passing through the mind. And in *Strange Interlude,* Eugene O'Neill revived the aside on a grand scale, all sicklied o'er with the pale cast of "psychology."

In addition to addressing each other, all the characters in *Strange Interlude* communicated to the audience everything which they did not say but only thought. In performance, the actors immobilized themselves while uttering their asides; in the printed text, these utterances were distinguished from the rest of the play by the use of a different type. It cannot be denied that *Strange Interlude* was very effective in performance. As one looks back upon it, however, it takes on something of the character of a phenomenally successful "stunt." Mr. O'Neill did not permanently enrich our dramatic technique, for other playwrights have not taken up the devices he employed here. Neither has he himself made use of them in subsequent plays.

When *Strange Interlude* was at the height of its success, the phrase most frequently applied to it by its admirers was "the great American novel"! But even in such a play, the amount of psychological analysis that can be attempted is severely limited by the medium. The mere fact that the play must be presented before people assembled in theaters imposes a limitation. For one thing, every word spoken must be clear as it falls from the actor's lips, and this in spite of the normal amount of distraction that must be allowed for in a theater. No playwright who has any sense will permit anything that cannot safely be missed to be uttered during the first few moments after the curtain rises; he will allow time to permit the audience to quiet down and become accustomed to the actors' voices; he must also allow for the first sentence spoken by the star actress to be lost in the burst of polite applause which will greet her entrance. One of Dion Boucicault's rules for playwriting was: "Begin with a good, loud front scene!"

The Unpsychological Drama

In a novel you may miss the significance of certain speeches and incidents altogether, then turn back and re-read. There is no turning back in the theater; what is lost once, is lost forever. Jane Austen can permit us, at the beginning of *Pride and Prejudice,* to misunderstand Mr. Darcy as completely as Elizabeth Bennet does: she has 500 pages coming, and that will be ample to permit correction of initial misapprehensions. But the brief time and space at the playwright's disposal does not allow comfortably for such readjustments.

Furthermore, man as an individual differs in many aspects

from man as a member of a larger unit. Aldous Huxley shows clearly, in his great book, *Ends and Means*, that as the group is often above the level of the individuals composing it, so the crowd is always below that level. No play can hope to be successful unless it concerns itself with subjects sufficiently basic to appeal to the average humanity of the theater-going public in its country, community, or time. The drama is not an esoteric form of art.

This is no doubt the reason why some critics now hold that the drama is moribund, is, in fact, a dying form. As the epic was the natural form for prose fiction to take during the Homeric age—when people had grown sensitive to spiritual values but with their ideals still in the realm of action—and as the drama was the ideal form for the Elizabethans—who had achieved a rather reasonable balance between the world without and the world within—so, it is urged, the predominant, often even morbid, "inwardness" of modern man demands novelistic expression. Chronology alone would make it impossible to deny that the novel is characteristically a modern form, but what, then, are we to say of the even more recent development of the cinema, which reaches more modern men than all the other arts together, yet which places a heavier emphasis upon action than the epic itself?

That the drama is at present in a bad way, her best friends could not deny. But is this due to the limitations of the form itself? Or is it due to accidental and external matters? —the competition of cinema, radio, and television; the prohibitive prices which have followed upon the unionizing of the theater; the collapse of the "road" and the local "stock" company, with the inevitably resultant limitation of large-scale, commercial theatrical production to a few large cities, and the consequent catering of playwrights to the "specialized" tastes of big city sophisticates, which, in its turn, results in cutting the umbilical cord which joins an art form to the life of the people? It is too early to answer any of these questions positively and until they have been answered, the notion that the drama as such is an out-moded form cannot be said to have been established.

Closet Drama

Everything that has been written here applies, of course, to plays intended for production, not to the so-called "closet drama"—works ilke *The Dynasts,* by Thomas Hardy, and Longfellow's *Christus,* cast in a loose dramatic form but incapable of staging and addressed to the reading-rather than the theater-going public. Such works manifest the workings of a dramatic imagination, though not always to a greater degree than prose fiction, but while they may sometimes be works of very high literary quality, they tend to appeal to a more select public than either the novel or the "regular" drama.

Of course, many plays become "closet dramas" in spite of themselves, for the simple reason that no producer will put them on, and sometimes the playwright knows this in advance, or suspects it strongly enough so that he neglects all practical theater considerations in his composition. Most successful plays have been written by people of practical experience in the theater, and very few have reached the stage in quite the form in which they left the playwright's study. Shelley's poetic drama, *The Cenci,* was barred from the nineteenth-century theater by its subject-matter, which involved incest, but such scattered performances as it has achieved since would seem to indicate that it has consider-able dramatic vitality.[3] Browning began with the hope of

[3] Cf. *Stage Version of Shelley's "Cenci,"* by Arthur C. Hicks and R. Milton Clarke, based upon the Bellingham [Wash.] Theatre Guild's Production of the Tragedy, March 6-9 and 12, 1940 (Caldwell, Idaho: The Caxton Printers, 1945).

success on the boards, and some of his plays were acted by Macready, but after his break with that great, but very difficult, man, he had no theater-outlet and came increasingly to disregard dramatic exigencies. A. H. Thorndike called this disagreement one of the most unfortunate things that happened to English dramatic literature during the nineteenth century.

It must be added that any play is a closet drama to him who reads it instead of seeing it acted, and no twentieth-century student of the drama can speak authoritatively of most of the great dramatic literature of the past for the simple reason that the contemporary theater hardly ever gives us the opportunity to see any of it. It would be an overstatement to say that a printed play is only a scenario. It is considerably more than that. But it is certainly not the complete work in the sense that a novel is a complete work. To read a play successfully a reader must have the dramatic imagination, must be able to produce the drama in the theater which lies under his hat. Playwrights who intend their work to be read as well as seen, as most playwrights do nowadays, often supply the reader with a good deal of explanatory matter which the theater audience does not get at all; this is intended to serve as a surrogate for production. Some of Barrie's printed texts approximate a form which lies part way between drama and novel.

Conventions

In no branch of story-telling are the basic assumptions which we call conventions more important than they are in the theater. We sometimes think of modern realistic plays as having come very close indeed to putting actual life upon the stage. Sometimes we are even tempted to think of them as having dispensed with dramatic conventions. Actually they have done nothing of the kind.

Let us begin with the simplest illustration. On the stage drawing rooms have only three walls, and not so long ago two of these were only "wings." But in life, all drawing rooms have four walls. The three-walled drawing room is a dramatic convention, and the audience accepts it because if the stage carpenter were to build up that fourth wall, nobody in the audience would be able to see anything which happens on the stage.

But this is not the only convention which you accept in drawing-room comedy. You permit the actors to talk far more interestingly—and more consecutively—than anybody ever talked in any actual drawing room. You permit them to develop a theme and to concentrate upon that theme. You limit them to talking one at a time. You also allow them to talk loud enough, even in confidences, so that everybody in the theater can hear what they are saying.

Special conventions apply to special kinds of drama. In the Chinese theater, the property man may appear on the stage, bringing in various articles which the actors are going to need to carry on the action of the play, and removing others which are no longer of use to them. But the audience pretends not to see him because he is not a part of the play.

There are many Renaissance comedies, including some of Shakespeare's, in which a girl disguises herself as a boy and runs away. Once she is disguised, nobody recognizes her. Nobody knows that she is a female, and nobody knows that she is herself. In life, of course, everybody would know both, just as the audience does.

To apply a realistic test to such a situation is nonsense, though so great a Shakespearean as Richard Grant White once foolishly attempted it. White wanted Rosalind disguised so thoroughly—her face stained with umber, her figure padded, her hair tied up in knots—that the disguise would really seem plausible! He forgot that the first duty of a romantic heroine is to be attractive to the audience. He forgot, too, that he was dealing with a convention, and that conventions ask merely to be accepted. (In the Elizabethan theater, of course, we had a boy actor, playing a girl who was disguised as a boy!) This particular convention simply assumes that when a girl is thus disguised she is unrecognizable. This is the element of "given." It is a "just suppose" situation. You do not argue about it. You accept it, and follow out the logical consequences of the assumption.

There are more serious problems, in Shakespeare and elsewhere, which have to be approached in the same way. No king would divide his kingdom up into three portions as King Lear does—except a stage king. But that is exactly what Lear is! Would he do it? Why, he did do it! You saw him do it! Suppose it did happen. What would follow?

In actual life, probably nobody who had accepted an obligation to avenge a father's murder would delay as long as Hamlet does. But the basic reason for Hamlet's delay was grounded not in his character but in the nature of the drama. It was the convention of the revenge drama that the crime should be made known at the outset and avenged at the end. If Hamlet had killed the king any sooner than he did, he would also have killed the play!

In life, misers do not keep servants and carriages. But Molière's miser does. Why? Because Molière is striving to make secret impressions of generosity upon us? On the contrary, as Professor Stoll has said, Harpagon keeps servants that he may have the pleasure of starving them, and a carriage so that he may get up of nights to steal the horses' oats. It is not life. It is a play. It is on the stage. And being a stage miser, Harpagon must have something to do; he must act out his miserliness.

Othello tells us he is "rude of speech," after which he proceeds to talk some of the most magnificent blank verse that Shakespeare ever wrote. Why? Because the dramatist wishes to suggest that Othello is a liar? Not at all. Because he wishes to convey the idea that Othello is a modest man? Not that either. Othello talks magnificent blank verse because the play of which he is the hero is a great poetic drama. But Othello is also a soldier, and it is fitting that a soldier should be "rude of speech." So Shakespeare has Othello *tell* us that he is "rude of speech," and we are intended to take this at face value. But the medium in which the dramatist is working makes it impossible for him to illustrate this aspect of Othello's character.

In *The Merchant of Venice* the bond story needs three months. The love story needs about three days. But the bond must run out at just the moment when Bassanio has won Portia. The action could not have been managed on any other basis. So Shakespeare has just that happen. He uses good stage arithmetic: Three days equals three months. And in the theater nobody has ever minded.[4]

A World of Illusion

In a sense, then, the world of the drama *is* a world of artifice, of illusion. Life itself is rarely dramatic, even in highly dramatic situations. Real battle scenes are always a deadly bore. If you want the thrill of battle, you have to

[4] The influence of Professor Elmer Edgar Stoll's books upon my interpretation of Shakespeare's plays will be clear to those who have read these books. In addition to the monographs on *Othello* and *Hamlet* (University of Minnesota, 1915, 1919), Professor Stoll's papers have been collected in *Shakespeare Studies* (Macmillan, 1927); *Poets and Playwrights* (University of Minnesota Press, 1930); *Art and Artifice in Shakespeare* (Cambridge University Press, 1933); *Shakespeare's Young Lovers* (Oxford University Press, 1937); *Shakespeare and Other Masters* (Harvard University Press, 1940); *From Shakespeare to Joyce* (Doubleday, 1944).

stage a battle; you have to go to *The Birth of a Nation.*
After Mussolini was executed, his body was hung up by the
feet in an Italian marketplace and abused by the mob. None
of us can ever have supposed that life would bring us so
perfect an example of "poetic justice." But when that
hideous scene was photographed for the newsreels, it was
not dramatic at all; it was merely disgusting. We shall never
get any drama out of it until, sometime, it may perhaps be
staged by a film director of imagination.

This quality of heightening, or intensifying, life belongs
to all art, but as the term "dramatic" itself shows, it belongs
to the drama first of all. You may call it "theater" if you
like, or even "hokum," but whatever you call it, the continued existence of the drama depends upon it. I am quite
convinced myself that one reason for the decline of the
drama in our time is this silly fear and mistrust of "theater"
that has grown up among sophisticated people, this total
misconception of the theater's nature and purpose which
actuates those earnest souls who insist upon treating it as
if it were a clinic or a temple. It is quite true that we have
less "hokum" in our theater than the nineteenth century
had. It is also true that we have less theater. Some of our
contemporaries are beautifully prefigured in the old farmer
who tried to train his horse to get along without oats. In
itself, this course of training was quite successful. But just
as the "durn critter" had completed it, he "up and died,"
out of sheer "cussedness."

There are worthy people in the world who are revolted
by all "hokum" and who find all make-believe childish.
They are generally very dull people, but this does not mean
that there is no useful place for them in our world. They
don't have to go to the theater. They can always stay home
and read the latest books on government and sociology.
Incidentally they will find quite as many fairy tales there

as they would find in the theater, but they will not know that they are fairy tales, and so it will not matter.

It may as well be admitted freely that it is not possible to be an artist, or even to understand either art or artists very profoundly, without having something of the child in you, or without enjoying make-believe for its own sake. In this sense, those who find artists childish are quite correct. "Who deniges of it, Betsey?" And who would have it otherwise? And if the artist understands himself, then he knows, as the great spiritual masters have known, that something of the child must be permitted to survive in every man who is not content to have himself immersed in a morass of cold worldliness.

Structure

When the curtain rises on a play, the dramatist's first job is to make the existing situation clear to the audience. The part of the play which achieves this is known as the "exposition." Sometimes, in the older drama, this was done through a prologue. Such devices in Shakespeare as Aegeon's address to the Duke of Ephesus at the beginning of *The Comedy of Errors*, or Richard III's opening soliloquy, are only slightly less formal than this.

In modern plays, portions of the exposition are often entrusted to servants or travellers or confidants, who can reasonably ask questions which will enable somebody else to give them the kind of information the audience needs. Many nineteenth- and twentieth-century plays open with a scene between the butler and the parlormaid. Clyde Fitch uses this device in *The Girl With the Green Eyes,* but very skilfully infuses drama into it. Modern playwrights dislike "utility" characters, but if they know their business, they are also aware that obscurity is even more likely to be fatal to a play than artificiality.

In the old five-act play, it used to be said roughly that the first act was given over to exposition. But it should be remembered that it may often be necessary to "feed" additional exposition to the audience from time to time, all through the play. The "flashback," popular in modern drama since Elmer Rice's effective use of it in *On Trial* (1914), is often an expository device; see, in this connection, the use Arthur Miller made of it in *Death of a Salesman*.

The thing that starts the action of the play moving is called "the exciting force." In *Romeo and Juliet* this enters when the hero and heroine meet and fall in love with each other. In *Hamlet* the Ghost's commission is the exciting force. In *Macbeth* it is the temptation to murder King Duncan. Iago's plot furnishes the exciting force in *Othello*.

Sometimes it is difficult to distinguish between the exciting force and "the initial incident." When the initial incident occurs, then the exciting force has begun to express itself in action.

Sometimes, too, it is difficult to distinguish between the initial incident and the preparations for it. In *Romeo and Juliet* the preparation is somewhat leisurely. The whole Rosaline affair is part of the exposition. The preparations of Romeo and his friends to go to the ball merely lead up to the initial incident. Romeo might have continued to "crash" Capulet parties and meet charming Capulet girls until he was an old man, but unless he and one Capulet girl had fallen headlong in love with each other, there would have been no play.

Ordinarily it is necessary to determine the theme of a play before you can be sure of the initial incident. Sometimes the theme is merely the subject, as in *Charley's Aunt* the amusing complications which develop when, under the given circumstances, a lively young man disguises himself as a woman. In other plays, it may be a problem or a thesis. In Barrie's *Dear Brutus*, the theme is suggested by the title, but the title is meaningless unless you understand the quotation from *Julius Caesar* from which it has been derived:

> The fault, dear Brutus, is not in our stars,
> But in ourselves, that we are underlings.

People are always saying that if they had a chance to live their lives over again, they would conduct themselves very differently. In *Dear Brutus*, Midsummer Eve enchantment brings a hand-picked group the opportunity to live through crucial decisions once more, but most of them make exactly the same choice they made the first time. What the playwright is saying is that our choices are determined by our characters, and that since these are constant, our choices are relatively predetermined.

Divisions of Material in Drama

Older books on the drama, like Gustav Freytag's, which Elisabeth Woodbridge popularized in this country in her long-standard *The Drama: Its Law and Its Technique*, were more inclined to be formal and dogmatic in their discussion of structure than we are today. The structure of the drama has, of course, tended to become much freer in modern times. Early in the twentieth century the four-act play was standard. Then came the three-act play. Now there is a tendency to present plays in two long acts, and many plays are not divided into acts at all but only into "scenes." It should be noticed, however, that a two-act play with two scenes in each act is virtually the old four-act play under a new name. Robert Nathan's *Jezebel's Husband*, is an example of this.

Divisions in plays are motivated by two considerations: the desirability of presenting the materials of which the play is composed in terms of logical divisions and the inability or unwillingness of audiences to sit through a whole play without a break. Shaw, who believed that an all-night sitting in a theater would be far more profitable than in the House of Commons, wrote both *Getting Married* and *Misalliance*, each in one long act, but these plays are generally presented in two or three divisions each, with the actors "frozen" each time the curtain falls.

An act is supposed to mark a logical division of a play. In English usage, a scene indicates a subdivision of an act. When a play is divided into scenes alone, like Robert Sherwood's *Abe Lincoln in Illinois*, a more episodic type of structure is indicated. In continental usage, a new scene begins every time a new character enters.

Logically, the ideal would be to allow each play (by the nature of its material), to determine its own structure. Such freedom has been more or less achieved in the novel, but the drama is less free. Only an O'Neill at the height of his vogue would dare a nine-act play, beginning at five o'clock, with an interval for dinner. Of late years, plays which logically demanded a four-act division have either been crowded into three acts or else they have remained unwritten.

In Elizabethan plays, the "climax" occurred generally about the end of the third act. In the four-act play, the climax is still at the end of the third act, in the three-act play, at the close of the second. The three-act play is the most symmetrical form of drama we have achieved: Act I—Exposition; Act II—Development; Act III—Unravelment.

The climax is the point of highest complication, where the development ends and the unraveling begins. In a tragedy, the climax is the point where the hero's enemies gain the upper hand; from that point he is doomed. Until now the action has been "rising"; from here on, it is said to "fall." The killing of Tybalt is the climax in *Romeo and Juliet*, the play scene in *Hamlet*, in *Macbeth* the villain-hero's failure to strengthen his position at the killing of Banquo. In *Othello* the climax is reached when Iago convinces Othello that Desdemona is guilty.

Protagonist and Antagonist

The hero of a play is the "protagonist." The "villain," or leader of the opposition, is his "antagonist." The action of a tragedy may be begun by the hero (as in *Hamlet* and *Macbeth*), or by the opposition (as in *Othello*).

In the first type, there is no difficulty about holding the interest up to the climax; the test comes in the fourth act, where the hero is more acted against than acting. Hamlet is in England, Macbeth in seclusion, and the foreground is occupied by people we do not know so well and who interest us much less. Shakespeare bolsters the fourth act of *Hamlet* by causing Ophelia to go mad—upon what seems to many students of the play an insufficient motivation. When you have an outstanding Ophelia, like Jean Simmons in the Olivier film, the mad scene may well be the most absorbing thing in the play. It remains, nevertheless, something of a device.

In the *Othello*-type of play, the fourth act is likely to be the most interesting part of the play, for here, for the first time, your hero comes into full activity. But you pay for this by running the danger of having him seem weak at the outset, where he has little or nothing to do. Shakespeare "saves" *Othello* by the very daring device of making the antagonist nearly as interesting as the hero; in less skilful hands, this would surely have resulted in a divided unity. Even as it is, some actors prefer to play Iago, and in Latin countries, where the intriguer-hero has always been popular, he is sometimes considered the principal character.

There are, of course, special cases. In *Coriolanus*, Shakespeare has ingeniously combined the *Macbeth*-type with the *Othello*-type; structurally, *Coriolanus* is surely his masterpiece, though the hero himself is much less interesting than his other tragic heroes. In *King Lear*, the climax of the Lear story (the Gloucester story is structurally complete), is in the first scene, at the division of the kingdom. The whole rising action precedes the beginning of the play. Gordon Bottomley seems to have felt this so strongly that he wrote *King Lear's Wife* to explain how Lear and his daughters "got that way!" [5]

The "falling action," as already indicated, is the portion of the play which follows the climax. At the "denouement" —the untying of the last knot—all suspense comes to an end. In Elizabethan tragedy, the term "catastrophe" is sometimes applied to the event which brings about this final equilibrium—the killing of Hamlet, the suicide of Romeo and Juliet, etc.

The Nature of Tragedy

The two noblest and most important types of play are indicated by the terms "tragedy" and "comedy."

A tragedy is a serious play involving a conflict in which the hero is destroyed. The conflict may be between the human will and the gods (or the nature of things), as in the Greek drama. It may be between man and man. It may be between man and social forces. It may even be a conflict within the man himself.

The ancients insisted on unity of tone in drama: a play must be all serious or all comic. The Elizabethans did not so insist. The Elizabethans classified their plays by reference to the ending. If the play ended happily it was a

---

[5] For further discussion of some of these matters, see Albert H. Tolman, *Falstaff and Other Shakespearean Topics* (Macmillan, 1925).

comedy; if it ended with the hero's defeat and death, it was a tragedy.

Dante was not an Elizabethan; neither did he write plays. But the Elizabethans would have understood why he called his great poem a *Comedy* and not a tragedy. It was a comedy because it ends happily—with the triumph of God and His righteousness. Justice prevails. This is a safe universe.

All good tragedies leave the spectator with a feeling of inevitability. A great tragic situation is a hopeless situation; it could not end except in death. Suspense is achieved by including a number of scenes in which the hero seems to have a chance, but in each case our hopes are dashed and the tragic effect deepened. Thus, in *Romeo and Juliet* the lovers might have been saved if Friar Laurence's letter had been delivered. This is an "accident," and there has been much discussion as to whether *Romeo and Juliet* is a faulty tragedy because of the role that accident plays in it. In the more realistic types of tragedy, it is difficult to avoid accident entirely, but the tragedy is usually considered imperfect if accident becomes the determining element.

The "Tragic Flaw"

Aristotle said that though the tragic hero must be noble, he should not be perfectly good. Many later critics have said substantially the same thing. He must have a weak spot, an Achilles heel, a place where the lime leaf clung to Siegfried. It is through this weakness that fate overtakes him. This is the doctrine of the "tragic flaw." Meredith expresses it perfectly in *Modern Love*, XLIII:

> In tragic life, God wot,
> No villain need be! Passions spin the plot:
> We are betrayed by what is false within.

This need not always be, in the ordinary sense, a moral

weakness. It may be an excess of a quality noble in itself, which yet disqualifies its possessor—or its possessed—from coping with the particular situation in which he finds himself. The hero with a tragic flaw is not necessarily foredoomed in *any* situation: he is simply foredoomed in this one.

Eighteenth-century critics, who believed in "poetic justice," which is the doctrine that each character gets his just deserts, overemphasized the doctrine of the tragic flaw. Dr. Johnson felt that *King Lear* was an unsatisfactory play because in it the innocent perish with the guilty. Some Elizabethan plays were rewritten in the eighteenth century to bring them into harmony with these doctrines. Denton J. Snider, the renowned St. Louis Hegelian critic of the nineteenth century, argued that Romeo and Juliet deserved their fate because they loved each other instead of being devoted to the family as an institution! He also believed that Desdemona deserved to die because she lied to Othello about the handkerchief! But the truth of the matter is that Shakespeare did not always use the tragic flaw. Macbeth, Lear, Coriolanus, and Antony possess it (in varying degrees), but Hamlet, Othello, Desdemona, and Romeo and Juliet are innocent victims of the world's evil.

Style and Stature

At its best, tragedy demands exalted utterance. Hamilton Wright Mabie once made the interesting remark that the drama was born in ancient Greece at the foot of the altar, and that, centuries later, in Christian Europe, it was born again at the foot of the altar. Since it originated as a part of religious ceremonial, its association with verse may, at the outset, have been accidental, but if so, the instinct was right. Though prose is used in most modern tragedies, it is doubtful that any of these achieve Shakespearean power. It was on this ground that John Drinkwater, writing at a time when we were more hopeful for our drama than we are today, judged modern drama still inferior to the Elizabethan.

Tragic characters must have stature also. Mediaeval people thought of a tragedy as the story of a great man, cast down by fate from a high estate, as Chaucer's "Monk's Tale" shows. Renaissance writers were a little more psychological about it, but in general they continued to feel that, even in the conventional sense, the tragic protagonist must be a great man. Shakespeare uses common people in his tragedies only as servants and for comic relief. Marlowe was not quite orthodox when, in *The Jew of Malta*, he made a money-lender the hero of a tragedy.

Since the eighteenth century, very few critics have maintained that the tragic hero must be a great man in the eyes of the world. Perhaps Fielding's *Jonathan Wild* made "great men" in general seem somewhat less praiseworthy than they had hitherto appeared. Somewhat earlier, Nicholas Rowe had been taunted with having written "she-tragedies." *Romeo and Juliet*, *Macbeth*, and *Antony and Cleopatra* are the only Shakespearean tragedies in which a woman is as important as a man; no Shakespearean tragedy is carried by a woman alone. Fielding's great rival novelist, Samuel Richardson, dissolved all Europe in tears over the tragic fate of Clarissa Harlowe.

Many critics would still be prepared to maintain, however, that though humble people may serve as tragic protagonists, people lacking spiritual stature cannot. If *Death of a Salesman* and Theodore Dreiser's novel, *An American Tragedy*, deserve to be called tragedies, they are certainly a new type of tragedy. Renaissance critics would not have considered them tragedies. The protagonists are too ignoble; they are not capable of suffering a tragic fall; a sufficiently aristocratic critic might even say that the saddest thing about them is not that they die but that they ever lived. A famous actress rejected the feminine "lead" in *Death of a Salesman* because she thought the play bound to fail; the public, she said, could not possibly be expected to interest itself in the doings of such ignoble people.

The Villain-Hero

There are tragedies, of course, in which the hero is a villain, but these are never successful unless the villainies in question are heroic villainies. *Macbeth* is the greatest of all villain-hero plays because Macbeth is a great man who destroys himself, spiritually and materially, when he takes the wrong turning. On a lower level, *Ladies in Retirement*, by Edward Percy and Reginald Denham, is the best of all recent murder plays because it shows a good and unselfish woman setting her feet on the road to hell. Even so, such plays are very tricky to handle. *Richard III* is less moving than *Macbeth* because the hero is less a man and more a monster. There is a liberal mixture of melodramatic sensationalism in *Richard III*. Even so, the hero always holds our psychological (as strictly distinguished from our moral), sympathy. He is not great but he is fascinating. The contemplation of his villainies becomes tolerable in the exact degree to which the dramatist succeeds in directing attention away from his merely repulsive qualities and fastening it upon his energy, his will, his executive force, and his endurance. It is only in very degraded forms of dramatic art that monsters are interesting merely because they are monsters, and such interest is only a step, and not a very long one, above that inspired by a visit to the bearded lady and the two-headed boy at the county fair.

Tragedy Secular Not Sacred

On the other hand, it is not necessary for tragedy to take up the religious attitude toward life. Most tragedy does not. There is only one religious tragedy: to lose your soul. The Christians who died in the Colosseum did not think of themselves as dying a tragic death. They were going, through sudden, brief agony, into the very presence of God; if they perished for Christ's sake, they were sure of salvation. On the other hand, a sufficiently sympathetic pagan spectator, unable to share this belief, might very well have found an element of tragedy in their death. "How tragic," we may fancy we hear him murmur, "that men should be capable of such self-deception, that they should throw their lives away, and inflict horrible sufferings upon themselves, for a delusion and a dream!"

To view the great tragic literature of the world from this point of view would be to exclude most of it. *Macbeth* might qualify. Browning's *Soul's Tragedy* might qualify. But most tragedies could not qualify. Modern tragedy in general is secular, not religious, in its point of view. The curtain falls at death, and, as Hamlet says, "The rest is silence."

This does not mean, however, that modern tragedies have no religious meaning. There are many plays which seem, from this point of view, to be reaching out toward the religious position, even if they do not quite achieve it. *King Lear* is a story of spiritual redemption through suffering. The bereft monarch who staggers on in the last act with the dead Cordelia in his arms has lost everything that ever made life worth living—except one thing: he is a far greater and better man now than he ever was in the days of his glory, and he has found, deep within himself, a source of spiritual strength, and even comfort, that he never knew he possessed.

Comedy

Comedy is far more difficult to define than tragedy. Nobody really knows why we laugh, and many writers are suspicious of a too clear-cut distinction between the tragic and the comic. Socrates said, "He who is by art a tragic poet is also a comic one." It was Horace Walpole's opinion that "Life is a comedy to those who think, a tragedy to those who feel." And Byron declares:

> And if I laugh at any mortal thing
> 'Tis that I may not weep.

The same phenomenon may be comic or tragic depending upon the angle from which it is viewed; thus the spectacle of the drunken man who staggers home on pay day, singing ribald songs through the streets, may well be amusing to the street urchins whom he encounters but it can only be tragic to his wife who has no money to buy her children milk. Vice itself may furnish comedy, as in Falstaff. In the Old Testament, the writers of the Wisdom Literature inculcated righteousness by teaching that the sinner makes a fool of himself.

No complete theory of comedy need be suggested here. Aristotle suggested incongruity ("what is out of time and place without danger") and degradation ("some device of ugliness which is not painful or destructive"). Bergson suggested what he called automatism, by which he meant to suggest characters who are not in control of themselves but who are pulled hither and yon by exterior forces, a conception which, as we shall see, comes much closer to what is generally meant by farce.

Incongruity may be seen in Titania and Bottom in *A*

Midsummer Night's Dream (the dainty fairy enamored of the ass-headed yokel); in *Mutt and Jeff;* in the pompous, self-vaunting, frock-coated, silk-hatted dignitary who slips on a banana peel and collapses in the gutter; in the stargazing philosopher who tumbles into a ditch. In rural New England "ridiculous" has often been used to convey extreme moral disapprobation, and in popular American speech "How funny!" still means "How strange!" or "How odd!"

Falstaff's bulk, Bardolph's nose, Malvolio's cross-gartered yellow stockings, Katherine's shrewishness, Mrs. Malaprop's "nice derangement of epitaphs"—all these might well come under the heading of degradation. All are due to some fault or weakness in the character involved. We cannot laugh at Mrs. Malaprop's misuse of words unless we know the true meaning of the words she misemploys. The widespread use of indecency as a source of comedy connects here also. Santayana says, "Things called indecent or obscene are inextricably woven into the texture of human existence; there can be no completely honest comedy without them."

Comedy and Sympathy

But all these notions have appealed mostly to those who see comedy largely in terms of satire. Voltaire, himself a great satirist, did not see it thus. "Laughter," said Voltaire, "arises from a gaiety of disposition, absolutely incompatible with contempt and indignation." And at this point Voltaire was perhaps closer to the genial spirit of Shakespeare's comic world than Aristotle was.

Modern comedy is more inward, more sympathetic than comedy used to be. We do not laugh at cripples, as the ancients did, for sympathy gets in the way of the amusement which their incongruity, taken by itself, might well inspire. Neither do modern Londoners take their guests to Bedlam that they may laugh at the antics of the lunatics, as their eighteenth-century forebears did. We do still laugh at the pompous gentleman who slips on the banana peel, but that is because we feel that he "had it coming" to be reminded that he was still a child of earth. We should not laugh at a feeble, humble old woman who slipped on a banana peel, and for that matter we do not laugh at the pompous gentleman if he seems to be really hurt. Except in slapstick (which is farce), action declines in modern comedy, and characterization increases. Yet you cannot admit too much sympathy, too much emotion into your comedy; if you do, you will destroy it. Thus the "sentimental comedy" of the eighteenth century became at last a quite tearful thing. Comedy need not be cynical, but it does need to be clear-headed, reasonable, and level-eyed.

Comedy and Social Standards

Comedy, too, is a social art: it presupposes social standards, and a social background, by and against which the figure involved is judged. A great tragic figure may be a solitary like Ethan Brand in Hawthorne's tale, but it would be difficult to conceive a comic character in these terms. Molière tests men by their ability to live in society. Meredith says, in his Essay on Comedy: "To love Comedy you must know the real world, and know men and women well enough not to expect too much of them, though you may still hope for good." And again: "You may estimate your capacity for Comic perception by being able to detect the ridicule of them you love, without loving them less: and more by being able to see yourself somewhat ridiculous in dear eyes, and accepting the correction of their images of your purposes."

A sense of humor is a balance wheel, a safety valve on

the machinery of life. But we must have moderation, even in humor! The man who sees first of all the humorous aspect of every situation will never accomplish much. He will forever be restrained from exerting himself in any cause by the fear that he might appear ridiculous. St. Paul once said that the preaching of the Cross of Christ was foolishness to those that perish, and Henry Brooke's delightful eighteenth-century novel, *The Fool of Quality*, describes the education of one who was content to be a fool for Christ's sake. Dickens, himself one of the greatest humorists who ever lived, understood all this well. When Scrooge was converted, he tells us,

Some people laughed to see the alteration in him, but he let them laugh, and little heeded them; for he was wise enough to know that nothing ever happened on this globe for good, at which some people did not have their fill of laughter at the outset; and knowing well that such as these would be blind anyway, he thought it quite as well that they should wrinkle up their eyes in grins, as have the malady in less attractive forms.

Comedy, therefore, can hardly be called a champion of righteousness, though it might well be called an enemy of vice. But comedy opposes vice less because it is wicked than because it is excessive, immoderate, unbalanced—and therefore ridiculous. As a matter of fact, it opposes excessive virtue on the same ground. "Be not righteous overmuch," says the Book of Ecclesiastes; "neither make thyself over wise: why shouldst thou destroy thyself? Be not overmuch wicked, neither be thou foolish: why shouldst thou die before thy time?" This view is far more in harmony with the comic spirit than it is with the more earnest, sometimes impractical nobilities of tragedy. *Love's Labour's Lost* is a good example of a comedy devoted to the favorite comic theme of the discrepancy between the real and the ideal.

Tragicomedy

The term "tragicomedy" indicates the existence of a type of play lying midway between tragedy and comedy and partaking of the characteristics of both. A tragicomedy is a play whose basic action is too serious for comedy, but which does not end tragically.

Shakespeare's so-called "problem plays" or "sombre middle comedies"—*Measure for Measure, All's Well That Ends Well,* and *Troilus and Cressida*—are in this class. So, in a different way, is *The Merchant of Venice,* where the main plot—the love story—is comedy, while the bond story skirts tragedy, and in Shylock's case might even be said to achieve it.

Mixed types of this kind always create special problems. The audience must never feel that the author has lacked the courage necessary to develop a tragic situation logically; if it does, the play will be spoiled. Some have felt this about O'Neill's *Anna Christie;* I myself cannot share this view. In many respects tragicomedy lies closer to life experience than either pure comedy or pure tragedy, and it is no accident that it developed along with the realistic movement.

Melodrama

"Melodrama" and "Farce" might be described as the poor relations of tragedy and comedy respectively. These terms indicate serious and amusing plays respectively, with the emphasis on sensation, situation, rather than upon character. The essential difference between tragedy and comedy, on the one hand, and melodrama and farce on the other, is that the action of tragedy and comedy is grounded in character. The people in tragedy and comedy do what they do because they are what they are. In melodrama and farce, the situation is all-important, and the playwright is not satisfied until he has extracted the utmost "thrill" or the last heave of belly-shaking laughter that it can be made to yield.

The spirit of the older American melodrama is well exemplified in Augustin Daly's famous play, *Under the Gaslight* (1867), in whose "big scene" a wounded soldier is tied to a railroad track and rescued by the heroine, a few seconds before the locomotive of the approaching train would have run over him. Other plays used buzzsaws and kindred devices in similar situations. Old-time melodrama survived in the United States until World War I and in the "movies" considerably longer; indeed, it has never wholly died, but has merely grown more sophisticated, taking on new and more "hard-boiled" themes and a more realistic dialogue. The present writer will always be grateful that he was "brought up" at the People's Theater, in Chicago, whose fine stock company, headed by Marie Nelson, must have been almost the last to do such plays seriously. As late as 1920, D. W. Griffith made a tremendously successful film out of Lottie Blair Parker's *Way Down East*, at whose climax, the heroine, played by Lillian Gish, was rescued from a floating ice cake, only a few seconds before it toppled over the falls.

The absurdities of this type of drama are clear enough so that they need not be labored here. Yet I think nobody who really knows the old melodramas can fail to be made thoroughly angry by the absurd burlesque performances of them which are sometimes perpetrated nowadays. Such "smart aleck" behavior is altogether too easy to be amusing. It manifests a failure of imagination on the part of actors and audiences alike; it wars on theater itself—for the melodramas were pure theater, theater unadulterated by the admixture of other elements, to an extent to which we have

little pure theater nowadays—and upon the basic illusion
on which all art rests. "Do you care for the play?" Thackeray once asked an acquaintance? "Ye-e-s," drawled the
other man, "I like a *good* play." "Pshaw, man!" exclaimed
the great novelist, "I asked you if you *cared* for the *play!*"
Exactly. And the trouble with far too many of the theater's
patrons and critics today is that they do not. That is why
they are everlastingly trying to pretend that the theater is
not a theater but something else altogether. If I were the
editor of a newspaper, I should take my drama critic to the
best performances of *Charley's Aunt* and *The Fatal Wedding* that I could find, and if he were too refined to guffaw
very rudely over the first, and sit on the edge of his chair
and chew his tongue some time during the performance of
the second, I should either "fire" him or assign him thereafter to the financial page.

Farce

Farce, too, got a new lease on life through the films,
entering upon a new and fantastic stage of its development
with the so-called "slapstick comedy," developed principally by Mack Sennett, first at the old Biograph studio, and
after 1913 with his own firm, Keystone. Sennett's slapstick
had its obvious points of affinity with the old pantomime
and the *commedia dell' arte*, but the resources of the camera
opened up developments in the way of both violence and
fantasy of which he was not slow to take advantage. In the
course of time, the comic police force became Sennett's
trademark; later he added bathing girls, in what the period
regarded as very daring undress. But his prime glory was
a company of excellent low comedians, including Ford
Sterling, "Fatty" Arbuckle, and Mabel Normand. Chaplin
himself began his screen career with Sennett, though he
never felt really at home with him and did not stay long.

Slapstick reached its highest point of development during World War I, and its ferocious, but harmless, violence has been interpreted as at once a reflection of and a protest against the real violence of the time. When men were being blown up in earnest all over Europe and the high seas, it may well have given the spectator a reassuring sense of man's superiority over material forces to watch Sennett's lunatics drive a crowded automobile over a cliff, sink through the water, and come up smiling to continue their utterly senseless business in the world as if nothing untoward had taken place.

Other Types of Drama

Many other terms have been used to indicate different types of drama, but these need not be considered here at length.

Thus the term "Neoclassic Tragedy" refers to plays like Racine's *Phèdre*, characteristic of French seventeenth-century tragic dramatists. These are plays written in imitation of the Greek and Roman classics, marked by extreme decorum, in which the classical unities of time, place, and action are observed, and all violent activity is reported from off stage. The English genius never took kindly to this type of play, and Addison's *Cato* is the only important British example.

Lope de Vega, Calderon, and others in sixteenth-century Spain, and Victor Hugo (*Hernani*), much later in France, exemplify "Romantic Tragedy," which breaks with the unities and other austerities of neoclassical tragedy, and uses all the sensational properties and imagination-stimulating settings that romanticists have always loved. The French "Heroic Comedy," as represented by Rostand's *Cyrano de Bergerac*, employs similar materials, but the atmosphere is not so heavy.

The "Comedy of Intrigue," popular in sixteenth-century Italy, is intricate, artificial, and highly plotted, principally concerned with the construction of an elaborate situation, or series of situations, designed to keep a pair of lovers apart. Many of Aphra Behn's plays, in Restoration England, were comedies of intrigue. This type appears also in early American drama, as in *Tortesa the Usurer*, by Nathaniel Parker Willis. The French bedroom farce is a later modification of the comedy of intrigue.

The "Comedy of Manners" generally presents a group of sophisticated people, involved in situations reflecting the foibles of a particular set or a particular age. The emphasis is likely to be upon brilliant dialogue, and the tone is brittle. The great Restoration comedies of Congreve, Wycherley, and their contemporaries are the best examples of this type.

It may be worth noting that serious, non-tragic plays are sometimes called merely "dramas," which is an unsatisfactory term because, properly speaking, "drama" has a much wider connotation. The French *drame* was a well-made serious play, with a strongly-developed plot, leading up to a "big scene" which made a powerful appeal to the emotions. The term was used more widely in America before 1910 than it is today, being generally applied to such plays as *Paid in Full* and *The Easiest Way*, by Eugene Walter; *The Lion and the Mouse*, by Charles Klein; and *The Woman in the Case*, by Clyde Fitch. Today, the term "serious comedy" is sometimes applied to serious plays which do not end in tragedy. Serious comedies, however, have less "theater" in them than most of the old "dramas" and show a greater tendency toward indeterminateness. Like many of Ibsen's plays, they show a tendency to pose a problem and, at the final curtain, to leave it hanging in the air.

"Problem plays" go a step beyond this by devoting themselves to some controversial matter of current interest. A problem play may or may not be directly didactic. Thus Shaw generally wanted his audiences to do something about the abuses with which he was concerned, while Galsworthy, who did not believe that anything much could be done, was content to probe the situation and observe it with sympathy and understanding.

The Beginnings of the American Film

The films have already wormed their way into this chapter several times, notably in connection with the discussion of slapstick comedy. But it would not seem reasonable to close the chapter without some more systematic commentary on the kind of theater which contemporary Americans know best.[6]

Edison's interest in motion pictures was a by-product of his work on the phonograph. The great inventor recorded photographic images on wax cylinders as early as 1888, the year before George Eastman invented photographic film. Though there has been some controversy about it, films seem to have been projected upon a screen at the Edison laboratories on October 6, 1889. Edison's own interest at this time was not in projection but in the peep-show, and the first Edison films were made for peep-show machines. The first public exhibition of motion pictures in New York was on April 23, 1896. The program included a scene from one of Charles Hoyt's farces, some dancing girls, and Robert Paul's pictures of the surf at Dover. The theatrical

---

[6] Among the multitudinous books about the cinema, the reader might consult, for world cinema, *The Film Till Now*, by Paul Rotha and Richard Griffith (Funk and Wagnalls, 1950), and, for the domestic variety, *The Rise of the American Film*, by Lewis Jacobs (Harcourt, Brace, 1939). The best book about technique is Ernest Lindgren, *The Art of the Film* (Allen and Unwin, 1948). The best picture book is Daniel Blum, *A Pictorial History of the Silent Screen* (Putnam, 1953).

producer, Charles Frohman, who was in the audience, is supposed to have realized that this was an historic occasion. "That settles scenery," he is quoted as saying. "Painted trees that do not move, waves that get up a few feet and stay there, everything in scenery we simulate on our stages will have to go."

On October 12 of the same year, the Biograph Company put on a show at Hammerstein's Music Hall. These pictures showed William McKinley, Republican candidate for president, in a parade at Canton, Ohio, and "at home." "Major McKinley," said a contemporary "review," "was seen to come down the steps of his house with his secretary. The secretary handed him a paper which he opened and read. Then he took off his hat and advanced to meet a visiting delegation." But even more sensational were the terrifying pictures of the Empire State Express rounding a curve.

For some years motion pictures were used as "chasers" between the acts at vaudeville theaters. Little cinematic progress was registered, but it was of some value that films should be kept alive and supplied with a small market while production got under way. The first picture theater is said to have been the one established in a store at Newark, New Jersey, in 1897, but it was not a success because the supply of films was not yet steady enough to enable the producer to change the bill often enough to build up a clientele.

The first real film producer of aesthetic significance was a Frenchman working in Paris, George Méliès, the Walt Disney of his day. His best-known, though not his most elaborate, film was *A Trip to the Moon* (1902), still frequently seen on Museum of Modern Art film programs. Méliès discovered the principle of what he called "artificially arranged scenes." From now on, in other words, producers are not going to be satisfied to photograph what happens;

they are going to make it happen. Méliès exploited the resources of the camera as nobody had ever dreamed of exploiting them before, and created effects which would have been impossible in any other medium. On the other hand, he knew nothing about film construction. Each "shot" in his films was a "scene" in the stage sense, played from start to finish before a stationary camera and shot from eye level. For this reason, and because his films, being fantasies, lacked the vitality of real-life subjects for the average viewer, he soon forfeited his leadership to Edison's Edwin S. Porter, who gave a kind of pre-view of his talents in *The Life of an American Fireman* (1902) and went on from there to establish some of the basic principles of cinema art in *The Great Train Robbery* (1903) which laid the foundations on which the whole motion picture industry was erected.

New producing units mushroomed through the first decade of the century. In 1908, D. W. Griffith, greatest of all film directors, came to work for Biograph, for whom he produced more than 100 films, some of them works of great vitality and visual appeal. Griffith also developed a remarkable company of young ac?ors, including Mary Pickford, Lillian and Dorothy Gish, Florence Lawrence, Mae Marsh, Henry B. Walthall, Arthur Johnson, and Lionel Barrymore. But Biograph opposed the "star system" and denied the player the privilege of seeing his name on the screen. Concurrently, the Vitagraph Company, in Brooklyn, was exploiting the personal angle for all it was worth. Their Maurice Costello became the first "matinee idol" of the screen, their John Bunny its first great comedian. And their leading woman, Florence Turner, was loved all over the world as "The Vitagraph Girl," before people even knew her name.

The Coming "Features"

Vitagraph did a five-reel *Life of Moses* as early as 1908 and a more important *Tale of Two Cities*, in three reels, in 1911. There were other long films, notably Kalem's *From the Manger to the Cross* (1912), produced in Palestine by Sidney Olcott, and shown for a generation. But films in general were brief during this period, and film programs were brief also, consisting of three or four reels, shown in small theaters, often with store fronts, at a five- or ten-cent admission. Other famous screen personalities of the periods included G. M. Anderson, the first screen cowboy, who produced a "Broncho Billy" film every week for 376 weeks, beginning in the spring of 1908—a still unequalled record; Max Linder, a dapper little French comedian of international vogue; and Pearl White, who was soon to become a famous "stunt woman" and "serial queen."

The real impulse toward feature-film production came, however, from abroad, notably from Italy, with the first important *Quo Vadis?* in 1913, promptly followed by the overwhelming twelve-reel *Cabiria*, made from a scenario by Gabriele D'Annunzio. In 1912, Adolph Zukor began his long career as a producer of "Famous Players in Famous Plays" by importing Louis Mercanton's four-reel production of *Queen Elizabeth*, in which the most famous actress in the world, Sarah Bernhardt, gave the still-despised "movie" an important prestige shot-in-the-arm. Zukor promptly followed *Queen Elizabeth* with American productions, featuring famous stage personalities, all "presented" by Daniel Frohman.

Unwilling to permit his leadership to be wrested from him by foreign competitors, Griffith now turned to a four-reel production of *Judith of Bethulia*, from the Apocryphal story and the play by Thomas Bailey Aldrich, a heavy, brooding film, of rich Oriental splendor, still impressive to see. But *Judith* was made against the advice of his conservative and penny-wise employers, and he left Biograph before it had been released, to set his feet on the road which led to *The Birth of a Nation* (1915).

This Civil War and Reconstruction spectacle—the most influential as well as the most controversial of all films—was the first motion picture to be "roadshowed" at a scale of prices running up as high as two dollars for the best seats. It was followed, next year, by the even more grandiose *Intolerance*, still often called the greatest film ever made. A financial failure, *Intolerance* carried Griffith to heights he was never quite to reach again except, perhaps, in a very different mood, in an intimate tragic film called *Broken Blossoms*, in 1919.

With *The Birth of a Nation* and *Intolerance*, "feature-length" films were at last established (though five reels, not twelve, was for some time to be standard); mechanical excellence steadily improved but there were no more radical innovations until the coming of sound. The prestige of the films increased enormously during World War I, when the government took them up as a propaganda arm, and the industry became "big business," so big, indeed, that Wall Street finally took over, and all the pioneers lost control. Mary Pickford, "America's Sweetheart," became a national idol and a national ideal, like no other actress, before or since. Douglas Fairbanks, the athletic hero whom she married in 1920, popularized Theodore Roosevelt's gospel of "the strenuous life." William S. Hart was the greatest of all Western "bad men" or "cowboy heroes," and Theda Bara made the verb "to vamp" a part of the English language. More important was Charlie Chaplin, busily engaged during these years, in building himself up into a world figure, perhaps the one universal man of our time.

"Sound"

Disregarding early experiments which never caught on, the first motion picture with recorded sound accompaniment (not on the film, but on records synchronized with it), was John Barrymore in *Don Juan*, presented by Warner Brothers in the summer of 1926. The film itself was silent, but it was shown with a number of talking and singing "shorts," featuring opera singers and vaudeville actors. The first feature film in which the star was allowed to talk— or rather, sing—was *The Jazz Singer*, with Al Jolson (1927). Most of this film was silent; it merely contained "sound sequences." But it became one of the great financial successes of motion picture history, and from that moment the silent film was doomed. In the early days of the "talkies," it often seemed as though cinema art itself was doomed also, for the early sound films were not motion pictures: they were photographed plays. Overnight, too, a good deal of the old personnel was thrown out, and Broadway actors substituted for it. In time, the native vitality of the cinema reasserted itself, though there are still those who are unconvinced that the sound film has ever possessed itself of either the fluidity or the distinctive originality of the "silents" at their best. To sound, color was soon added, and as these lines are written, the film industry seems to be facing another crisis while producers try to make up their minds what to do about the new three-dimensional processes.

Cinema and Drama

This extremely brief résumé of motion picture history in America has been no digression: for one thing, it furnishes necessary background for an understanding of the difference between films and drama. Because both media employ actors, they are often thought of as being much closer together than they actually are. As a matter of fact, however, the film is not always acted. There were no actors in the early films, and there are no actors in most documentary films. As these lines are written, one of the current motion picture successes is *A Queen Is Crowned*, J. Arthur Rank's record of the coronation of Queen Elizabeth II, narrated by Sir Laurence Olivier. In just what sense is that either "theater" or "drama"?

Rossellini and other Italian directors have often used non-professionals; so did Griffith in his early days. In the work of such an artist, one often sees the director himself performing through other human beings whom he handles almost as if they were puppets. Often, too, in silent picture days, a director would simulate real emotion in a player by invoking considerations which had nothing whatever to do with the film itself and then photograph it, and since the performance did not need to be repeated, as on the stage, this often served his purpose very adequately.

The film has a range that the stage has never dreamed of. It can present any action which men are capable of performing and a great many besides, for, as Méliès discovered at the very beginning, almost anything that can be imagined can be made to happen before the camera. The film director does not need to strain the probabilities to bring his people together in the locality represented upon the stage: he can go wherever they are and take his camera along with him. The film has a fluidity equal or superior to that of the novel itself, equal (it sometimes seems) to that of thought: there were shots in *Intolerance* that were only five frames long. It can simulate epic action. Instead of being watched from a fixed position, as a play must be, the film places the spectator wherever a camera can be placed—in a swinging trapeze if necessary, or in an airplane. Moreover, the position of the camera can be changed as often as the director chooses to do so or the exigencies of the theme dictate. And by this means it can express many values identified not with any particular position but developed in terms of the contrasts between them.

The film can comment, too, not in words but in images. If the director wishes to convey the idea that a woman is a "cat," it is not necessary to have some other character apply that word to her. That would be doing it in terms of literature. Instead, he may "dissolve" the woman into a feline and back again, and if her "cattiness" is really dangerous, there is nothing to prevent him from using a black panther instead of a domestic cat. In Dimitri Buchowetzki's production of *Peter the Great*, starring Emil Jannings, many years ago, the director did not try to impress the wicked wastefulness and futility of war upon his audiences by moralizing about it in subtitles; instead, immediately the Battle of Poltava had been fought and won, he flashed a pyramid of skulls upon the screen, and then quickly took it off again. In King Vidor's production of *La Bohème*, starring Lillian Gish, the heartbreaking contrast between Mimi's health and happiness in the early days of her love affair and her utter desolation as she lay dying was accented by the use of a few skilfully chosen flashbacks as the film approached its termination. In George Sidney's recent production of Margaret Irwin's novel, *Young Bess*, dealing with the early life of Queen Elizabeth I, and starring Jean Simmons, the action alternates between the court, where the princess lives when she is in favor, and Hatfield House, to which she is banished when she is not. Each transition is marked, without verbal comment, by a long shot of the same scene, with the caravan of the princess travelling up the hill to the palace or down the hill toward Hatfield, and one of these is used with great skill. Having inherited her father's temper,

the princess has just been storming that she WILL NOT
return to Hatfield to please anybody. No response is offered
upon this declaration, but immediately it has been made,
we see the same familiar shot, with the cavalcade traveling
down hill.

Such effects as these are far removed from anything that
we can experience in the drama, and I think there are
aspects in which the film is farther from drama than it is
from either novel or epic, though it is never really anything
but cinema! There are times, too, when it resembles music
in its development, as the early realization that it needed
musical accompaniment showed. Take the four interwoven
stories of *Intolerance*, like the four "movements" of a
symphony—the Babylonian story, the Judean story, the
French Huguenot story, and the modern industrial story—
all developing the theme of man's inhumanity to man. In
the last two reels, all four reach their climax. Christ goes
to Calvary. The Mountain Girl drives madly to warn
Belshazzar of the approaching armies of Cyrus. The Huguenot lover searches distractedly for his sweetheart, caught in
the massacre of St. Bartholomew's. And the modern wife,
in an automobile, races to overtake the governor's train,
with proof of her husband's innocence, while he himself
is already ascending the gallows. Transitions from one story
to another become increasingly frequent, and tension
mounts to nearly unbearable heights. "History itself,"
writes Iris Barry, "seems to pour like a cataract across the
screen."

Does this mean, then, that the cinema is a superior
medium to that of the drama? This is a little like the question which, to her intense annoyance, American reporters
once addressed to Madame Curie: "Do you believe that
men are more intelligent than women?" She replied: "There
are intelligent *people*, and there are people who are not so

intelligent." There are good plays and there are good films, and I myself do not wish to be deprived of either. But I must add that it takes a great deal of technical splendor to make up to me for the absence of the artist's living presence and the consciousness that something is being created while I watch it.

Radio drama has had no such impressive development as the cinema, and now, with the coming of telecasting, seems destined to be relegated to an inferior status. From television itself, however, more may reasonably be hoped for. Early television dramas seemed working toward a form intermediate between the fluidity of the cinema and the immobility of the stage. It is to be hoped that the tendency to record television shows on films will not put an end to such experiments, for films on the small television screen can never compete with films projected under theater conditions.

The theater and the drama have experienced great vicissitudes during our lifetime, and of these trials there is yet no end in sight. Like life itself, the theater is forever in a state of transition and a condition of peril; that is how we know that it is alive. It is only those who lived in extinct civilizations who can be considered quite safe. But however widely it may change, and however painful these changes may be to some of us, there seems little danger that the theater itself can die so long as the histrionic impulse remains in human nature. And that means so long as human beings are what they are.

CHAPTER SEVEN

Why Poetry?

The Decline of Poetry

There is a delightful story about a big-city "drunk" who was very fond of the variety of beer known as bock. One spring day, on his way home from work, he stopped at every saloon he passed to regale himself with a fresh schooner. And as he imbibed renewed delight with each replenishment, he found his intellectual curiosity drunkenly stirring: he wished to define to himself the source of his great enjoyment. So, having ordered and been served once more, this time by a bartender with no admiration for drunks, he inquired gravely, "What *is* bock beer?" "What IS bock beer?" echoed the bartender, with withering, disgusted sarcasm, then scornfully waved a great paw toward the glass on the bar: "Why, *that's* bock beer!" It was a descent to earth as sharp and wholesome as Dr. Johnson's when he demonstrated the reality of matter of stubbing his toe against a stone.

To define bock beer would be no great business, but when we get to the great life-words, there is another tale to tell. There are as many definitions of "romantic" and "Shakespearean" and "Puritan" and "Christian" as there are definers, and of "life" itself—or the purpose of life— there is no satisfying definition anywhere, nor ever will be, for the simple reason that the whole cannot be defined in terms of its parts, and there is nothing outside of life by reference to which the definition can be framed. When Admiral Byrd returned from the South Pole and told about eating seal meat, he was asked what seal meat tasted like, to which he replied that it tasted like seal meat—another reply worthy of Dr. Johnson.

But though this chapter will be largely concerned with the definition of poetry—and of the varied types and aspects of poetry—[1] its title is not "What Is Poetry?" but "Why Poetry?" This is the more fundamental question. For poetry is much distrusted in our time.

It is true that a few poets like Robert Frost and the late Edna St. Vincent Millay still command large audiences, but generally speaking, the vast body of readers upon which Byron and Mrs. Browning, Tennyson and Longfellow, found it safe to rely has gradually melted away. Longman offered Tom Moore £3,000 for *Lalla Rookh* before the poet had completed it or the publisher read a line of it: could anybody match this today?

Prose has preëmpted both narrative and drama. Such exceptions as (in the first area), *John Brown's Body*, by Stephen Vincent Benét, *At Midnight on the Thirty-First of March*, by Josephine Young Case, and *Tristram*, by Edwin Arlington Robinson, only accentuate, by contrast, our general poverty. And when a Maxwell Anderson, a T. S. Eliot, or a Christopher Fry does succeed in getting a verse-play on the stage, the lines are spoken exactly as if they were prose, and a large share of the audience would be greatly

[1] Bliss Perry, *A Study of Poetry* (Houghton Mifflin, 1920) is a good general introduction. Lawrence J. Zillman, *Writing Your Poem* (Funk & Wagnalls, 1950) is an exceptionally useful book on poetic technique. Edith Rickert, *New Methods for the Study of Literature* is the best book for the analysis of style. The author of the present study expresses his thanks to Professor Zillman (of the University of Washington) for his friendly and helpful critical reading of this chapter.

surprised, perhaps even horrified, if somebody were to inform them, as they left the theater, that they had been exposing themselves to "poetry."

Is Poetry Unnatural?

In the light of such a situation, "Why poetry?" is no idle question. Modern prose is an infinitely varied and supple instrument. We cannot handle it more brilliantly than the Elizabethans did, nor surpass the rich orchestrations of Sir Thomas Browne and his contemporaries, but we can certainly do a great many things which they could not. Poets themselves have been complaining for centuries about the "slavery of rime" and of the hobbling, crippling effect of a regularly recurrent beat which forces them to leave unsaid what they wish to say and to say instead something which suits the measure. The hobble skirt is in the museum. In our time, girls are free, if they choose, to discard skirts altogether and take to shorts, which, there is no denying, are as becoming to some as they must be comfortable for all. Why, then, should anyone wish to subject his brains and his language to Mr. Iambic Pentameter?

The violence of the question betrays, I fear, the desperation of the case it poses. For, even now, there are many who do so wish, and if they do, then there must be something in the nature of things effectually to prompt such a desire. The fact is that "Why poetry?" is only one form of the "Why must such things be?" type of question. Why sex? Why pain? Why physical death? Why the mysterious perversity that so heartbreakingly negatives so many of humanity's best efforts? Who can answer such questions? But the wise man is not he who expends all his energy wringing his hands over them. He is the man who sets to work to achieve the maximum realization of his aims and the maximum satisfaction of his desires possible against the frame of reference which exists in a world where such mysteries rule.

No art is "natural"; the only art which even approaches being natural is bad art. But the need to create art *is* natural, as basic as the need to feed or to sleep, and between expression in verse and expression in what we call prose, there can be no question that the first comes much closer to nature than the second. It lies closer to the rhythm which is life itself—the coming of the seasons, the alternation of day and night, the throbbing of the blood in heart and pulses. Rhythm is no invention of the prosodists; without it, neither you nor I would be alive. "The father of rhythm," says an old sage, "is God."

If moderns have so far forgotten this that poetry often seems to them a marginal concern of human beings, or one which makes its appeal only to fantastically cultivated or freakish people, the basic reason for this curious misapprehension is that they themselves are so out of tune with the basic rhythm of life that they do not really know what "natural" means. They are all rather like the young critic of whom C. S. Lewis tells, who had got so tired of second-rate pictures of moonlight on the water that he dismissed a real moon shining on a real lake as "conventional"! Nor is it only in criticism that such ignorance threatens us. Let us never forget—for he deserves immortality—the Washington bureaucrat who, in the early days of the New Deal, refused to change a directive when Western farmers complained that they could not possibly carry it out during the lambing season. "We suggest," he telegraphed, "that you change, this year, the lambing season," thus giving an harassed and depression-cursed nation the best laugh it had had in years.

Poetry and Civilization

The Greek heroes whom Homer celebrated, the dragon-killers of *Beowulf*, and the Vikings who harried Alfred's England were not "sissies" exactly, but they wrote, and when they wrote they wrote verse. In their time, verse was the language of all literature, and prose was used, as in the *Anglo-Saxon Chronicle* only for keeping records. What we call aesthetic prose marks a late stage in the development of literature, signifying, as the reader may choose, an attempt to infuse factual writing with imaginative significance, or marking the invasion of the realm of the imagination by a less imaginative spirit than poetry could tolerate.

"Poetry," says Dr. Walter Russell Bowie, "belongs first to children and to simple folk. For poetry begins with the open-eyed and wondering regard which sees the world with fresh eyes, and takes spontaneous delight in that un-hurried seeing." A man may begin writing fiction as Defoe and William De Morgan did, at sixty, and all the criticism worth reading has been written by mature men, but I know of no mature writer who has commenced poet. Even in very good poets, like Matthew Arnold, the poetic vein sometimes dries up as the man gets older: the ability to pour out first-rate lyric verse uninterruptedly from youth to age, as Robert Herrick and Walter de la Mare have done, is a rare achievement indeed, and one all the more miraculous in Mr. de la Mare's case because he has concurrently been producing prose works which have called for the most mature and discriminating critical taste. Poets, says Max Eastman, "are lovers of the qualities of things. They are not engaged . . . in becoming adjusted to an environment, but they are engaged in becoming acquainted with it." And Rupert Brooke, who ought to have known if anybody knew in our time, said that being a poet was simply seeing things and people as they are.

In an interesting passage in *Language in Action*, Dr. Hayakawa has shown that, on a degraded level—only that qualification, Dr. Hayakawa himself would not, I am sure, accept!—the makers of slang employ their imaginations quite as the poets do. "Rubberneck," "out like a light," "keep your shirt on"—here is the same use of metaphor and simile that we find in the great poets. And it is significant, I think, that slang expressions are not often coined by the conventionally cultured classes or by those who live closer to books than they do to common life experience.

So far, indeed, are the intellectuals from being the special patrons of poetry that they are likely to attack it far more uncompromisingly than the bruisers do. Indeed, the boy or girl who thinks he "hates poetry" ought to scrutinize very carefully the company he is getting into! The alternative, my friend, may well turn out to be test tubes or the dizzy heights of the higher mathematics!

It was as early as 1825 that Macaulay wrote:

We think that as civilization advances, poetry almost necessarily declines. . . . Language, the machine of the poet, is best fitted for his purpose in its rudest state. Nations, like individuals, first perceive and then abstract. They advance from particular images to general terms. Hence the vocabulary of an enlightened society is philosophical, that of a half-civilized people is poetical. . . . In proportion as men know more and think more, they look less at individuals, and more at classes. They therefore make better theories and worse poems. . . . In an enlightened age there will be much intelligence, much science, much philosophy, abundance of wit and eloquence, abundance of verses and even of good ones, but little poetry.

"In proportion as men know more and think more, they look less at individuals, and more at classes." It has a curious

—and sinister—modern ring. It reeks of all the concentration camps of Europe and Asia. Macaulay cannot possibly have known, when he wrote that sentence, with what horror we, his descendants, would read it today, in the light of our experience, happily denied to him, of dictatorships and threatened dictatorships, from the left and from the right. Cardinal Newman, on the other hand, tells us that the destruction of the world itself would be a lesser evil than the contamination of one human soul, and Hawthorne, brooding over poverty-stricken, outcast English children, about a quarter of a century after Macaulay had written his words, wonders, "if they are to have no immortality," what "superior claim" he can enter for his own. "If a single one of those helpless little ones is lost," then, he cannot but feel, "the world is lost" too. Did Hitler and Stalin really "think" more than these men? Were they more "intelligent"? more "advanced"? If so, some of us will have to make shift to get along with the poor brains we have, while we cling to the childish individualism fostered by Christian humanism and the spirit of poetry. Samuel McChord Crothers did not need to wait for the horrors of a world war to teach him that there is no tyranny so cruel as that which must result from the rule of theorists and philosophers. "For the philosopher is concerned with general laws and is intolerant of exceptions, while it is the quality of mercy to treat each person as in some degree an exception. . . . We should look back with envy to the good old times of Nero and Tamerlane." There are some things that not even the worst of men will do in his own interest, but what bounds are set to even good men's depredations when they serve that which is larger than self? If the world is ever destroyed, it will not be blown up for private gain. It will be blown up for a "cause."

Poetry and Passion

There is another force which makes powerfully for the continuance of poetry, and that is the passion of the human heart itself. For poetry is more intense, more concentrated than any other kind of literature. Carried beyond a certain point, intensity of experience and utterance simply demands poetic expression. Look at a stanza from Keats's "Ode to a Nightingale":

> Darkling I listen; and, for many a time
> I have been half in love with easeful Death,
> Called him soft names in many a musèd rhyme,
> To take into the air my quiet breath;
> Now more than ever seems it rich to die,
> To cease upon the midnight with no pain,
> While thou art pouring forth thy soul abroad
> In such an ecstasy!
> Still wouldst thou sing, and I have ears in vain—
> To thy high requiem become a sod.

You cannot say that in prose. If you try, you will come up with something about as impressive as "I wish I were dead!" or "Wouldn't this be a lovely place to die!" In other words, you can only go so far with the expression of emotion in prose. Nobody knows why, and you yourself can discover where the boundaries lie for you only by patient experimentation. But if you attempt to go beyond them, you proceed at your own peril. Your pathos will turn to bathos, and instead of moving your reader you will only repel him. Willa Cather once said that she could not imagine anything worse than the story of *Romeo and Juliet* would be, rewritten in prose by D. H. Lawrence. But you can go on in verse a considerable distance beyond the point at which you must leave off in prose, for the measured rhythm of the verse at once softens and reinforces the effect you seek. When Dickens was writing that portion of *The Old Curiosity Shop* which deals with the death of Little Nell and its aftermath, the force of his emotion carried him over into blank verse, without he himself being at all aware of what had happened. Now if you are going to junk poetry, or deny writers the privilege of writing poetry when they rise to the poetic level of experience, then, obviously, all those areas which lie beyond the prose-range will simply have to be abandoned or left unexpressed.

Rime and Metre

So far, in this discussion, the terms "poetry" and "verses" have been used, for convenience, almost interchangeably. But they are not interchangeable, for versecraft is merely the mechanics of poetry, a means to an end and not the end itself.

Are rime and metre necessary to poetry? A good deal of high authority can be mustered to support the view that they are not. Sidney holds that "One may be a poet without versing, and a versifier without poetry." Shelley, including Plato and Bacon among the poets, declares that "The distinction between poets and prose writers is a vulgar error." And even Emerson, considerably less extreme, says that "it is not metres but a metre-making argument that makes a poem. . . ."

To follow Shelley for the purpose of this exposition would not, I fear, make for clarification. We should be left with a vague general impression that all highly imaginative literature was somehow "poetry," but, so far as all technical considerations were concerned, we should come out by that same door where in we went. It is true that Plato is, in a sense, a poet, and even those who are offended by Shelley's "vulgar error" would, I think, understand what was meant if they heard him called a poet. But that, surely, does not mean that there is no value in differentiating between what we mean when we call Plato a poet and what we mean when we apply the same term to Shelley himself. For that matter, the poet has his affinities with writers who are very unlike Plato. When he is at his best, his powers of observation are equal to the scientist's, his probing of human conduct and motive as keen as the trained psychologist's, his insight into life as deep as the prophet's. But he is not scientist or psychologist or prophet, for all that, or when he is, it is because he is something else besides a poet. The countryman in Mrs. Gaskell's *Cranford* was convinced by Tennyson's keen powers of observation—he knew that ashbuds were black in March—that Tennyson was a great poet. But Paul Elmer More is quite just when he declares that it would have been more to the point, upon that evidence, to settle for his being a good botanist.

For my money, Emerson's "not metre but a metre-making argument" comes closer to it than Shelley does. If you can say it as well in prose as you could in verse, then the chances are that you can say it better in prose; only, there are some things you cannot say in prose at all! But I am not saying that there are "poetical" subjects per se, and that other subjects are not "poetical." The poetry is less in things than in the poet's eye and brain. Says Lytton Strachey, "There is poetry to be found lurking in the metaphysical system of Epicurus, and in the body of a flea." There is probably no phase or aspect of human experience in which *no* imagination may conceivably stake out a claim, no arid tract where we can safely post a sign of "No Thoroughfare" which every wayfarer can be expected to honor. "Poetry," says one definer, "is passional beauty in rhythmic patterns," and another, "the concrete and artistic expression of the human mind in emotional and rhythmic language." Any subject which can be vivified and intensified by the writer's imagination, and exalted to such a height as to demand, to be susceptible of, the kind of expression which is poetry, that is, for that poet, a poetic theme. Poetry may, or may not, exist without versecraft, but it is certain that versecraft can exist without poetry. Otherwise, many of us would be as great as Shakespeare! It is said that Browning's father could write verses faster than his famous son.

The Goose-Pimple Test

We began this chapter with the story of the bartender who defined bock beer by refusing to define it. A. E. Housman, though himself a gifted poet, was capable of being equally practical about it: he never dared, he said, to allow a line of real poetry to come into his mind while he was shaving, for if he did he would be sure to cut himself. Here is what I call the goose-pimple test in poetry, and I know of none better.

Lo, here, then is poetry! And if the goose-pimples never rise—well, there are always some very good courses in economics!

> Look, love, what envious streaks
> Do lace the severing clouds in yonder east.
> Night's candles are burnt out, and jocund day
> Stands tiptoe on the misty mountain tops.
> > William Shakespeare: *Romeo and Juliet*

> But, look, the morn, in russet mantle clad,
> Walks o'er the dew of yon high eastern hill.
> > William Shakespeare: *Hamlet*

> At last he rose, and twitched his mantle blue:
> Tomorrow to fresh woods, and pastures new.
> > John Milton: "Lycidas"

'With an host of furious fancies
  Whereof I am commander,
With a burning spear and a horse of air
  To the wilderness I wander.
By a knight of ghosts and shadows
  I summoned am to tourney
Ten leagues beyond the wide world's end,
  Methinks it is no journey.
             Anon: "Tom o' Bedlam's Song," before 1615

Tiger! Tiger! burning bright
In the forests of the night,
What immortal hand or eye
Could frame thy fearful symmetry?
            William Blake: "The Tiger"

I strove with none, for none was worth my strife:
  Nature I loved, and next to Nature, Art:
I warmed both hands before the fire of Life;
  It sinks: and I am ready to depart.
        Walter Savage Landor:
           "On His Seventy-Fifth Birthday"

Life, like a dome of many-coloured glass,
Stains the white radiance of Eternity,
Until Death tramples it to fragments.
        Percy Bysshe Shelley: "Adonais"

  Now sleeps the crimson petal, now the white;
Nor waves the cypress in the palace walk;
Nor winks the gold fin in the porphyry font:
The fire-fly wakens, waken thou with me.
        Alfred, Lord Tennyson:
           "Now Sleeps the Crimson Petal"

Cold in the earth—and the deep snow piled above thee,
Far, far removed, cold in the dreary grave!

Have I forgot, my only Love, to love thee,
Severed at last by Time's all-severing wave?

> Emily Brontë: "Remembrance"

It lies in Heaven, across the flood
  Of ether, as a bridge.
Beneath, the tides of day and night
  With flame and darkness ridge
The void, as low as where this earth
  Spins like a fretful midge.

> Dante Gabriel Rossetti: "The Blessed Damozel"

When I am dead, my dearest,
  Sing no sad songs for me;
Plant thou no roses at my head,
  Nor shady cypress tree:
Be the green grass above me
  With showers and dewdrops wet;
And if thou wilt, remember,
  And if thou wilt, forget.

> Christina Rossetti: "Song"

It was many and many a year ago,
  In that kingdom by the sea,
That a maiden there lived whom you may know
  By the name of Annabel Lee;—
And this maiden she lived with no other thought
  Than to love and be loved by me.

> Edgar Allan Poe: "Annabel Lee"

In broad daylight, and at noon,
Yesterday I saw the moon
Sailing high, but faint and white,
As a schoolboy's paper kite.

> Henry Wadsworth Longfellow:
> "Daylight and Moonlight"

Here lies a most beautiful lady,
Light of step and heart was she;
I think she was the most beautiful lady
That ever was in the West Country.
But beauty vanishes; beauty passes;
However rare—rare it be;
And when I crumble, who will remember
This lady of the West Country?

Walter de la Mare: "An Epitaph"[2]

Now I have deliberately chosen these varied passages out of the large treasure-trove of the most familiar British and American poems, taking special care to avoid selections which present special problems of interpretation or require a special taste. Two—the Landor and the de la Mare—are complete poems; a number are stanzas; some are only fragments. I do not expect that any reader will like all these passages equally well. But the reader who has, in general, found beauty and passion in these verses may be forthwith assured that, however much or little he may *know* about poetry, the root of poetic appreciation and understanding and enjoyment is in him. The door to the treasure-chamber is on the jar.

That is much more important than it would be to possess at this point a perfect theoretical knowledge of the mechanics of poetry—of prosody, of metrics. Only, it is better still to have both, for the full beauty of such work as has been quoted here cannot be savored until emotional response has been supplemented by intellectual understanding. For the mechanics of poetry is the means by which the poet creates beauty. Moreover, it is the only means by which such beauty can be created. To this, then, we must now turn.

[2] From Walter de la Mare, *Collected Poems* (Henry Holt and Company). Copyright, 1920, by Henry Holt and Company, Inc. Copyright, 1948, by Walter de la Mare. Used by permission of the publishers.

268 • WHY POETRY?

The Means

What we shall study, of course, will be the mechanics of modern English verse. But these are not the only means that have been used in the world to achieve the kind of pattern—the variations in repetition—upon which poetry depends. Ancient Hebrew poetry, for example, employed the basic device of parallelism:

> Bless the Lord, O my soul:
> And all that is within me, bless his holy name.
> Bless the Lord, O my soul,
> And forget not all his benefits,
> Who forgiveth all thine iniquities,
> Who healeth all thy diseases . . . .

The Anglo-Saxon poet, on the other hand, depended for his rhythm upon four heavily stressed syllables in each line, plus an undefined number of unstressed syllables. Thus the *Beowulf* begins:

> Hwæt! we Gar-Dena   in gear-dagnum
> þeod cyninga   þrym gefrunon,
> hu þa æþelingas   ellen fremedon.
> Oft Scyld Scefing   sceaþena þreatum,
> monegum mægþum   meodo-setla ofteah.

Professor J. Duncan Spaeth has reproduced the effect of this in modern English:

> List to an old-time lay of the Spear-Danes,
> Full of the prowess of famous kings,
> Deeds of renown that were done by the heroes;
> Scyld the Sheaf-Child from scourging foemen,
> From raiders a-many their mead-halls wrested.[3]

This much, as the saying is, for the sake of the record.

[3] From J. Duncan Spaeth, *Old English Poetry* (Princeton University Press, 1921).

But our concern is with the way our poetry is written in modern English, even though we must use the Latin nomenclature to describe it, having none of our own. This will cause no difficulty, provided only we remember that in Greek and Latin, the rhythm of the verse depends (with reservations) upon the alternation of "long" and "short" syllables, while in English it depends almost entirely upon stress and the absence of stress.

It must not be supposed that there is no rhythm in prose. Prose which lacked rhythm would make very rough reading. But the rhythms of prose, being much less "regular" than those of verse, are harder to describe or to analyze.[4]

"Feet"

In English poetry, each "verse" or line[5] is divided into "feet." And each "foot" normally contains one stressed syllable and either one or two unstressed syllables.

The two-syllabled feet are called "iambic" and "trochaic." Most English poetry is iambic.

In iambic verse, the unstressed syllable stands first:

$$\overset{\times}{\text{I}}\,\overset{\prime}{\text{strove}} \mid \overset{\times}{\text{with}}\,\overset{\prime}{\text{none,}} \mid \overset{\times}{\text{for}}\,\overset{\prime}{\text{none}} \mid \overset{\times}{\text{was}}\,\overset{\prime}{\text{worth}} \mid \overset{\times}{\text{my}}\,\overset{\prime}{\text{strife.}} \mid$$

In trochaic verse, the stressed syllable stands first:

$$\overset{\prime}{\text{Com}}\overset{\times}{\text{rades,}} \mid \overset{\prime}{\text{leave}}\,\overset{\times}{\text{me}} \mid \overset{\prime}{\text{here}}\,\overset{\times}{\text{a}} \mid \overset{\prime}{\text{lit}}\overset{\times}{\text{tle,}} \mid \overset{\prime}{\text{while}}\,\overset{\times}{\text{as}} \mid \overset{\prime}{\text{yet}}\,\overset{\times}{\text{'tis}} \mid$$
$$\overset{\prime}{\text{ear}}\overset{\times}{\text{ly}} \mid \overset{\prime}{\text{morn:}} \mid$$

The three-syllabled feet are called "anapaestic" and "dactylic."

---

[4] For methods to be used in charting and analyzing prose rhythms, see Edith Rickert, *op. cit.*

[5] A verse is a single line of poetry; a stanza is a group of verses. The clergyman who asks the congregation to sing the first, third, and last "verses" of a hymn would be greatly nonplussed if he were taken at his word.

In anapaestic verse, the stressed syllable stands last:

$$\overset{\times}{\text{And}}\ \overset{\times}{\text{the}}\ \overset{\prime}{\text{sheen}}\ |\ \overset{\times}{\text{of}}\ \overset{\times}{\text{their}}\ \overset{\prime}{\text{spears}}\ |\ \overset{\times}{\text{was}}\ \overset{\times}{\text{like}}\ \overset{\prime}{\text{stars}}\ |\ \overset{\times}{\text{on}}\ \overset{\times}{\text{the}}\ \overset{\prime}{\text{sea}}\ |$$

In dactylic verse, the stressed syllable stands first:

$$\overset{\prime}{\text{This}}\ \overset{\times}{\text{is}}\ \overset{\times}{\text{the}}\ |\ \overset{\prime}{\text{forest}}\ \overset{\times}{\text{pri}}\ |\ \overset{\times}{\text{meval.}}\ \overset{\prime}{\text{The}}\ |\ \overset{\times}{\text{murmur}}\ \overset{\times}{\text{ing}}\ |$$

$$\overset{\prime}{\text{pines}}\ \overset{\times}{\text{and}}\ \overset{\times}{\text{the}}\ |\ \overset{\prime}{\text{hem}}\ \overset{\times}{\text{locks}}\ |$$

If there are two feet in a verse, the verse is called "dimeter." If there are three, it is called "trimeter." If there are four, it is called "tetrameter." If there are five, it is called "pentameter." If there are six, it is called "hexameter." And so on.

Thus, the first example quoted above would be called "iambic pentameter." The second is "trochaic octameter." The third is "anapaestic tetrameter." The fourth is "dactylic hexameter."

Variations

But very little verse above the level of jingles and Mother Goose rimes is quite regular. Take two lines as simple as these:

$$\overset{\prime}{\text{Only}}\ \overset{\times}{}\ |\ \overset{\times}{\text{to}}\ \overset{\prime}{\text{hold}}\ |\ \overset{\times}{\text{you}}\ \overset{\prime}{\text{close,}}\ |\ \overset{\times}{\text{my}}\ \overset{\prime}{\text{dear,}}\ |$$

$$\overset{\prime}{\text{Never}}\ \overset{\times}{}\ |\ \overset{\times}{\text{to}}\ \overset{\prime}{\text{let}}\ |\ \overset{\times}{\text{you}}\ \overset{\prime}{\text{go.}}\ |$$

Blank verse is, by definition, iambic pentameter—a line of five feet, with the stresses falling on the second, fourth, sixth, eighth, and tenth syllables. But if you were to try to read any good piece of blank verse according to this definition—say, Portia's "Mercy Speech" in *The Merchant of Venice*, for example—you would come up with an utterly ridiculous and indefensible reading. Instead, you would probably read the lines something like this:

The qual | ity | of mer | cy is | not strain'd. |
It drop | peth as | the gen | tle rain | from heaven |
Upon | the place | beneath. | It is | twice blest: |
It bless | eth him | that gives | and him | that takes. |
'Tis might | iest in | the might | iest; it | becomes |
The thron | ed mon | arch bet | ter than | his crown. |
His scep | tre shows | the force | of temp | oral power, |
The at | tribute | to awe | and maj | esty, |
Wherein | doth sit | the dread | and fear | of kings; |
But mer | cy is | above | the scep | tred sway; |
It is | enthron | ed in | the hearts | of kings; |
It is | an at | tribute | to God | himself | . . . .

"Something like this" I say you would probably read it, but I am not saying that you *must* read it exactly like this. There is only one way to read Latin quantitative verse correctly, but English accentual verse leaves much more room for variety of interpretation. I have phonograph records of the "Mercy Speech" by Ellen Terry, Julia Marlowe, and Viola Allen, and no one of these distinguished actresses gives a reading that agrees in every particular with that of the others nor yet with mine. Moreover, I myself might read the lines differently upon another occasion, as wishing to stress another aspect of Portia's meaning.

But let us look at the lines as I have marked them here. Only two—the fourth and the seventh—are entirely regular. The last two lines each begin with a trochee. The very first line contains both a "pyrrhic" substitution (two unstressed syllables in a foot) and a "spondee" (two stressed syllables in a foot). And though each of the twelve lines contains five feet, only four lines contain five stresses each, even counting the lines in which the stresses are irregularly distributed.

There are, as it happens, no six-stressed lines in this passage, but there are many such in Milton's blank verse, and there is one famous line in *Paradise Lost* which contains eight stresses:

Rocks, caves, | lakes, dens, | bogs, fens, | and shades | of death. |

How, then, can we call such a passage blank verse? Well, we can call a passage blank verse (or anything else) only to the extent that the underlying norm is (though sometimes only by a hair) preserved. We can call it blank verse only if, despite all the variations, the iambic pentameter base predominates. When the variations are numerous enough so that the pattern breaks down, then the result is either prose or something midway between prose and verse which is actually neither fish nor fowl nor good red herring. This happened frequently among the later Elizabethans, and it destroyed blank verse until Milton came along to resurrect it.

Syllabization and the Caesura

But there are many other forms of metrical variation, and they cannot all be illustrated here. If you will look back at the trochaic and dactylic examples which have been given above, you will notice that in each one the last foot is one unstressed syllable short. The omission of an unstressed syllable at the end of a line is called "catalexis." When the same phenomenon occurs at the beginning of a line, it is called "truncation." The *addition* of an extra syllable at the beginning of a line is "anacrusis." "Syllabization" is a general term covering the addition or omission of unstressed syllables anywhere in the line. Such variations may be used to relieve monotony or secure special effects.

The same is true of the pause within the line known as the "caesura." This, it should be understood, is a pause made deliberately, and not a mere breath-pause. Look at Ben Jonson's caesuras in the last line of the lovely poem, "Have You Seen But A White Lily Grow?"

O so white,—O so soft,—O so sweet is she!

The breathless adoration of the lover in the presence of his beloved could be so effectively suggested in no other way.

But Milton is after a very different effect when he uses pauses in his description of the fall of Mulciber toward the close of the first book of *Paradise Lost:*

Nor was his name unheard, or unadored,
In ancient Greece, and in Ausonian land
Men called him Mulciber: and how he fell
From Heaven they fabled, thrown by angry Jove
Sheer o'er the crystal battlements; from morn
To noon he fell, from noon to dewy eve,
A summer's day; and with the setting sun
Dropt from the zenith like a falling star,
On Lemnos, the Aegean isle.

Why not "from morn to eve he fell"? Or even "All through a summer's day he fell"? The meaning would be quite the same. Ah, yes, but the effect would be altogether different!

It takes as long to say "from morn to noon he fell" as it would take to say "from morn to eve he fell." So you say "from morn to noon he fell," and all the while you are saying it, Mulciber, in your mind, is falling. Then you pause before embarking upon the second stage of his falling— "from noon to dewy eve"—which takes as long again. At this point a second pause occurs, and only after that do you utter the final phrase, which takes almost as long to say as either of the others, and which exercises a kind of summarizing effect—"a summer's day." And Mulciber is still falling. Even without the pauses, which add much, we have made Mulciber's fall seem nearly three times as great as it would have seemed if he had fallen merely "from morn to eve." And it is important to remember of all these poetic devices with the fearsome names that what matters is not what they are called but how intelligently the poet uses them. In the hands of a Milton the effect of so slight a thing as a pause may be dizzying, overwhelming.

Stanzas: Couplets

But verses do not stand alone in poetry: they are gathered into "stanzas," which is an Italian word meaning "rooms." Not, to be sure, always. Blank verse runs on indefinitely without stanzaic divisions, and many poems not in blank verse are arranged in what can only be described as free metrical paragraphs of irregular length. But let us look at some characteristic English stanza forms.

For convenience, we shall begin with the simplest form, the "couplet," that is to say, two verses which rime with each other. Since individual couplets are not generally printed apart from each other as separate units but run on indefinitely, like blank verse, it might be argued that the couplet is not really a stanza. It is, nevertheless, a very important form, and it should be illustrated here.

English couplets are usually iambic pentameter—the "heroic couplet" must be—though there are tetrameter couplets also, and these may be either iambic or trochaic.

The heroic couplet was invented by Chaucer, but it found its most elaborate development in the eighteenth century with Alexander Pope, and, as Lytton Strachey has well said, Pope's heroic line, at its highest point of development, comprises "four main words arranged in pairs," as follows. The letters in the right-hand margin, here and in later examples, indicate end-rimes:

See how the world its veterans rewards!	a
A youth of frolics, an old age of cards;	a
Fair to no purpose, artful to no end,	b
Young without lovers, old without a friend,	b
A fop their passion, and their prize a sot;	c
Alive ridiculous, and dead forgot!	c

But couplets may be used very differently from this, as in Keats's "Endymion":

A thing of beauty is a joy for ever:	a
Its loveliness increases; it will never	a
Pass into nothingness; but still will keep	b
A bower of quiet for us, and a sleep	b
Full of sweet dreams, and health, and quiet breathing.	c

It is worth while to look at lines like these if only to break down the common notion that the rimed couplet is necessarily a tight or inflexible form.

Quatrains, etc.

The four-line stanza known as the "quatrain" is familiar in popular ballads and in hymns. Thus, the first stanza of that most moving of supernatural ballads, "The Wife of Usher's Well," reads:

There lived a wife at Usher's Well,	a
And a wealthy wife was she;	b
She had three stout and stalwart sons,	c
And sent them o'er the sea.	b

Here, as will be seen, the second and fourth verses, which are trimeter, rime, but the first and third, which are tetrameter, do not. This 4-3-4-3 pattern is known as "common measure."

But look at the ballad of "The Twa Corbies":

As I was walking all alane,	a
I heard twa corbies making a mane;	a
The tane unto the t'other say,	b
"Where sall we gang and dine today?"	b

This is "long measure" (4-4-4-4), and there are no un-rimed lines. Still other hymns and ballads are in "short measure" (3-3-3-3). An "abab" rime scheme is also admissible. This is the meaning of the familiar abbreviations in hymn-books: L.M., C.M., and S.M. But there is no necessary correlation between any particular measure and any particular rime scheme.

There are other, more specialized types of quatrain. Consider the dignity of the "heroic quatrain" (iambic pentameter, riming "abab"), as already illustrated in Landor's poem on his seventy-fifth birthday, quoted on p. 265.

In *In Memoriam*, Tennyson used a special "envelope" type of quatrain:

I stretch lame hands of faith and grope,	a
And gather dust and chaff and call	b
To what I feel is Lord of all,	b
And faintly trust the larger hope.	a

Here the second and third verses are, as it were, tucked into a kind of protecting cover made of the first and the last. This was a distinct advantage in a long philosophical poem, for it made each stanza almost literally a little "room," just large enough to turn a thought around in. At the end of every four verses, we have arrived at a real termination; had the rime scheme been "abab" or even "abcb," the poet would have given the impression of running on indefinitely, with no real terminal facilities in sight.

But look at the quatrain Edward FitzGerald used for his

famous translation of the agnostic Persian poem, *The Rubáiyát of Omar Khayyám:*

O Thou, who Man of baser Earth didst make,	a
And ev'n with Paradise devise the Snake:	a
For all the Sin wherewith the Face of Man	b
Is blackened—Man's forgiveness give—and take!	a

Is there not, in the unrimed, slightly dissonantal third verse, a subtle suggestion of the disharmony of the universe itself, which is the very theme of the poem? How beautifully appropriate this stanza is for FitzGerald's poem, and how utterly out of place it would be in the affirmative *In Memoriam!*

Many stanza-forms must be omitted from our discussion, for lack of space, or passed over very hastily. Thus "rime royal" is Chaucer's seven-line stanza, named in honor of the royal poet, King James I of Scotland, from its use in *The King's Quair* (Book). Here is the first stanza of Chaucer's *Troilus and Criseyde*, in rime royal:

The double sorwe of Troilus to tellen	a
That was the kyng Priamus sone of Troye,	b
In lovynge, how his aventures fellen	a
Fro wo to wele, and after out of joie,	b
My purpos is, er that I parte fro ye.	b
Thesiphone, thow help me for t'endite	c
Thise woful vers, that wepen as I write.	c

"Ottava rima" is an eight-line, iambic-pentameter stanza, used by the Romantic poets, and especially by Byron in *Don Juan:*

It was the cooling hour, just when the rounded	a
Red sun sinks down behind the azure hill,	b
Which then seems as if the whole earth it bounded,	a
Circling all nature, hushed, and dim, and still,	b
With the far mountain-crescent half surrounded	a

On the one side, and the deep sea calm and chill   b
Upon the other, and the rosy sky,   c
With the one star sparkling through it like an eye.   c

The Spenserian Stanza

More important for English poetry, however, is the "Spenserian stanza," invented by Edmund Spenser for *The Faerie Queene*, and later employed by James Thomson in "The Castle of Indolence," by Byron in *Childe Harold's Pilgrimage*, and by Keats in "The Eve of St. Agnes." Here is a stanza from *The Faerie Queene:*

The noble heart, that harbours vertuous thought,   a
And is with childe of glorious great intent,   b
Can never rest, until it forth have brought   a
The' eternall brood of glorie excellent: b
Such restlesse passion did all night torment   b
The flaming corage of that Faery knight,   c
Devizing how that doughtie turnament   b
With greatest honour he atchieven might: c
Still did he wake, and still did watch for dawning light.   c

The beauty and variety of this stanza form has never been surpassed in English. Spenser built upon the rime-royal basis, but his apparently slight additions produced a wonderful effect. Unlike most stanza forms, this one has been so subtly built and curiously interwoven that it cannot be divided at any point. It is rich, too, in ever-varying rime music: each rime occurs a different number of times. Finally, the first eight lines are iambic pentameter, but the ninth line has an extra foot (making it hexameter, or an "alexandrine"); this provides a real termination and furnishes the reader a point of rest after about as long a stanza —or as large a "room"—as he can manage to be comfortable in.

Moreover, the stanza is ideally adapted to Spenser's

purpose in *The Faerie Queene*, to his genius, his temperament, and his type of mind. For though *The Faerie Queene* is an epic, Spenser is not essentially a narrative poet. All his great "purple passages" are descriptive, meditative, or philosophical passages. As de Selincourt says, the "sustaining principle" of his verse was "a slow circling movement that continually returned upon itself." And he quotes Wordsworth:

> Sweet Spenser moving through his clouded heaven
> With the moon's beauty and the moon's soft pace.

You would not want *The Lady of the Lake* in Spenserian stanzas: they would get in the way of the furious, exhilarating rush of action. For Scott *is* essentially a narrative poet! But they are just right for Spenser.

Yet, even as I write these words, I remember that other poets have used them very differently. It would be difficult to find a poet more different from Spenser than Byron was, but Byron made a pretty good job of the Spenserian stanza in *Childe Harold's Pilgrimage*. At least, there is nothing slow or circling or meditative about his description of the bull fight in the first canto. I can quote only one stanza here:

Sudden he stops; his eye is fixed: away,	a
Away, thou heedless boy! prepare the spear:	b
Now is thy time, to perish, or display	a
The skill that yet may check his mad career.	b
With well-timed croupe the nimble coursers veer;	b
On foams the bull, but not unscathed he goes;	c
Streams from his flank the crimson torrent clear:	b
He flies, he wheels, distracted with his throes;	c
Dart follows dart; lance, lance; loud bellowings speak	
his woes.	c

The Sonnet

But the most important of all the elaborate forms in English is unquestionably the "sonnet," which, really, is not a stanza at all, but a complete poem, becoming part of a larger unit only when it appears in a "sonnet sequence," which is a series of sonnets, often a very lengthy one, developing a theme or telling a story.

The sonnet is a fourteen-line, iambic pentameter poem, of Italian origin. The word sonnet comes from the Italian *sonetto*—a little song. The early sonnets were frequently accompanied by music.

The Italian sonnet was divided into octave (eight lines) —to place the thought—and sestet (six lines)—to draw the conclusion. The rimes in the octave were fixed: abba, abba. The rimes in the sestet were not inflexible, but cde, cde and cd, cd, cd were favorite patterns. The Italians avoided a rimed couplet at the close because they did not wish to emphasize the last two verses at the expense of the rest of the poem.

The Italian sonnet was both amatory and religious. It celebrates the mistress, but the mistress may herself be a symbol of heavenly beauty and holiness. It was marked by extreme idealism; it was learned in mood and temper; its style was full of figures and conceits; it employed many illustrations drawn from classical culture.

Though Chaucer was familiar with Petrarch's work, the real task of translating and adapting his sonnets into English did not get under way until Sir Thomas Wyatt and Henry Howard, Earl of Surrey came along, during Henry VIII's reign. Sir Philip Sidney's *Astrophel and Stella*, which may or may not have reflected the poet's real love for Penelope Devereux (Lady Rich), was the first sonnet-sequence. It was not published until 1591, five years after the death of Sidney, but it existed as early as 1580. Whether Shakespeare's *Sonnets*, published in 1609, were intended as a sonnet-sequence cannot now be determined. They lack a title; their publication seems to have been unauthorized; and we are not sure that the order in which we have them is that of the author's devising.

No other English stanza-form has been subjected to such an intensive "development" as the sonnet. Wyatt imitated the Petrarchan form, but he sometimes ended with a rimed couplet. Longfellow, the most distinguished American sonneteer, was more faithful to Petrarch. Here is the touching sonnet Longfellow wrote about his second wife, who died by fire:

THE CROSS OF SNOW

In the long, sleepless watches of the night,	a
A gentle face—the face of one long dead—	b
Looks at me from the wall, where round its head	b
The night-lamp casts a halo of pale light.	a
Here in this room she died; and soul more white	a
Never through martyrdom of fire was led	b
To its repose; nor can in books be read	b
The legend of a life more benedight.	a
There is a mountain in the distant West	c
That, sun-defying, in its deep ravines	d
Displays a cross of snow upon its side.	e
Such is the cross I wear upon my breast	c
These eighteen years, through all the changing scenes	d
And seasons, changeless since the day she died.	e

Many English writers, however, have simplified the sonnet, destroying its tight Italian structure, and making it consist merely of three quatrains in alternate rime, followed by a rimed couplet. Surrey is generally given credit for having originated this form, and this was the form adopted by Shakespeare:

Let me not to the marriage of true minds	a
Admit impediments. Love is not love.	b
Which alters when it alteration finds,	a
Or bends with the remover to remove:	b
O no! it is an ever-fixed mark,	c
That looks on tempests and is never shaken;	d
It is the star to every wandering bark,	c
Whose worth's unknown, although his height be taken.	d
Love's not Time's fool, though rosy lips and cheeks	e
Within his bending sickle's compass come;	f
Love alters not with his brief hours and weeks,	e
But bears it out even to the edge of doom.	f
If this be error and upon me prov'd,	g
I never writ, nor no man ever lov'd.	g

Beyond this, I do not care to go in defining stanza-forms here. It seems more convenient to speak of the ode later in another connection, and the French forms—ballade, rondel, triolet, villanelle, etc.—which have been used in English with notable success by Swinburne and other writers, would require more space than I can afford to give them. But there are other technical devices which must still be considered.

Some Poetic Devices: Rime and Repetition

The first of these—rime—I have already been forced to take up, or at least to illustrate, in describing the various stanza forms. By definition, rime refers to the agreement of terminal sounds (final vowel plus succeeding consonants). Ordinarily, it is single, but it may be double (as often in -*ing* words), or even triple (as in -*ingly* words, or when, for example, Thomas Hood rimes "stains of her" with "remains of her"). Though ordinarily thought of as exact, rime may be approximate. Ordinarily, too, we think of rime as standing at the end of the verse, but some poets use internal rime also, as Poe does repeatedly in "The Raven," e.g.:

Ah, distinctly I *remember*, it was in the bleak *December*.

Identical rimes are not in favor with modern poets, though in Middle English it was considered rather clever to rime a word with itself, provided you could find a word that had two different meanings. Thus Chaucer ends the first metrical paragraph of the Prologue to *The Canterbury Tales:*

The hooly blisful martir for to seke, (seek)   a
That hem hath holpen whan that they were seeke. (sick) a

"Repetition," too, may be employed as a poetic device. Like approximate rime, it can be very annoying when it seems unskilfully or involuntarily done. But what could be more charming and reassuring than these lines of Frederic Adrian Lopere?

WORLD WISDOM

I

From out the temple's pillared portico,
Thence to the gardens where blue poppies blow
The gold and emerald peacocks saunter slow,
Trailing their solemn ennui as they go,
Trailing their melancholy and their woe.

II

Trailing their melancholy and their woe,
Trailing their solemn ennui as they go,
The gold and emerald peacocks saunter slow
From out the gardens where blue poppies blow
Thence to the temple's pillared portico.[6]

[6] From *The International*, September 1915. Quoted by Bliss Perry, *A Study of Poetry*, pp. 191-192.

Repetition on such an elaborate scale as this is rare in poetry, but it occurs as an incidental and less important device in many poems which do not stake so large a share of their effect upon it. In the form of the "refrain"—sometimes with variations—it has been well known in song literature from the days of popular balladry to tin-pan alley. Particularly good examples will be found in the various texts of the ballad "Edward," which is Number 13 in Child's collection of *English and Scottish Popular Ballads*.

Alliteration and Assonance

"Alliteration" indicates the repetition of a sound—generally consonantal—either at the beginning of a word, or in some other emphatic position, as the beginning of a stressed syllable.

"Assonance" indicates the agreement of vowel sounds.

These may be illustrated—and repetition too—from Shakespeare's great description of Cleopatra's barge:

> The barge she sat in, like a burnish'd throne,
> Burn'd on the water. The poop was beaten gold;
> Purple the sails, and so perfumed that
> The winds were love-sick with them. The oars were silver,
> Which to the tune of flutes kept stroke, and made
> The water which they beat to follow faster,
> As amorous of their strokes. For her own person,
> It beggar'd all description: she did lie
> In her pavilion—cloth-of-gold of tissue—
> O'er-picturing that Venus where we see
> The fancy outwork nature. On each side her
> Stood pretty dimpled boys, like smiling Cupids,
> With divers-colour'd fans, whose wind did seem
> To glow the delicate cheeks which they did cool,
> And what they undid did.

I do not propose to analyze this rich passage in detail. But let us look at a few points in the first four lines.

"Burn'd," of course, repeats the first syllable of "burnish'd"—with great intensifying effect.

We have b-alliteration in "barge," "burnish'd," "Burn'd," and "beaten," and p-alliteration in "poop," "Purple," and "perfumed."

Assonance occurs in the first syllables of "Purple" and "perfumed."

How much farther can you carry this analysis?

"Tone Color"

"Tone-color" is familiar to all in its grosser form of "onomatopoeia," which refers to words like "click," "scratch," "grunt," etc., which actually imitate the sound of the thing described. But there are many passages in poetry—and sometimes in prose too—which do not go so far as that, and yet in which the meaning of the words is subtly reinforced by their sound, by the rhythm of the lines, or by both. This effect is often, somewhat inaccurately, called tone color.

Pope states the principle in "An Essay on Criticism":

'Tis not enough no harshness gives offence;
The sound must seem an Echo to the sense:
Soft is the strain when Zephyr gently blows,
And the smooth stream in smoother numbers flows;
But when loud surges lash the sounding shore,
The hoarse, rough verse should like the torrent roar:
When Ajax strives some rock's vast weight to throw,
The line too labours, and the words move slow;
Not so, when swift Camilla scours the plain,
Flies o'er the unbending corn, and skims along the main.

Note the softening influence of the s's in lines 2-4. In line 6, "hoarse," "rough," and "roar" are as violent in their sound as in their meaning. But look at lines 7-8:

When Á | jax strives | some rock's | vast weight | to throw, |
The line | too lab | ours, and | the words | move slow. |

Here the accumulation of stresses on syllables which contain good, mouth-filling vowels slows up the reading to such an extent that the reader plows through them with an effort comparable to that exerted by Ajax himself. Note how the last two lines fly along in contrast.

In these lines from "The World," by Henry Vaughan, note how the vowels, in such words as "Eternity," "great," "pure," "all," "calm," "round," etc., suggest the roundness, vastness, and turning movement which is the poet's special theme. Then see how the writer speeds up his motion in "Driven by the spheres."

> I saw Eternity the other night
> Like a great ring of pure and endless light,
>   All calm as it was bright;
> And round beneath it, Time, in hours, days, years,
>   Driven by the spheres,
> Like a vast shadow moved, in which the world
> And all her train were hurled.

"The Passing of Arthur," by Tennyson, is full of marvelous tone-color passages. Look at these lines, considering especially the way in which the words which I have taken the liberty of italicizing *express by their sound*, entirely apart from their meaning, the ideas which the poet wishes to convey:

> So, saying, from the ruined shrine he stept,
> And in the moon athwart the place of tombs,
> Where lay the mighty bones of ancient men,
> Old knights, and over them *the sea-wind sang*
> *Shrill, chill*, with flakes of foam. He, *stepping down*
> By *zigzag paths*, and *juts of pointed rock*,
> *Came on the shining levels of the lake.*

There drew he forth the brand Excalibur,
And *o'er him, drawing it,* the winter moon,
Brightening the skirts of a long cloud, ran forth
And *sparkled keen with frost against the hilt;*
For all the haft *twinkled with diamond sparks,*
Myriads of topaz-lights, and jacinth work
Of subtlest jewelry. He gazed so long
That both his eyes were *dazzled* as he stood,
This way and that dividing the swift mind,
In act to throw: but at the last it seemed
Better to leave Excalibur concealed
There in the *many-knotted waterflags,*
That *whistled stiff and dry about the marge.*
So strode he back slow to the wounded King.

Then spake King Arthur to Sir Bedivere:
"Hast thou performed my mission which I gave?
What is it thou hast seen? or what hast heard?"

And answer made the bold Sir Bedivere:
"I heard the *ripple washing in the reeds,*
And the *wild water lapping on the crag.*"

Tone Color and Dramatic Effect

And now, for an impressive example of the use of tone color for dramatic effect, for characterization, look up two of Browning's best dramatic monologues, "Fra Lippo Lippi" and "Andrea del Sarto." The beginning of each is given below.

Both these men are artists—and both are sinners—but their temperaments are very different, and Browning has chosen to characterize them not only by what they say but by the way they say it. Moreover, he has chosen to treat the first sympathetically and the second most unsympathetically.

Fra Lippo Lippi, the unfaithful monk who had no vocation, and who accepted the cloister as the only alternative to starvation, is as full of faults as an old shoe, but that which he came into the world to do—that is, to paint—he does with all his might. But Andrea del Sarto, a far more celebrated painter, is a man whose soul is dead. Aspiration has faded out of his life and his work together: only his marvelous technique—dull, dead, soulless perfection—remains.

Here is the quick, nervous, vigorous, enthusiastic style of Fra Lippo Lippi's utterance:

> I am poor brother Lippi, by your leave!
> You need not clap your torches to my face.
> Zooks, what's to blame? you think you see a monk!
> What, 'tis past midnight, and you go the rounds,
> And here you catch me at an alley's end
> Where sportive ladies leave their doors ajar?
> The Carmine's my cloister: hunt it up,
> Do,—harry out, if you must show your zeal,
> Whatever rat, there, haps on his wrong hole,
> And nip each softling of a wee white mouse,
> *Weke, weke,* that's crept to keep him company!
> Aha, you know your betters! Then you'll take
> Your hand away that's fiddling on my throat,
> And please to know me likewise. Who am I?
> Why, one, sir, who is lodging with a friend
> Three streets off—he's a certain . . . how d'ye call?
> Master—a . . . Cosimo of the Medici,
> I' the house that caps the corner. Boh! you were best!
> Remember and tell me, the day you're hanged,
> How you affected such a gullet's-gripe!

But Andrea's rhythms are as lifeless and meaningless as his own paintings:

> But do not let us quarrel any more,
> No, my Lucrezia; bear with me for once:
> Sit down and all shall happen as you wish.

You turn your face, but does it bring your heart?
I'll work then for your friend's friend, never fear,
Treat his own subject after his own way,
Fix his own time, accept too his own price,
And shut the money into this small hand
When next it takes mine. Will it? tenderly?
Oh, I'll content him,—but tomorrow, Love!
I often am much wearier than you think,
This evening more than usual, and it seems
As if—forgive now—should you let me sit
Here by the window with your hand in mine
And look a half-hour forth on Fiesole,
Both of one mind, as married people use,
Quietly, quietly, the evening through,
I might get up tomorrow to my work
Cheerful and fresh as ever. Let us try.

Read these two passages aloud, allowing your own dramatic sense to determine pitch, emphasis, tempo, etc. Then reverse your styles, reading each passage (if you can!), in the style that rightly belongs to the other. I know of no other way in which you may more unerringly realize how a great artist achieves characterization through speech-rhythms and choice of words.

Intention or Accident?

At this point, somebody is sure to ask whether the poet did all this consciously or deliberately. Strictly speaking, this is a question of psychological rather than aesthetic interest. We know much less than we should like to know about what goes on in a poet's mind while a poem is being born, though Phyllis Bartlett's fascinating *Poems in Process* (Oxford University Press, 1951), brings together considerably more information on this subject than most readers have ever supposed to exist.

To the question as a whole no categorical answer can be

given. Poets differ widely in the use they make of instinctive and deliberative methods respectively, as they differ in other things. We do know, however, that poets have discussed these things as far back as the time of Dante. One interesting example is Poe's paper on "The Philosophy of Composition,"[7] in which he offered an elaborate description of how he wrote "The Raven."

This account is too long to be quoted in its entirety here. But Poe says that "the work proceeded, step by step, to its completion with the precision and rigid consequence of a mathematical problem." He seems to have had no fear that he might be accused of working too mechanically: "The sound of the *refrain* being . . . determined, it became necessary to select a word embodying this sound and at the same time in the fullest possible keeping with that melancholy which I had predetermined as the tone of the poem." And, further: "The next desideratum was a pretext for the continuous use of the one word 'Nevermore.'" Nor did he confine his deliberateness to the tone-color side of the poem:

I made the night tempestuous, first, to account for the Raven's seeking admission, and secondly, for the effect of contrast with the (physical) serenity within the chamber.

I made the bird alight on the bust of Pallas, also for the effect of contrast between the marble and the plumage—it being understood that the bust was absolutely *suggested* by the bird; the bust of *Pallas* being chosen, first, as most in keeping with the scholarship of the lover, and, secondly, for the sonorousness of the word, Pallas, itself.

It is true, of course, that this is an analysis after the event, and many readers have refused to take it seriously. But though afterthought may well have operated in a de-

[7] The quotations are from Volume VI—*On Poetry and the Poets*—of the Stedman-Woodberry Edition of Poe.

gree, it is impossible to believe that the intricate sound-effects which do exist in poems like "The Raven" or "Ula-lume" or "The Bells" "jes' growed," Topsy-fashion, or came into being spontaneously.[8]

Sense and Sound

One point in passing should be made here. Among the literary experimentalists of our time have been a number of writers—and Gertrude Stein is the patron saint of many of them—who have frankly given over the idea that litera-ture means anything, and who concern themselves alto-gether with the manipulation of sound-effects for their own sake. This tendency did not begin with Gertrude Stein; it tempted much more important writers before her—Swin-burne, for example, who often seems more interested in the verbal harmonies he could create with such great skill than in the idea he might wish to communicate through them. Swinburne even wrote a poem, "Nephelidia," in which he achieved a delightful burlesque of his own style at its worst:

> From the depth of the dreamy decline of the dawn through
>   a notable nimbus of nebulous moonshine,
>   Pallid and pink as the palm of the flag-flower that flickers
>   with fear of the flies as they float,
> Are the looks of our lovers that lustrously lean from a
>   marvel of mystic miraculous moonshine,
>   These that we feel in the blood of our blushes that thicken
>   and threaten with throbs through the throat?

[8] Robert Louis Stevenson's "On Some Technical Aspects of Style in Literature" is an important study in this field; it will be found in Volume XXII of the "Thistle Edition" of Stevenson (Scribners): *Sketches, Criticism*, etc. See, too, Albert H. Tolman, "The Symbolic Values of English Sounds," in *The Views About Hamlet and Other Essays* (Houghton Mifflin, 1904). A more elaborate consideration of these matters is given by Edith Rickert, *op. cit.*

And, of course, the thing has been done again and again in
nonsense verses, never more consummately than in Lewis
Carroll's "Jabberwocky":

> 'Twas brillig, and the slithy toves
> Did gyre and gimble in the wabe;
> All mimsy were the borogoves,
> And the mome raths outgrabe.

Nobody can say there is no appeal to the imagination in
that! If it does not "mean" anything, it *does* create an atmosphere. And at least you can be sure of a good many
things it does *not* mean!

Why is this enjoyed by many people who are only annoyed by the cult of Stein, whether in prose or in verse?
May it not be because Stein and her followers give no
indication that they know they are writing nonsense? Now
the "man in the street," confronting this phenomenon—
"A rose is a rose is a rose" and all the rest of it—disposes
of the matter very briefly and efficiently. "The dame," he
says, "is nuts." This seems to me admirably effective for all
practical purposes. Actually, however, the thing that appears to have happened is that Gertrude Stein was trying to
do in literature something that can be done with complete
success only in music. This confusion of genres is always
likely to be characteristic of aesthetic experimentalists. The
composer of a love song may, if he likes, confine himself
altogether to liquid, melting, voluptuous sounds; the composer who wishes to give the impression of a battle would
be permitted by the nature of his medium to employ only
cacophonies. But the poet cannot do better than try to
achieve a harmony between sound and meaning. Sometimes
he will have a choice between *this* word which possesses
tone color and *this other* which does not, but if he wishes
to be understood, there will be instances in which he must

use *this* word and *only this word* because it alone conveys
his meaning, even though its color may be all wrong or
lacking altogether. It is true that a skilful writer may sometimes make a virtue of necessity by using even a structural
word in such a way as to enhance an emotional effect.
Frank Norris did that with the colorless and unromantic
word "and," in a famous description of a ship becalmed at
sea; the ocean, he wrote, "stretched out and around and
before and behind us. . . ." Structurally, he needed only
one of those "and's"; he repeated the word because he
wanted the monotonous effect of the repetition as a means
of expressing the maddening loneliness of the people on the
ship, and he wanted, too, the lonely *sound* of the vowel
contained in it. But this is a minor tour-de-force, and, in
any event, writers often have to use one "and" anyway,
or whatever the word may be, whether it "sounds right"
or not.

Imagery

Nothing has, as yet, been said of "imagery," but nothing
in poetry is more important. As has already been said, the
poet concerns himself with the concrete; his is a vivid,
picture-making imagination. Here, again, images are not
peculiar to poetry: where in literature will you find more
of them, more dynamically and imaginatively used, than
in Henry James's last great novels: *The Wings of the Dove,
The Ambassadors,* and *The Golden Bowl?* Nor is imagery
limited to artistic prose, written by great artists. We ourselves find it in the prose that we speak, and very ordinary
people often surprise themselves and others by the vividness
of their speech in moments of passion or sudden insight.
In days of war and turmoil, the man of no imagination may
content himself by observing that "These are terrible times
to live in," but surely we shall get a much more vivid sense

of terror if we hear him say, "Our world is crumbling under our feet." In 1914, Sir Edward Grey's imagination functioned on a higher, though still, unmistakably, a prose level, when he observed that "The lights are going out all over Europe, and we shall not see them lighted again in our time." But when Cleopatra's world crumbles around her, Shakespeare puts into her mouth one of the most imaginative lines in all literature:

> darkling stand
> The varying shore o' the world.

And now there is no doubt that we *have* entered the realm of poetry!

Some of these examples, it will be noted, are figures of speech, and it is true that images are often developed in figurative terms. But this is beside the point for our analysis here, and the two things—imagery and figurative language —should not be confused. "A red rose bloomed near the corner of the fence" is not a figurative statement, but it is as much an image as if it were. The creation of a mental picture is the essential point, though, as we shall see, the appeal to sight is not necessarily involved in every image.

Some writers speak as if poetry were all imagery, or poetry impossible without it. This is not true. In this sonnet by John Addington Symonds, the imagery is indeed nearly 100 per cent of the poem:

THE JEWS' CEMETERY

Lido of Venice

> A tract of land swept with the salt sea foam,
> Fringed with acacia flowers, and billowy-deep
> In meadow grasses, where tall poppies sleep,
> And bees athirst for wilding honey roam.
> How many a bleeding heart hath found its home

Under these hillocks which the sea-mews sweep!
Here knelt an outcast race to curse and weep,
Age after age, 'neath heaven's unanswering dome.
Sad is the place, and solemn. Grave by grave,
Lost in the dunes, with rank weeds overgrown,
Pines in abandonment; as though unknown,
Uncared for, lay the dead, whose records pave
This path neglected; each forgotten stone
Wept by no mourner, but the moaning wave.[9]

On the other hand, there is very little imagery in this famous song of Shakespeare's, and what there is is too vague to contribute much to the total effect:

> Who is Silvia? What is she,
>   That all our swains commend her?
> Holy, fair, and wise is she;
>   The heaven such grace did lend her,
> That she might admired be.
>
> Is she kind as she is fair?
>   For beauty lives with kindness.
> Love doth to her eyes repair
>   To help him of his blindness,
> And, being helped, inhabits there.
>
> Then to Silvia let us sing
>   That Silvia is excelling;
> She excels each mortal thing
>   Upon the dull earth dwelling.
> To her let us garlands bring.

Analyzing Imagery

Images may be either simple or complex (according as they appeal to one or more of the five senses), and either

---

[9] It is illuminating to compare this poem with Longfellow's treatment of an almost identical subject in "The Jewish Cemetery at Newport," which will be found in his collected poems.

still or moving. Let us analyze a few of the many images in Coleridge's "The Rime of the Ancient Mariner":[10]

1. (I, 12)

> . . . who pursued with yell and blow
> Still treads the shadow of his foe
> And forward bends his head.

The predominant appeal here is to sight-form (in the whole picture) and sight-color (in the word "shadow"). But sound is present also ("yell," "blow"), and touch, tactual and kinesthetic both ("blow," "treads," "bends"). The whole is a complex, moving image, in which the appeal to sight predominates. Next in importance is touch-kinesthetic —the sense of strain.

2. (I, 13)

> . . . ice, mast-high, came floating by,
> As green as emerald.

Sight-form is general throughout this image, being especially strong in the words "mast-high," which form a subsidiary image. Sight-color is used in the simile "as green as emerald." Some readers will find a suggestion of sound (the movement of the water and the crackling of the ice), but this is not presented directly, and many will not be conscious of it at all. More, probably, will insist that they are conscious of touch-thermal in "ice" and in the general feeling of coldness which prevails. This is a moving image, but whether it is simple or complex will depend upon whether the reader gets the suggestions of sound and touch which I have suggested. There can be no question, however, that

---

[10] These analyses follow Edith Rickert's methods in *New Methods for the Study of Literature*. In some cases, the image analyzed here appears in the poem as part of a larger image.

sight predominates. If complexity be admitted at all, then touch-thermal is next in importance.

3. (I, 15)

It [the ice] cracked and growled and roared and howled.

Here we have sight-form and color again, and sound ("cracked and growled and roared and howled"). If touch-thermal has been admitted in analyzing the previous image, it must be admitted again here; many readers will, I think, feel a kinesthetic sensation here, whether they have felt it previously or not. In any case, we have a complex, moving image, in which, for once, not sight but sound predominates.

4. (II, 7)

> All in a hot and copper sky,
> The bloody Sun at noon,
> Right up above the mast did stand,
> No bigger than the Moon.

This elaborate image has clearly been built up synthetically from a number of subsidiary images: a hot, copper-colored sky, the bloody Sun, the mast, and the Moon. The appeal to sight-form is very strong, both in the picture as a whole and, specifically, in the words "sky," "Sun," "mast," and "Moon." But sight-color is very strong also—see "copper sky," "bloody Sun," and "Moon." Touch-thermal certainly appears in "hot," probably also in "bloody Sun." There may be some kinesthetic in the word "stand." Some readers will probably insist that they get smell in "copper" and "bloody." This is a complex, still image. Sight predominates; color is very strong. Of the other sense-appeals, I should call touch-thermal the most important.

5. (II, 10)

> Yea, slimy things did crawl with legs
> Upon the slimy sea.

Sight-form appears vaguely throughout the picture. "Legs" is the most specific form-word, but we are given no indication of the particular shape of the legs in question. Touch-tactual is very strong in the word "slimy," which appears twice. Touch-kinesthetic is equally strong in "crawl." This is a complex, moving image. Touch predominates. The words "slimy" and "crawl" dominate the image.

Narrative Poetry: The Ballad

We have now spoken, though in a shockingly fragmentary fashion, of the technique of poetry, but nothing has yet been said concerning the various types of poetry. From time immemorial a three-fold division has been made: narrative, dramatic, and lyric.

Two forms of narrative are peculiar to verse—the ballad and the epic.

In the course of English literary history, almost every kind of short poem has been called a ballad. The word comes from the Provençal *balada*—a dancing song. In Chaucer's time, a ballad was a lyric poem from the French, a carol-dance song. In Shakespeare's time, the term seems to have been applied loosely to any lyric verse. The present meaning dates from the eighteenth century. It has never been better stated than in the words of Robert Shafer: "A popular ballad is 'a song that tells a story,' and that has come out of the past through oral tradition."

Though both Sidney and Addison were interested in ballads, they were not seriously studied in England until the second half of the eighteenth century. In 1765 Bishop

Percy published the first important collection, *Reliques of Ancient English Poetry*. Scott collected Scottish ballads at the close of the century and published his *Minstrelsy of the Scottish Border* (1802-1803). But it was left for an American scholar to make the definitive collection of British ballads. This was the *English and Scottish Popular Ballads* (1882-1898), of Francis James Child.[11] The transcribing of ballads from the singing or reciting of people in out-of-the-way places has continued to our own time.

Because ballads were preserved in the memory, in some cases for centuries, before it occurred to anybody to write them down, it has sometimes been assumed that they were composed, as well as preserved, by the folk. "The folk poetizes," said Grimm (*"Das Volk dichtet"*), and picturesque hypothetical pictures have been painted of a community gathered to sing and dance about the fire, with one member of the group and then another contributing a verse or an image which spontaneously "came," so that by the time they had finished, a ballad had been composed which was the product of the community, and it would have been impossible to tell who was the "author" of it, even had anybody wished to do so.

"Communal Composition"?

This theory of the "communal composition" of ballads was eloquently urged in the writings of Francis B. Gummere, an influential scholar in his day, but it has now fallen out of favor. In 1921 it was energetically attacked by Miss Louise Pound, in her *Poetic Origins and the Ballad*, and though many of the older scholars wrung their hands vio-

[11] Child's work now appears in an abridged edition, edited by Kittredge and Sargent, in the "Cambridge Poets" series (Houghton Mifflin). For American ballads, see John A. Lomax, *American Ballads and Folk Songs* (Macmillan, 1934) and other books; also Carl Sandburg, *The American Songbag* (Harcourt, Brace, 1927).

lently at the time, some of these have now swung more than halfway round to Miss Pound's position. Professor Gordon Hall Gerould, for example, reviewed *Poetic Origins and the Ballad* very bitterly, but by 1932, when he published *The Ballad of Tradition*, now the best general book on the subject, he was willing to grant that "neither a melody nor the outline of an imagined story can well emerge from more than a single mind."

It is still true, however, that so long as ballads were preserved in the memory, the folk imagination did introduce many intentional and unintentional changes into them. Some ballads even achieved an international circulation, so that different texts reflect different cultures. In a survey course in the history of English literature, the writer once had a student who had grown up in Brazil and had there become familiar with the English and Scottish ballads in the Portuguese language! Her home was in a part of Brazil to which, long ago, a group of North Carolinians had emigrated. When they came, they brought the ballads with them—in their minds—and in the course of time they translated them, except for the proper names—into their adopted tongue. This young lady had never connected the ballads with "literature," and it was one of the surprises of her life when they turned up in her "English course."

The obviously impersonal "style" of the ballads has made it easier to believe that they were composed by the community. They deal with primal themes: love, hate, conflict, fear of the unknown; and they are full of superstitions and folk-beliefs, obviously, in many cases, of pre-Christian origin. Sometimes, as in "Edward," they begin in the midst of the action, as Horace said an epic should begin. "Edward" also uses dialogue freely. It is often amusing to look at the variant texts of the older ballads. In its oldest form, "Riddles Wisely Expounded" (Number 1 in Child's collection) is a dialogue between a girl and the devil, whom she puts to flight by answering his riddles correctly. But in the later "A" text, the situation has been rationalized: here the demon has been replaced by a human lover. And this time the girl's object is not to get rid of him but to hold him!

I have been speaking so far of folk balladry—popular balladry—but the making of ballads did not come to an end with the passing of whatever the conditions may have been which brought folk-literature into being. Later writers have often imitated the style of the folk ballads. Scott and Coleridge were notable workers in this field, and Coleridge's "The Rime of the Ancient Mariner" probably vies with Rossetti's later poem, "The King's Tragedy," for the title of the most elaborate "literary ballad" in the language. Among the standard American poets, Longfellow was the most important for balladry. Kipling's *Barrack-Room Ballads* introduced a more robust type of ballad toward the close of the nineteenth century. Among twentieth-century ballads in English, none has enjoyed, or deserved, wider vogue than "The Highwayman," by Alfred Noyes.

The Epic

The epic has nothing in common with the ballad save that the origins of both are lost in time, and both have, therefore, been made the subject of considerable theorizing. Until the nineteenth century, it was taken for granted that the *Iliad* and the *Odyssey* were the work of an individual writer who was one of the great poets of world literature. Then, as Carl Van Doren sarcastically remarked, a school of critics arose who found it difficult to believe that so great an artist could have existed at this early period, but who found no difficulty whatever in believing that a whole group of such great artists should have existed at this same period! Close kin to these was the probably apocryphal, but delightful, schoolboy who finished an examination on the Homeric problem with the immortal sentence: "The Homeric poems were not written by Homer but by another poet of the same name, living at about the same time."

A good simple definition of the epic is the one made by Thomas Arnold, of Rugby: "a poem telling the story of a great complex action, in the ground style, and with fulness of detail." C. M. Gayley is a bit more elaborate when he speaks of it as "a dispassionate recital, in dignified, rhythmic narrative, of a momentous theme or action, fulfilled by heroic characters and supernatural agencies, under the control of a sovereign destiny."

The "grand style" is the heart of the matter. The epic poet does not strive for realism. He does not want the reader to "feel with" his characters or to put himself in their place, but merely to admire them. They are off somewhere against the horizon, like the demigods in a Wagnerian opera, each at least eight feet tall, and with virtues and vices to correspond to their physical stature. In the ancient epics, the hero is more than himself: he is a tribe or a people or a nation. Aeneas, for example, is Rome. Such later epics as *The Divine Comedy* and *Paradise Lost* are not epics in the classical sense, but if the term is to be applied to them at all, it will have to be justified on the ground that they dramatize a creed or a world-view, and that this larger interest takes the place of the national or tribal outlook of the *Iliad* and *Odyssey*, the *Aeneid*, the *Song of Roland*, the *Kalevala*, the *Niebelungenlied*, and the rest of them. A merely personal interest, as in most novels and plays, will not do.

Gayley stresses the fact that the epic heroes perform their mighty deeds "under the control of a sovereign destiny." The stars in their courses fought against Sisera. In the

Greek epics, the action shifts, from time to time, from earth to heaven, that we may observe the gods taking sides in the conflicts of mortals. No poet can achieve a mood of epic grandeur unless he can make his reader believe that what the characters do matters supremely, not only to them but to the cosmos itself.

"The Grand Style"

It is this atmosphere of high seriousness which necessitates the "grand style." Speeches are long and elaborately organized, and much figurative language is employed. Not only are all important personages treated with portentous dignity; even the things they use take on a quality of magnificence. So we get the detailed descriptions of weapons and armor in the epics which strike the martial note. All this is given in great detail; time is no factor. The psychological effect is quite sound; if it is worth while to take a couple of hundred lines to tell how the hero was armed, then surely the contest in which he participated must have been a very grand affair! The hero must be praised, too, not only by his friends, but by his enemies, and Beowulf is lauded by the Danish coast guard before the latter knows whether he comes as friend or foe.

The tendency toward formalism reaches its highest point in the development of "stock" ways of saying things: "wine-dark sea," "far-shadowing spears," "bright-eyed goddess," "gold-frontleted steeds," etc., or, with variations, "Diomedes of the loud war cry" and "Odysseus of many wiles." ("Swift-footed Achilles," says Lessing, "even when he is asleep.") Epic formulae are developed, too, on a more elaborate scale: "So they stretched forth their hands to the good cheer that was set before them"; "He of good intent spake to them and said"; "So he fell with a crash and his armor clanged upon him"—this last, perhaps, the direct ancestor of the American dime-novel formula: "Thus another redskin bit the dust."

Epic style was nowhere more beautiful than in the Homeric simile, which, usually beginning with "like" or "as," developed an elaborate description of some aspect of natural beauty, then applied it briefly, for purposes of vividness and elucidation, to the material in hand. Matthew Arnold made brilliant use of this stylistic device, again and again, in his "Sohrab and Rustum":

> Like some young cypress, tall, and dark, and straight,
> Which in a queen's secluded garden throws
> Its slight dark shadow on the moonlit turf,
> By midnight, to a bubbling fountain's sound—
> So slender Sohrab seemed, so softly reared.

The Epic and Modern Life

Why do we have no epics any more? In the first place, of course, it is not quite accurate to say that. Charles M. Doughty wrote a whole series of epics—*The Dawn in Britain, The Cliffs, The Clouds*, etc.—but the world has preferred to read his *Travels in Arabia Deserta*. Alfred Noyes tried the epic in *Drake*, and epic claims have been made for works as different as *The Dynasts*, by Thomas Hardy, and *John Brown's Body*, by Stephen Vincent Benét. But nobody would call the epic, in any form, a characteristic product of our age, and whatever the explanation may be, it is certainly not that we have lost our capacity for epic action. Lindbergh's flight across the Atlantic was an epic feat, if ever there was one, but there was no poet of consequence to praise it, though earlier in the century, Percy MacKaye had struck the note of epic exaltation briefly, in a little poem glorifying Colonel Goethals, the builder of the Panama Canal—

A man stood up in Panama,
And the mountains stood aside.[12]

Coming somewhat closer to the materials of the Greek epics, our bloody wars have produced their quota of epic action, but while a great deal of literature was the result, very little of this is in the epic mood, or concerned with those aspects of the conflict that the epic could conveniently have embraced. Except for the conscientious objectors, we are not living in the spirit yet, and when we kill we make a much more efficient job of it than our ancestors ever did. If we do not ask "Whom first, whom last, did he slay?" may not the reason be that no epic could be long enough to contain the answer? But it does not seem too much to say that our attitude toward all this kind of thing —and perhaps toward action itself—has changed.

Narrative poetry is not confined to ballad and epic: these are merely the types which need most clearly to be defined, and which submit most gracefully to such definition. There is no example of either, however, in that greatest of all treasure-houses of poetic narrative, Chaucer's *Canterbury Tales*. For humorous and satirical effect, the "mock epic" applies the epic style to a trifling theme: the best-known example is "The Rape of the Lock," by Alexander Pope, where the theft of a lock of hair from a girl's head is described in a manner more suitable to the fall of Troy. The Middle Ages had the metrical romance, which was a long narrative poem only less elaborate than the epic, less serious, less national in its embodiment of group ideals. Modern poets, too, have experimented freely with various types of narrative. There have even been novels in verse, like Mrs. Browning's *Aurora Leigh* and *A Prophet of Joy*, by Gamaliel Bradford.

[12] From *The Present Hour*, by Percy MacKaye (Macmillan, 1914). Used by permission of the publishers.

Poetic Drama and Dramatic Monologue

The technique of the drama, of course, is the same, whether the play be written in prose or in verse, and this technique has already been considered. The older poetic drama held its place on our stage well into the nineteenth century; during the early twentieth century, it shrank, for the most part, to the more popular plays of Shakespeare. New playwrights, however, became increasingly timid about using verse, and when they did use it, they found increasing difficulty in getting their plays produced. The most successful American poetic play of the early twentieth century was Josephine Preston Peabody's *The Piper*, a social drama, based upon the old legend of the Pied Piper of Hamelin. Percy MacKaye was a valiant and indefatigable crusader for the poetic drama; perhaps his best "break" on Broadway came in 1906, when Sothern and Marlowe produced his *Jeanne d'Arc;* two years later, they performed a similar service for a poetic drama of the French Revolution, *The Goddess of Reason*, the work of the American novelist, Mary Johnston. But the poetic drama did not win any really important successes in the modern commercial theater until the coming of Maxwell Anderson and Christopher Fry.

Distinctly "modern," on the other hand, is the "dramatic monologue," which was Browning's characteristic type of poem, though Tennyson also used it with distinguished success, and it has been handled successfully by later poets, including Edwin Arlington Robinson. The dramatic monologue differs from the soliloquy in that, though we hear but one voice, the presence of a listener is assumed, and the listener's reactions, gestures, unheard queries, etc., may have a very important effect upon its development. Naturally the poet generally chooses to present his hero in some moment of spiritual crisis, or to show him engaged in some

crucial action, in the course of which an important revelation or realization of character can be made. The most
familiar, though certainly not the greatest, of Browning's
dramatic monologues, "My Last Duchess," presents that
moral monster, the Duke of Ferrara, in marriage negotia-
tions with the envoy of the nobleman whose daughter he
next proposes to honor with his title. In the course of
displaying his treasures, he exhibits the prized portrait of
his

> last Duchess painted on the wall
> Looking as if she were alive,

a work in which he takes a pure aesthetic pleasure, quite
unmodified by any remorse for having destroyed her with
his own merciless cruelty and jealousy.

> Even had you skill
> In speech—(which I have not)—to make your will
> Quite clear to such an one, and say, "Just this
> Or that in you disgusts me; here you miss,
> Or there exceed the mark"—and if she let   5
> Herself be lessoned so, nor plainly set
> Her wits to yours, forsooth, and made excuse,
> —E'en so would be some stooping; and I choose
> Never to stoop. Oh sir, she smiled, no doubt,
> Whene'er I passed her; but who passed without   10
> Much the same smile? This grew; I gave commands;
> Then all smiles stopped together. There she stands
> As if alive. Will't please you rise? We'll meet
> The company below, then. I repeat,
> The Count your master's known munificence   15
> Is ample warrant that no just pretence
> Of mine for dowry will be disallowed;
> Though his fair daughter's self, as I avowed,
> At starting, is my object. Nay, we'll go
> Together down, sir. Notice Neptune, though,   20
> Taming a sea-horse, thought a rarity,
> Which Claus of Innsbruck cast in bronze for me!

At line 9 of the portion quoted, the envoy must have made some move which caused the duke to suppose that he expected a fuller explanation of the late duchess's attitude toward her husband. At line 13, we get the suggestion that the envoy has been so overcome with horror by the callous revelation that has just been made that he forgets to rise from the seat before the picture where he and the duke have been sitting until the latter gives him a specific direction. At line 19 the envoy has stepped back to permit the duke to precede him down the stairway, as befits his rank, but the hideous monster is in an excellent mood after having written himself down a murderer; he also wishes to make a good impression upon the envoy whose report may be expected to have some influence upon the success or failure of his suit. So he lays aside the prerogatives of his rank; he and the envoy descend the stairs together, as if they were equals. Perhaps he even affectionately takes the envoy's arm; if so, the man must have shuddered as at the touch of a snake. Then, in the last three lines, comes the crowning revelation of the speaker's heartlessness: he turns, in passing, from the exhibition of one art treasure, the portrait of the wife whom he destroyed, to another, a bronze depicting a mythological subject. He treasures both these beautiful objects very highly; he would not have the envoy miss either one!

Browning has told us nothing specific about the character of the envoy, but hints, given here and there between the lines, suggest that he is a rather sensitive man, and as the poem comes to an end, we hope that we may trust him not to give his master a report friendly to the duke's suit. The duke himself is, however, quite unaware of the possibility that he has created an unfavorable effect. It is the crowning revelation—and the crowning punishment—of his infamy that he should have lost the power to understand how decent people react to the revelation of monstrous villainy.

Browning's most elaborate development of the dramatic monologue was in his masterpiece, *The Ring and the Book*, in which the dramatic monologue expands to the proportions of an epic. "The epic of free speech," as Chesterton called it, and the first important work of art to build up its capital out of the relativity of human judgments, *The Ring and the Book* tells the story of a domestic scandal eventuating in murder, as many times as there were people involved or interested in it. It is an interesting commentary on the fluidity of literary types that, many years later, Virginia Woolf should have done something similar, with a completely different kind of material, in the series of monologues which make up the book called *The Waves*, which was published as a novel, and which is generally considered a nearly ultimate expression of the "stream-of-consciousness" technique. It is also interesting to note in passing that, in our own time, the dramatic monologue itself has become a full-scale dramatic entertainment. Though lyceum and Chautauqua entertainers had been using it for years, Ruth Draper was, I think, the first successfully to invade the "regular" theater with a one-woman show. She was followed shortly by Cornelia Otis Skinner, who, in such entertainments as *The Wives of Henry VIII* and *Paris '90*, has worked out a style of presentation involving settings, costumes, and properties, the whole adding up to what is distinctly a virtuoso type of performance.

The Lyric

I come finally, then, to the last of the Greek divisions—the "lyric" poem. By definition, this is a poem which expresses the poet's feelings; in practice, the definition has to be stretched a little, for there are many "dramatic lyrics," in which, instead of giving us what he himself feels, the poet uses his imagination to enter into the mind and heart of another human being, and writes from that other's point of view. "Ye Banks and Braes o' Bonnie Doon" is the utterance of a betrayed girl, but Robert Burns wrote the poem. Browning was a "liberal," but he wrote his "Cavalier Songs" from the point of view of loyal supporters of King Charles I in the seventeenth century.

This does not mean that poets "lack sincerity," or that they are "liars," because various works express different moods which are not, necessarily, in every aspect, reconcilable by the laws of formal logic. The poet's utterance does, as a whole, "mean" something. If it is any good, it is the projection and the expression of a personality and a point of view which is the poet himself and nobody else on earth. There is a difference, nevertheless, between a poem and a sermon. Strictly speaking, as Keats observed, the poet has no opinions; he only has perceptions. And he is not necessarily obliged to stake his soul's salvation upon every perception which he has expressed. And this is the same Keats who testified that he could not see a sparrow alight outside his window without, through his imagination, taking part in its activities, even to the extent of pecking about the gravel.

As a matter of fact, the same thing is true, in a more limited degree, of the preachers themselves, for no preacher who knew his business ever tried to express the whole truth in a single sermon. "What is truth?" is nearly as large a question as "What is life?" and when Pilate asked it, Christ himself attempted no answer. What the intelligent preacher does is to express the particular truth which his own experience has vitalized for him at this particular time, or which the needs of his congregation seem to require. Emerson realized all this clearly—Emerson, himself a poet, whose preaching, and whose essays, came about as close to lyric poetry as prose can come. Emerson said that a foolish consistency was the hobgoblin of small minds, and this is forever being quoted out of context by people who do not know what it means. Emerson was not afraid of inconsistency because he was in no danger of it. Everything he talked about was dipped deep in the colors of his own mind, acclimated in the world of that mind; in the sense that every word he wrote expressed his own sense of life, few writers have ever been more consistent that he was, under all his reckless surface inconsistencies. Most preachers, however, feel the need of referring their perceptions to a set of beliefs held more rigidly and unchangingly than anything Emerson held before himself; few find their own temperament an adequate criterion to the extent that he seems to have found his. Indeed, it is at this point that Emerson is more poet than preacher, as much the poet when he preaches as when he is writing poems. And the poet's effort is generally extended in the direction of expanding, not constricting, the area of his perceptions. He is a man, and nothing human is alien to him. But simply because he is a man, his perceptions have been limited by his own temperament and experience, and most poets feel that this natural range, which has been imposed upon them, is quite limited enough. What they are forever trying to do is to take in a larger and larger segment.

It was remarked earlier that the definition of one poetic form, the "ode," would be postponed until we reached the discussion of lyric poetry. It would be more accurate to say that the form of the ode in English cannot be defined, for the excellent reason that it has none. In classical poetry a very different situation prevailed. The so-called Pindaric ode was very complicated in its structure. Written for choral performance, it had a strophe, which was chanted by one group of performers, an antistrophe, chanted by another group, and an epode, which was chanted by the chorus as a whole. There are English odes in which these divisions—and terms—have been retained (see, for example, "The Progress of Poesy" and "The Bard," by Thomas Gray), but, like many of the Latin terms retained in what Richard Grant White called our "make-believe" English grammar, they do not mean a thing. And about all one can say of the ode in English poetry is that it is a serious and dignified form of lyric utterance which is long enough to permit the progressive development of a theme.

Descriptive and Philosophical Poetry

It may be objected that I have said nothing about "descriptive" or "philosophical poetry." Yet most of this is lyrical in effect. Thus, Wordsworth devoted much of the first three stanzas of "I Wandered Lonely as a Cloud" to his description of the daffodils—

> Beside the lake, beneath the trees,
> Fluttering and dancing in the breeze.

But the real point of the poem is in the subjective last stanza:

> For oft, when on my couch I lie
> In vacant or in pensive mood,
> They flash upon that inward eye
> Which is the bliss of solitude;
> And then my heart with pleasure fills,
> And dances with the daffodils.

This is what we really want to know, and this is what we have to go to Wordsworth to get—the impression which the daffodils made upon his mind. If it was merely information about the flowers that we were after, we could do much better by going to a botanical handbook, or perhaps, even, an illustrated nurseryman's catalogue. Wordsworth, of course, was a notoriously subjective poet, and therefore, very likely, not quite a fair case. But what shall we say of James Thomson, in *The Seasons?* Thomson does give his readers a vast array of fairly objective and generalized observation. Actually, however, he is not out to give us information, any more than Wordsworth is. For he subjects all that he has observed to the expression of various moods of grandeur, terror, glory, etc. in nature, which, in turn, appeals to kindred moods in his readers. Only upon some such basis could so non-subjective a piece of work as *The Seasons* be called a poem.

Quite the same thing is true of philosophical poetry, or any poetry seemingly devoted to the expression of an idea. The immortality of the soul, for example, is not a poetic subject insofar as it is an article of the Christian faith; it is rather a theological subject, and a theological subject it remains, unfortunately, in many verses which obstinately refuse to become poetry! But give it to John Donne, let him submit it to the alchemy of his own passions, and express it, not as an article of his creed, but as a lyrical utterance, a *cri de coeur*, and you may get something so splendid as this:

> Death, be not proud, though some have called thee
> Mighty and dreadful, for thou art not so;
> For those whom thou think'st thou dost overthrow
> Die not, poor Death, nor yet canst thou kill me.
> From rest and sleep, which but thy pictures be,
> Much pleasure, then from thee much more must flow,
> And soonest our best men with thee do go,
> Rest of their bones and souls' delivery.
> Thou art slave to fate, chance, kings, and desperate men,
> And dost with poison, war, and sickness dwell,
> And poppy, or charms can make us sleep as well,
> And better than thy stroke; why swell'st thou then?
> One short sleep past, we wake eternally,
> And Death shall be no more; Death, thou shalt die.

"Modern" Poetry

Nothing has been said, so far, of "imagism," "free verse," or what is now called "modern" poetry. And insofar as they differ from older and more orthodox poetry, all these are sufficiently complex and specialized phenomena so that it is impossible to consider these in detail here.

Glenn Hughes's critical study of the imagist movement, *Imagism and the Imagists* (1931) embraced Richard Aldington, H.D., John Gould Fletcher, F. S. Flint, D. H. Lawrence, Amy Lowell, and Ezra Pound. Some of these were at the center of the movement, others toward the periphery; one even told Mr. Hughes that there never had been a "movement" at all, and that the term was invented because Miss Lowell had to have something to talk about! Semi-official manifestoes of the purpose of these writers were achieved, however, in the Preface to the anthology *Some Imagist Poets* (1915) and in Lowell's *Tendencies in Modern American Poetry* (1917). What they amount to is that the imagists insisted on freedom in choice of subject (extending this freedom specifically to embrace the distinctively modern); that because they were striving for hard, clear impressions (and, therefore, seeking to avoid everything that was blurred or indefinite), they searched also for the exact word and the word that would create a clean-cut picture; that they believed intensely in condensation; and that they were committed to the avoidance of conventional rhythms and the creation of new rhythms, congenial to, or determined by, the subject itself. "To understand *vers libre*," said Amy Lowell, "one must abandon all desire to find in it the even rhythm of metrical feet. One must allow the lines to flow as they will when read aloud by an intelligent reader." These poets also made something of a point of refusing to read subliminal meanings into nature; the intense partisanship which their work always awakened was due less to the failure of their opponents to appreciate the beauties they created than to a half-defined impression that there was a great deal of beauty in the world worth preserving to which the tenets of this group were somehow vaguely hostile.

Readers of this chapter will be well aware that if imagism was something new, imagery certainly was not; indeed the difference between imagism and imagery is a little like the difference between nudism and nakedness. Neither was free verse altogether new. Images as rich and clear as any that the imagists created may be found in the work of all good poets, and if the older members of the fraternity were not imagists in the technical sense, the only reason was that they had never been taught that it was immoral to think about the beauty which they had observed and recorded. With the free verse *ideal* nobody can sensibly quarrel either, for the poet who finds the form which is demanded by his subject has taken a long step toward creating an excellent poem. If Matthew Arnold's "Philomela" is not free verse, it would be difficult to say what it is, for Arnold has come as close as language can come to suggesting the ebb and flow of the nightingale's song:

> Dost thou once more assay
> Thy flight, and feel come over thee,
> Poor fugitive, the feathery change
> Once more, and once more seem to make resound
> With love and hate, triumph and agony,
> Lone Daulis, and the high Cephissian vale?
> Listen, Eugenia—
> How thick the bursts come crowding through the leaves!
> Again—thou hearest?
> Eternal passion!
> Eternal pain!

Moreover, Arnold is quite as successful as this, in more varied aspects, in a much greater poem, "Dover Beach."

In that most stimulating and exciting of all books about poetry, *Convention and Revolt in Poetry*, published originally in 1919, when the imagist movement was still exciting and new, John Livingston Lowes declared that "At no time, perhaps, in the history of this country at least, has there been so keen and widespread an interest in poetry," and again that "more people are reading poetry today than for a period of many years." This he found all to the good, though he also declared that "The poetic world is already too safe for democracy. And the daily prayer of free verse should be deliverance from the tender mercies of misguided friends."

Well, so far as the "modernist" poets are concerned, the poetic world has indeed been saved from the democratic ideal! But all the rest of the hopes Lowes cherished for poetry in 1919 have been as cruelly dashed as even the political hopes under whose inspiration he, quite clearly, wrote his last chapter. The typical "modern," "intellectual" poet, both in England and in America, is a coterie writer. Not only does he take no special pains to be understood; it is impossible for anybody to understand him without a "key."

I had a curious experience some months ago. [Desmond MacCarthy wrote these words in 1934, but they have only recently been reprinted in his posthumously-published book, *Memories*.] I was one of a small company who might, on the whole, be called distinguished; and one of them, a poet who certainly deserves the name, read out after dinner a composition by a young man in whose work he had faith. There was, at any rate, "something there," he thought; whether it would unfold or not he could not tell. Gravely, beautifully, he read the poem aloud—and not one of us understood a single line! We were

clever, we were well-read; we were experts in catching suggestions, in seizing and dropping adroitly imaginative clues,
and two of us at least had had practice in following intricate
trains of reflection. Yet, at the conclusion, from the nature of
the case, our comments could only be blurred expansions of
the statement that there *might* be "something there." Mysterious criterion! If at any point in its progress that poem had
conveyed some gleam of meaning, some trace of coherent sentiment, or even an image or two, we were an audience not
unqualified (hard as it is to estimate a poem on first reading),
to form a provisional opinion upon its value and genuineness,
and on the literary skill with which the words had been arranged. But none of the tests which, up till today, have been
applied to verse and prose since literature began were here of
use. As the reader pointed out, with the exception of the suggestion of a hawk, no passage was even visual in its appeal: the
poem was "abstract" from beginning to end. The demand made
upon the listener was that he should yield himself to a flow of
words conveying neither images nor sentiments nor thoughts,
in the faith that the whole would somehow wake in him an
emotion that was truly "poetical." The postulate of such productions is that "poetry" is an essence independent of what a
poem says—probably best taken "neat." The same postulate
underlies modern abstract painting.

Both Desmond MacCarthy and I have described modernist practices at their worst: readers who desire a more
"sympathetic" interpretation will find it in a number of
books, Louise Bogan's *Achievement in American Poetry,
1900-1950* (Henry Regnery Company, 1951), being one of
the best. And, of course, there are many contemporary
poets who are not modernists and to whom the strictures
which have been uttered here do not, in any sense, apply.

We have had poetical revolutions before. We had one in
the seventeenth century, when the so-called "metaphysi-
cals" threw over the Petrarchan stock-in-trade and mapped
out new poetic territories, new sets of poetic conventions,

and new avenues of appeal. Poetry, like other arts, progresses by revolution as well as evolution; the lunatic fringe has a way of wearing off in time, and sometimes the experiments they have conducted are themselves found, when used by better-balanced people than their inventors, to have enriched, in some measure, even the orthodox techniques against which the revolution was directed.

For there is one striking difference between an aesthetic revolution and a political revolution: In aesthetic revolutions, nobody gets killed. Neither is the work that "goes out" destroyed; it is still there for anybody who cares to take the trouble to look it up and read it. It is not necessary to reject Virginia Woolf in order to enjoy Defoe (whom Virginia Woolf also enjoyed), and it is perfectly possible to read both Tennyson and Hopkins with relish and enjoyment. We must never get so excited about the privileges of writers that we forget that readers have privileges also. Literature was made for man, not man for literature. I think we shall be very foolish if, in our annoyance over the vagaries of the moment, we allow ourselves to imagine that the progress of English poetry is over. What may be ahead of it in the years to come, nobody knows. But I do not believe that it will end in a *cul-de-sac*.

CHAPTER EIGHT

We Begin Again

The Essay

We have now finished our consideration of the most important literary types. But you will read a great many books during your life which do not come under any of these headings. How are they to be classified?

Of course, it is much more important to understand them and, above all, enjoy them than it is to classify them. Nor can they all be classified here. But let us look briefly at a few varieties.

Let us begin with the most informal of all—the Essay. Simply because of its informality, it is very difficult to define.

Here, on my desk, is a prospectus for a book of essays, which divides its material under the following headings:

Some Old Masters
Fundamental Issues
The American Scene
Literature and Life
Education
Personages
Creatures
Sketches
Bagatelles

Among the nearly forty titles listed are Lamb's "Dissertation upon Roast Pig"; Aldous Huxley's "War" (from *Ends and Means*); Jane Addams's description of "The Devil Baby at Hull-House"; Woodrow Wilson's defense of "Mere Literature"; Virginia Woolf's answer to her own question, "How Should One Read a Book?"; definitions of education by Matthew Arnold, Thomas Henry Huxley, and Cardinal Newman; Clemence Dane's heart-warming appreciation of Shakespeare's queen, "The Loved Elizabeth"; Elmer Davis's consideration of an unaccustomed theme, "On Being Kept by a Cat"; "A Clergyman," that most brilliant *jeu d'esprit*, by the most brilliant modern British essayist, Sir Max Beerbohm; and Robert M. Gay's playful speculations on the subject of "Noah's Wife."

If you were not bewildered before, you certainly have a right to be now! If these are all "essays," then what on earth can an essay be except "something to read"?

Well, perhaps they are not all essays, strictly speaking. Perhaps the right of some of these items to be included in a book of essays might be successfully challenged. But let us see. And let us begin, as all intelligent people always do, by consulting the dictionary.

Webster's New Collegiate Dictionary gives two unspecialized meanings for "essay" as a noun. The first is: "An effort to do something; attempt; trial." And the second: "A literary composition, analytical or interpretative, dealing with its subject from a more or less limited or personal standpoint."

Now these are excellent definitions. The last part of the second—"dealing with its subject from a more or less limited or personal standpoint"—will remind you of our fundamental distinction between literature and non-literature in Chapter II. In other words, it will help you to understand why the essay *is* literature, even though it does not ordinarily involve the fictional or imaginative materials which, by this time, you have become accustomed to associate with the thought of literary works. And even the first, intentionally non-literary, definition has more application to our theme than you might think. If an essay is "an effort to do something," an "attempt" or a "trial," then you would not expect from an essay on, say, Robert Burns (and both Carlyle and Stevenson wrote famous essays on Burns), the comprehensive, comparatively uncolored and impartial view of the subject that you would have a right to expect from the *Encyclopaedia Britannica*. You might, rather, expect to find almost as much Carlyle (or Stevenson), as Burns. You would not go to such an essay for basic information—not if you are an intelligent reader. It would be the essayist's response to Burns that you were after, the reaction of one writer to another. And this is exactly what you would get.

This is what you get even in the more formal essayists, and this is just what marks the difference between the essay on the one hand and the treatise or the critique on the other. "Plutarch, Cicero, and Bacon," wrote Hamilton Wright Mabie, "discuss the gravest problems of experience in a philosophic temper; but the attitude of each writer toward these problems is intensely individual." If Bacon's essays seem more reserved than those of Montaigne, the reason simply is that the man himself was more reserved. He did not wear his heart upon his sleeve; perhaps he did not have much to wear. But being what he was, his essays expressed his personality quite as adequately as Montaigne's expressed his.

The Author's Personality

All literary artists reveal their personalities in one way or another, but the essayist's self-revelation is the most direct of all. It is not necessary for a good essayist to be

an egotist, but he certainly cannot be a successful essayist
if he fears, or dislikes, to strike the personal note. Like no
other writer, he addresses his reader directly, companion-
ably. The essay is closer to good talk than any other kind
of writing. The writer takes his ease at his inn, and the
reader is at ease with him. He chooses a theme because it
interests him, and simply because he feels no obligation to
achieve a complete or comprehensive or definitive cover-
age of it, he is relaxed as no other writer is relaxed. He feels
free to emphasize the particular values he wishes to stress—
no matter whether anybody agrees with him or not—and
to arrange his materials in any order which seems to him
calculated to secure the maximum literary effects of emphasis and charm.

Readers, consequently, are more likely to feel personally
about essayists than they are about other writers. And,
quite obviously, the value of any expression of personality
is going to depend upon the quality of the personality that
is being expressed. In early American literature, Emerson
wrote essays with titles as impersonal as Bacon's own, but
no essayist ever succeeded more magnificently in giving the
reader his own particular "tap." What is generally meant
by the "personal essay," however, was more typically represented, for Emerson's contemporaries, by Oliver Wendell Holmes. Beginning in the first number of *The Atlantic
Monthly* in 1857, the papers later published in *The Auto-
crat of the Breakfast-Table* became "one of the great immediate successes of American literature"; Lowell, the first
editor, credited them with keeping the magazine alive.
When they came out in book form in 1858, they sold
30,000 copies in a few weeks. Holmes was the urbane,
worldly (though high-minded) gentleman, discoursing to
his fellow-boarders on a vast variety of themes and delivering himself of authoritative dicta on whatever happened

either to interest him or might be suggested by the needs of his listeners.

The *Atlantic Monthly, Harper's, Scribner's, The Century,* and other literary magazines long provided a market for that kind of essay, and a number of distinguished reputations were made. Probably the most important of these belonged to Samuel McChord Crothers (1857-1928) and Agnes Repplier (1855-1950). Crothers, a clergyman by profession, was the direct heir of the Holmes tradition, a genial humorist of earnest spirit but delightfully companionable instincts. Agnes Repplier, a Philadelphian and a Roman Catholic, was slightly more formal in her approach and considerably more astringent. Though essentially romantic in her literary tastes, Miss Repplier was a witty and incisive opponent of what she regarded as the wishy-washy sentimentalism of modern American life. It was her considered judgment of her contemporaries that it was not their hearts that were soft but their heads, and her insistence upon subjecting all well-meaning panaceas to the test of reason provided a wholesome discipline for many readers. Hers was a very distinguished style—polished, balanced, and enriched with a wide variety of remarkably apt quotations, chosen from the most diverse sources. She read phenomenally and apparently never forgot anything she read, so that when she chose to write upon any given topic, whatever anybody she knew had ever said upon the subject came into her mind. All this material she wove very skilfully into the fabric of her own style. The first book in her long career, *Books and Men,* appeared in 1888, the last, *Eight Decades,* comprising her own selection of the essays she had published in many different volumes, accompanied by a brief autobiographical commentary, not until 1937.

Though this chapter is not intended as a lament for past

glories, I cannot escape pointing out that there would be very little market today for such work as Crothers's and Agnes Repplier's, fine as it is. Most of the magazines that gave it sanctuary have perished, and those that survive have radically transformed themselves. American literary scholarship, it seems to me, is better today than it has ever been. Neither have we lost the power to produce distinguished criticism, though the best work in this field is rarely the most highly publicized. But the atmosphere of urgency under which the modern writer works is not friendly to the relaxed mood of the personal essay. The only considerable reputation in the field belonging distinctly to our time is that of E. B. White.

Biography

But if our times have given the death-blow to the essay, they have, on the other hand, made biography more popular than it has ever been before. There was a time, during the 1920's—when the Englishman Lytton Strachey, the American Gamaliel Bradford, the Frenchman André Maurois, and the German Emil Ludwig were all at the height of their vogue—there was a time when biography seemed to be jostling fiction itself for the place of preëminence upon the booksellers' tables. Though this is not quite true today, we still show considerably more interest in biographical writing—and especially in the technique of biographical writing—than our forefathers did.

Biography is the study of human character, and since we are human beings ourselves, there is no branch of human knowledge which we could more reasonably expect to find valuable to us. Moreover, biographies are written about men and women who, whether they were "great" or not, did all have something in them which made them an object of interest to their fellows. But all this being admitted, it may still be asked whether, and if so upon what grounds, biographical writing can be said to be literature, as the term was defined in the second chapter of this volume.

The ordinary biography, of course, is not literature. The old-fashioned double-decker, the "Life and Letters," repository of fact and record, was generally not literature. Again, as in Chapter II, I must insist that I am not speaking disparagingly of non-literary writing. The industry of the old-fashioned biographers was prodigious. They often had the solid virtue of honesty, and they would have scorned, as, alas! many of the new biographers do not, to use a subject as a mere excuse for exhibiting themselves. Furthermore, they had to do their work, accumulating the necessary materials, before anybody else could do his. Only, aesthetic considerations did not greatly trouble them. Poets and novelists were born, but biographers were made. Anybody who had the materials could write a "Life." How, indeed, could the biographer make use of creative gifts, even if he had them? His material had all been prescribed for him in advance. Certain things had happened; he studied them out and wrote them down. What else was there to it?

Well, there is a good deal more than that to it. There is, for one thing, all the difference between a good biography and a bad one. Desmond MacCarthy has called Cavendish's *Life of Wolsey* the first English biography that could be described as a work of art. It is no mere chronicle; neither was it written to glorify its subject, as most biographies are. Instead it has a theme—*sic transit gloria mundi*—and this theme "imposed a unity on the story and a disinterestedness towards the subject of it which was not to reappear again in biography for almost a hundred years." But it is true that the biographer's obligation to be faithful to "what really happened" and his inability to allow his imagination the free play of the novelist or dramatist impose limitations upon him. In his early days, specifically in *Ariel: The Life of Shelley*, M. Maurois permitted himself a blending of fact and fiction. But this was not sound biographical practice, and M. Maurois soon reformed and confessed his fault in the frankest and most winning manner possible, in a charming little book called *The Art of Biography*. Be it noted, however, that he did not, therefore, cease to believe that biography was an art. Boswell was faithful to the facts of his hero's career in his *Life of Johnson:* did he therefore cease to be an artist? Lytton Strachey, himself one of the most gifted of all biographical artists, once said that it was almost as difficult to write a good life as to live one. Perhaps it was the narrowly constricting limitations which the tyranny of the fact imposes upon the biographer's art that he had especially in mind.

"Psychography"

Our own time invented a new form of biographical writing in Gamaliel Bradford's "psychography." This New England writer—a direct descendant of the Pilgrim Governor Bradford—was born in Boston in 1863 and died in Wellesley Hills in 1932. After attempting various other forms of literary work, he finally hit his stride with a full-length "psychograph" of *Lee the American* in 1912, and came into his widest success and influence during the 'twenties. Bradford's psychographs, most of them papers twenty to twenty-five pages in length—there are more than 125 of them in all—were gathered into such volumes as *Confederate Portraits*, *American Portraits, 1875-1900*, *Damaged Souls*, *Bare Souls*, *Wives*, *Daughters of Eve*, and *Saints and Sinners*.

Of course the Bradford psychograph was not something absolutely new under the sun. The author himself avowed his indebtedness to the work of Sainte-Beuve. He had, too, a certain affinity of spirit to all writers of "character sketches" clear back to Overbury, Earle, and Hall in the seventeenth century, and even, for that matter, to Theophrastus. Yet he came closer to inventing a new biographical technique than any other man within living memory. Since he was not concerned to tell the "story" of a man's life, but simply to analyze his character, he threw over the conventional chronological arrangement of materials altogether, substituting therefore a topical arrangement, which left him as free in the matter of arrangement, emphasis, and climax as any creative writer is free. Quotations—brief and made an integral part of the text—from the subject and the writings of others about him, were used for evidence and also to give the color and flavor of the subject's personality.[1]

Nature Writings

Much further than this it does not seem desirable to carry the discussion of literary types in this book, but some mention of nature writing might well be made. I distinguish "nature writing" sharply from the work of the naturalists, which, as I understand it, belongs not to literature but to science. A good nature writer may, of course, be a trained naturalist, but if so, he writes from a literary man's point of view. Good nature writers are men like Thoreau and, more recently, John Burroughs (1837-1921), whose writings fill twenty-three delightful volumes.

It is true that Thoreau sometimes seemed more at home

[1] Gamaliel Bradford discussed psychography in chapters on the subject in his *Lee the American* (Houghton Mifflin, 1912), *A Naturalist of Souls* (Dodd, Mead, 1917), *Biography and the Human Heart* (Houghton Mifflin, 1932), and elsewhere. See, also, the present writer's discussion of it, in the appendix to his book, *The Man Charles Dickens* (Houghton Mifflin, 1929).

in the woods than he did in Concord, and that Emerson told him that if God had meant him to live in a swamp, He would have made him a frog. But in making that statement, Emerson showed something less than his usual perspicacity. "What is Nature," asks Thoreau, "unless there is an eventful human life passing within her?" Again he asserts: "Man is all in all, Nature nothing, but as she draws him out and reflects him." Burroughs, too, though unflinching in his opposition to sentimentalism and nature-faking, was interested in the human suggestiveness of nature and in the use that human beings can make of nature. "The facts of natural history," he says, "become interesting the moment they become facts of human history." Once get that point of view established with a writer, and the likelihood of his producing literature rather than mere scientific writing will be considerable. But little or nothing can be said about nature writing as form. If it is an essay, for example, it will not differ in form from other essays: the difference will be in subject matter.

Literature of Travel

The literature of travel is another popular kind of reading-matter for which no form can be prescribed. It goes back, of course, to Marco Polo—and beyond him—but its golden age, in this country, began after the Civil War, when peace, increasing prosperity, and a growing hunger for the kind of culture Europe held out, combined to drive Americans back and forth across the Atlantic in droves. Sometimes it seems as though most of these must have tried to recover their expenses by writing books about their experiences. Probably nobody else ever "recovered" quite so handsomely as Mark Twain did with *The Innocents Abroad* (1869), or ever insisted so uncompromisingly upon viewing Europe through American eyes, but Bayard Taylor

(1825-1878), poet, novelist, and man of letters, depended
for his livelihood largely upon his travel books and the
lectures he dug out of them, and he was, by no means, a
unique phenomenon. Nor was Europe the only hunting-
ground of these writers; two of the most successful travel
books of the 'seventies were Charles Dudley Warner's *My
Winter on the Nile* and *In the Levant*. Occasionally it even
happened that an East Coast writer would discover that the
North American continent did not end at the Alleghenies
and write about what he had found beyond with an exciting sense of discovery. Warner himself finally reached far-
away California, but it required the Santa Fe railroad and
its money to get him there.

Some travel-writers filled out their own observations
with reading and study, so as to give as "complete" a picture as possible. Melville had done that in writing about his
adventures in the South Seas, and Mark Twain, whose
methods were often much more "literary" than he is given
credit for, always "read up" his subjects and even quoted
considerably. It was, indeed, the bookish and fastidious
Henry James who insisted upon confining himself entirely
to his own impressions. James wrote a number of travel
books, the most distinguished of which is *The American
Scene* (1907), where, reversing the usual process, he gives
us the fruit of his observation of his native land, upon his
return here after having lived for many years in England.
Now there are a great many aspects of the American scene
—and the other "scenes" which he describes in other volumes—about which James knows nothing and consequently
cannot speak. But everything he does give us is his own
authentic impression; his travel books are the work of a
creator of literature whose imagination has gone to work
upon the materials of his travels in quite the same way as,

in his fiction, it came to bear upon the materials which life brought him in other aspects.

About Commencement

The title of this chapter is "We Begin Again," and it may be that you have regarded that as merely an eccentric straining for effect. But you will remember that the exercises which mark the end of the college year—or course— are called "Commencement." As a child, I once asked a university man of my acquaintance why this was so, and he replied, "Because that is when you commence to live."

I hope it means rather that you continue to live, expresses (shall we say?) a pious hope that the life that developed for you during your college years will not abruptly come to a premature end, a case of arrested development. "In my end is my beginning"—such was the legend embroidered on Mary Stuart's Chair of State—"*En ma fin est mon commencement.*" Her Majesty undoubtedly intended these words to be taken in their religious sense, but they have been fulfilled upon this earth also, for she has lived more triumphantly, and controversially, in the imaginations of men, and with far intenser vitality, since her death than she ever lived during her lifetime, and of that living there is no end in sight.

It does not take the intelligent student very long to learn that the mere fact that he has "taken a course" in a subject does not really mean that he knows anything about it. All that the course can do—and all that any single book can do—is to furnish him with a map (often as inadequate a map as those quaint medieval monstrosities which ended in unexplored territories with some such legend as "Here is the place where men fall off the earth"), and to indicate the direction in which explorations may be reasonably pursued. But that is a lifetime job—or delight—and the exploring party to which you have belonged hitherto will not have got very far. At the height of the depression, an American university president told his graduating class that he was less concerned for their economic welfare than for their integrity. The world is a very corrupt place, and to go from the college cloisters into the marketplace is, in a great many cases, to exchange the better for the worse. It is true that what college has given may serve as a very effective kind of amulet, but to achieve such service it must be used wisely and well. If you think you know "all about literature" because you have read this book, you would be much better off if you had never read it. The writer himself does not know "all about literature." Indeed, he does not know very much, though he is still learning. What he has learned, however, he would like to share, and here are the things which it seems to him most important to say in parting.

To read joyfully and successfully, you must learn how to ride two horses going in opposite directions at the same time. You must give yourself up to the author, and you must stand away from him, or sit in judgment on him. For if you fail to do the latter, you will be a jellyfish and a sponge. And if you fail to achieve the former, you will never get far enough into your author to make what you think—and feel—about him of any importance to anybody, least of all yourself.

One of these tasks will probably be easier for you than the other. Which is which will depend upon your own temperament. Some readers actually identify themselves imaginatively with the heroes of their favorite novels; others are always conscious that they are watching the spectacle from the cool distance of art. A combination of sympathetic comprehension plus a certain quality of disinterested detachment would seem to be the ideal.

A priori, then, it would seem very unlikely that a writer who had held the respectful or admiring attention of mankind for a considerable period has nothing to give to you if you approach him rightly. If you feel that there is nothing there, it is much more likely that you are wrong than it is that the writer is at fault and all the people whom he has pleased along with him! On the other hand, there is sound sense in the jaunty resignation of the old poet:

> If she be not [fair] to me,
> What care I how fair she be?

If you do not make a vital contact with your man now, let him alone for a while and then try him again later. Do not, above everything else, pretend that you enjoy something which you really do not enjoy. Above all, do not pretend to yourself. If you do, you will soon bring yourself to a place where you actually will not know what your reactions are, and once you arrive in that desolate country, the faculty of enjoyment will be destroyed altogether. But do not trust to the negative impression of a single contact or exposure either, or you may lose something that could be of lasting value to you. Even so, you will probably find in the long run that there will be some cases in which you will be obliged to content yourself with having acquired an intellectual appreciation of the writer in question, no vital contact between your spirit and his ever having really been established. You cannot expect every book you read to carry the quality of revelation for you. Even in a literary life, there are not many nights like that in which J. A. Symonds discovered Plato:

My hostess, a Mrs. Bain, who lived in Regent's Park, treated me to a comedy at the Haymarket. I forget what the play was. When we returned from the play I went to bed and began to read my Cary's Plato. It so happened that I stumbled on the

Phaedrus. I read on and on, till I reached the end. Then I began the *Symposium*; and the sun was shining on the shrubs outside the ground floor on which I slept before I shut the book up. I have related these unimportant details because that night was one of the most important nights of my life. . . . Here in the *Phaedrus* and the *Symposium* I discovered the revelation I had been waiting for, the consecration of a long-cherished idealism. It was just as though the voice of my own soul spoke to me through Plato. Harrow vanished into unreality. I had touched solid ground. Here was the poetry, the philosophy of my own enthusiasm expressed with all the magic of unrivalled style.

Who could have supposed that a youngster could completely forget the play at the Haymarket, which was the special "treat" his kind hostess had prepared for him, and then find his whole life made over by reading through the night in a "dry," "highbrow" book, written by a Greek who had been dead more than 2,000 years? Here, again, as Sarah Bernhardt said, "God was there." Could there be a better illustration of how little these things can be planned or prepared for?

Only, of course, it could have been the other way around. Even the greatest literature may grow stale sometimes to even the best students, and the meaning of life may be lost, only to be regained through a walk in the country or something in a cheap vaudeville show which seems quite pointless to everybody else. In Walter de la Mare's wonderful, and completely convincing, story, "The Wharf," a woman regains her sanity, and achieves her adjustment to life, by looking upon—of all things—a compost pile!

So you must not be afraid of the aristocrats in literature. Dukes and dustmen—it is all one here: whatever your status in the workaday world, you are free of the best society in the world of art, if only you have the capacity to enjoy it. For the great writers do not speak for themselves alone nor yet for a class; neither do they address you as an individual. They speak for humanity. Often they say what you feel better than you could say it yourself, so that they actually interpret you to yourself, and you see yourself forever after in the light of their revelation of you, and live by that light.

Art, said George Edward Woodberry, is "a means, by which . . . wisdom, which is the soul's knowledge of itself, is stored up for the race in its most manifest, enduring and vital forms." You will be cheating yourself of your rightful heritage if you neglect to take possession of such of the really great books of the world as may prove to belong to you. On the other hand, you must not neglect the humbler books altogether either. You do not want to be a "cowardly custard" in your reading, but neither do you want to be a prig or a snob. So fastidious a writer as Virginia Woolf speaks enthusiastically of the joys of "rubbish reading," of rummaging here and there in forgotten books which nobody ever reads anymore, and there finding, with a shock of surprise, something that seems addressed to you alone, and that is, for the time being, at least, your own particular discovery.

Probably most of the really great books that have been written upon this planet have, in greater or lesser degree, survived, but so far as merely good books are concerned, certainly there are many more of these dead than alive, and some of them could mean as much to you, if you were to find them, as any of the great books themselves. There are few experiences better worth having than picking up for twenty-five cents in a second-hand store a book by an author you never heard of before, and whom none of your friends ever heard of either, and discovering, by patient and enthralled perusal, that *this is your man!* Not only has a new pleasure come into your life, but a precious act of piety has been performed, and you have raised a phoenix out of dead ashes.

I know there are people who profess a keen interest in literature yet never buy books, but to my way of thinking, they are all humbugs. An intellectual understanding of literature they may have; that they love it, I frankly do not believe. If you love your friends you want to have them around you, and while none of us can afford to own all the books we read, we can own a fair percentage of the books we love best. I know that the usual complaint is that books cost too much. So they do, the new ones. So does everything else nowadays. But it seems to me that I often see the people who are most vociferous in making this complaint, spending their money very freely on many other things which they would be much better off without.

The fundamental difficulty with the people who tell you never to read a book until it is thirty years old—"When a new book comes out, read an old one," and all the rest of it—is that if we were really to follow their advice, the writing of books would come to an end. There would never be another book published. Lovers of literature ought to realize that they have a share in the responsibility for keeping literature alive, and it might be well to remember also that the library sale alone is not large enough to cover the publishing costs of any book.

In a university where I once taught, the university book store offered a prize for the best student library. The prize went to a Filipino student who was living, with his wife, on thirty-five dollars a month.

Human beings usually get the things they want most in this world—if they are willing to go after them. "God says, 'Here is the world. Take what you want—and pay for it.'"

The joys of literature are not among the things for which one pays highest.

Appendix: Of Book Reviewing

This Appendix aims to provide materials for a study of book-reviewing. If there is any area in which most American college students need help it is here. Many of them are under the impression that when you "review" a book, you "tell the story" and then call it a day. Nor is this heresy confined to students. The writer once heard a clubwoman exclaim, "I do love to hear Mrs. R—— review a book. She gives you so much that you don't need to read it at all."

A good review is not a résumé; it is a critical evaluation. It does not take the place of reading; it aims instead to guide reading and to enrich it. Compared to more formal and elaborate critical enquiries, reviews of individual works, published in newspapers and magazines, are exploratory, tentative; the conditions under which they are written and published are such that there is no opportunity to do more than give the writer's first impression. Such reviews have, too, an important practical purpose: they serve as sources of information to the reader, helping him to decide whether or not he wishes to buy or to see the work in question.

This Appendix opens with reviews of four novels. The first two are characteristic works by two of the established masters of the twentieth century. The third is an ambitious and monolithic fiction, more experimental in its technique.

The last work exemplifies the modern historical novel at its best.

Because a very different reviewing technique must be employed by the reviewer who is considering a collection of short stories from any that can be used in reviewing a novel, I have given next a review of the collected stories of one of the most celebrated writers of this genre in our time. It should be noted that Professor Belitt was not approaching Katherine Mansfield's work for the first time when he wrote this review; this fact made it possible for him to achieve a more definitive evaluation than generally lies within the scope of the reviewer.

From fiction we pass on, briefly, to poetry, with, first, a review of a very successful narrative poem, and then, another of an outstanding collection of lyrics, etc.

Space has been found here for only one "general" or "nonfiction" book. I have chosen Henry Hazlitt's review of Aldous Huxley's *Ends and Means* because both the book and the review are as stimulating and provocative as any that might have been chosen.

The Appendix closes with one review of an acted play, plus two film reviews. I thought the film should be represented, first, by one major effort or serious achievement—Laurence Olivier's *Hamlet* was the almost inevitable choice here—and, next, by a photoplay created in a less austere mood.

Many different types of critical approach, different types of mind, and different critical convictions are represented in these reviews. I purposely refrain from commenting upon these here in order that each teacher may be free to use this section in what seems the best way for his needs. Neither have I thought it wise to analyze in advance materials which the student may well be called upon to analyze himself. In view of what has been said in the first para-

graph, I should, however, like to call attention to the fact
that only Professor Baker's review of *The Old Man and the
Sea* tells much about the story. If the student is able to perceive how and why it becomes evident that this is nevertheless not a résumé, that the reviewer is not retelling the
story for story's sake, and that even such paragraphs as are
largely narrative in form are actually analytical in purpose,
he will have taken one long step toward mastering the
secret of successful reviewing of fiction.

The last three reviews illustrate what was said in the
body of this book about the complications of the dramatic
forms. A review of a book concerns the author, but the
drama reviewer is quite as much—sometimes more—concerned with actors, directors, designers, and technicians of
various kinds. Both Miss Marshall and Mr. Agee are more
casual, less systematic in their approach than any of our
book reviewers: they attempt a less comprehensive cover-
age. Mr. Agee does not consider *Meet Me in St. Louis* a
wholly satisfactory film; primarily he writes about one
extraordinary artist, Margaret O'Brien. (It is interesting to
remember that Miss O'Brien had reached the advanced age
of seven years when this film was made.) But note how the
genius of the player is interwoven with, dependent upon,
reinforced and handicapped by turns, by the technical
aspects of the medium in which she functions.

As for our reviewers: Joseph Wood Krutch has long
been a distinguished author and critic. Carlos Baker is
the author of the first full-length study of Ernest Hemingway: *Hemingway: The Writer as Artist* (Princeton University Press, 1952). The late Kelsey Guilfoil was associate
editor of the *Chicago Sunday Tribune Magazine of Books*.
Marchette Chute has written studies of Chaucer, Shakespeare, and Ben Jonson which combine sound scholarship
with popular appeal. Ben Belitt is Professor of English in

Bennington College. The late Hervey Allen wrote *Anthony Adverse*. Edward Wagenknecht is the author of this volume. Henry Hazlitt is at present editor of *The Freeman*. Claudia Cassidy is drama and music critic of the *Chicago Tribune*. Margaret Marshall, like Mr. Krutch, is one of the editors of the "American Men of Letters" series. James Agee was, at the time he wrote our review, film critic of *The Nation*.

The author of this book is grateful to the authors and publishers whose generosity made the inclusion of this section possible. Detailed acknowledgments are given hereinafter.

DEATH COMES FOR THE ARCHBISHOP, by Willa Cather. Alfred A. Knopf, 1927.

In one of his literary essays, Havelock Ellis drew a useful distinction between what he called the Nordic and the Celtic treatments of the past. The uninstructed reader of Homer might, he pointed out, very reasonably suppose that the poet was contemporary with the events which he described, whereas in the case of any Celtic epic it is always perfectly clear that the author is dealing with things which, for him as well as for the reader, are remotely picturesque. The Greeks, in other words, preferred to treat the past as if it were present because they were interested in a dramatic immediacy, but the Celts deliberately evoked the pathos of distance because that pathos was to them the essence of poetry.

Now I am by no means certain that this distinction upon the basis of race is valid; perhaps it would be safer to speak merely of the heroic and the elegiac moods; but certainly the distinction itself is of fundamental importance and it is, moreover, the one which serves better than any other to define the particular quality of Miss Cather's work. Though she is absorbed in what

From *The Nation*, CXXV, 390 (October 12, 1927). Reprinted by permission of the publishers.

would be to another the heroic past of our continent, her mood is that which Ellis would call the Celtic. She has upon occasion evoked her own memories, and one would expect to find in them the softness of remembered things, but even when her stories are rather documented than recalled she manages to invest documents with the wistful remoteness of recollected experience and to make past things vivid, less because they are present in the heat and sweat of actuality than because some softened memory of them seems to be. Not Calliope nor Melpomene is her muse but rather she who was called the mother of them all, and she is always at her best when that fact is most clearly recognized.

Certainly her newest story—concerned with the life of a missionary bishop in the newly-annexed territory of New Mexico—would be in the hands of another something quite different from that which she has made it. These were stirring, adventurous times; many writers might feel that they could be recaptured only in some exciting and dramatic narrative; but Miss Cather softens the epic until it becomes an elegy. In recounting the lives of her characters she chooses by preference their moments of calm reflection; when she wishes to throw the long tradition of the priesthood into relief against the primitive background of the new land, she seizes upon some contrast that is deep without being violent; and she sees everything as one sees it when one broods or dreams over the past. The tumult and the fighting reach us but dimly. What we get is the sense of something far off and beautiful—the picturesqueness and the fragrance of the past more than the past itself, pictures softened by time and appearing suddenly from nowhere.

In a garden overlooking Rome, a cardinal drinks his wine and discusses the appointment of a new bishop for a vague and distant see. That bishop, come all the way from the Great Lakes, struggles with the paganism of his priests, rides miles over the desert to perform a belated marriage ceremony over the Mexicans whose children he has baptized, or dreams of the cathedral which shall some day rise in the savage land; but at night he cooks himself a soup with "nearly a thousand years of history" in it and in the sense of these vanished contrasts lies the effect of the book. . . .

Even when Miss Cather strives most consciously to give to her books a narrative movement there is likely to be something static or picture-like about her best effects, and when she falters it is usually in the effort to carry the reader from one to the other of the moments which rise like memories before her. In the present instance she has nothing that could properly be called a plot, but she is wisely content to accept the fact and to depend upon the continuous presence of beauty rather than upon any movement to hold the interest of the reader. When things are recalled in the mood of elegy there is no suspense and they do not take place one after the other because all things being merely past, there is no time but one. And so it is in the case of *Death Comes for the Archbishop*. It is a book to be read slowly, to be savored from paragraph to paragraph, and it is quite the most nearly perfect thing which its author has done since *A Lost Lady*.

JOSEPH WOOD KRUTCH

THE OLD MAN AND THE SEA, by Ernest Hemingway. Charles Scribner's Sons, 1952.

The admirable Santiago, Hemingway's ancient mariner and protagonist of this triumphant short novel, enters the gallery of permanent heroes effortlessly, as if he had belonged there from the beginning.

Indeed he has. His story belongs as much in our time as that of Nick Adams. He is one of the men without women, fighting it out alone with only a brave heart for company. He is one of the winners who takes nothing. Though he does not die, he is one of those for whom the bell tolls. What Santiago has at the close of his story is what all the heroes of Hemingway have had—the proud, quiet knowledge of having fought the fight, of

From *The Saturday Review*, XXXV, September 6, 1952, pp. 10-11. Reprinted by permission of the author and the publishers.

having lasted it out, of having done a great thing to the bitter end of human strength.

Santiago, in the sum of things, is a tragic hero. His story, architectonically speaking, shows a natural tragic pattern. After eighty-four days without a strike, the old man rises in the cool dark morning and rows out alone towards the mile-deep Gulf Stream. It is the month of September, the time of the big fish. Towards noon of this eighty-fifth day, trolling his baits at various levels, he hooks a huge marlin down in the green dark of a hundred fathoms. Then through that long afternoon, and the night, and another day and another night, he hangs on with the line over his shoulder while his skiff is towed slowly northeastward through the calm September sea.

Living on strips of raw bonito, a flying fish, and part of a dolphin, washed down with nips from his water-bottle, Santiago takes and endures almost infinite pains. Twice the fish leaps clear of the water, trying to throw the hook. But it is not until noon of the third day out that Santiago manages to bring his great trophy finally to the surface and to drive his harpoon into that other fighting heart. The marlin is two feet longer than the skiff, too big to hoist abroad even if the old man's strength were still equal to the task. He lashes it alongside, comes about, and sets his patched old sail for home.

An hour later the first shark comes. The tragedy of subtraction begins. Number One is a handsome Mako, big and voracious, with eight raking rows of teeth. Santiago kills him with the harpoon, which is lost when the Mako sinks. Also lost, like a piece of the courageous old man's heart, is a great forty-pound bite from the side of the prize fish. What is worse, the scent of its blood spreads through the water like a lure for all the sea's rapacious attackers. Two or more presently close in—ugly, shovel-nosed Galanos sharks, rending and tearing what the old man has earned by the sweat of his brow, the blood of his hands, and the indomitable pride of his endurance. Like the first, these are killed. But others follow: one, then a pair, and finally in the night a whole anonymous pack. Santiago fights them off with all he has (his knife lashed to an oar-butt, the boat's club, the tiller) until these break or are lost and there are no more weapons. Yet now there is no more trophy either. If the old man were to look overside in the dark, he would see only the bony head, the proud perpendicular tail, and the picked white skeleton of his prize. The old man does not bother to look. He knows too well what has happened.

Once more, in his lengthening career as one of the few genuine tragic writers of modern times, Hemingway has memorably engaged a theme familiar to tragic literature. Santiago belongs among all those who have the strength and dignity to fight against great odds and to win moral victories, even though the tangible rewards may be lost in the process of the battle. On the heroic level, one thinks of Melville's Ahab, Whitman's Columbus, Sandburg's Lincoln. But the great skill here has been to take a simple fisherman and by setting his struggle against the background of the ancient and unchanging sea, and pitting him against an adversary worthy of his strength, to bring out his native ability and indomitability until, once having known him, we can never afterwards lose sight of him. Wordsworth's Michael and his leech-gatherer are pastoral types, artfully projected against the English hills and plains, and showing the resolution and independence which always tugged at Wordsworth's heart-strings, as Santiago's tug at ours. Yet the pitch here attained and held to is several degrees above the plane of pastoral tragedy. It approaches, as a tragic pattern, the story of King Lear, whose shark-hearted daughters bled him of his dominions and his hundred knights, yet left his dignity unimpaired and his native courage unshaken. "I will show him what a man can do," says Santiago of his marlin, "and what a man endures." The thousand times he has proved his worth before mean nothing. Now, climactically, he is proving it again, and earning nothing more tangible than our sympathy and admiration.

"One cannot hope to explain," says the publisher's commentary, "why the reading of this book is so profound an experience." One can, however, at least begin to explain the essence of the experience by making two related observations about it. The first is that the story not only shows a natural tragic pattern (which is no doubt why Hemingway was drawn to it); it develops also as a kind of natural parable. Like human life, for which it easily stands as an extended image, the struggle commences, grows, and subsides between one sleep and another. The parable of Santiago Agonistes works upon our sensibilities like a heroic metaphor achieved naturally and without manifest heroics. The result, a dividend above and beyond the pleasure of reading a fine story, is the discovery of an open-sided trope in which every man may locate some of the profounder aspects of his own spiritual biography.

The second point enters the region of religious experience. The theme of what is Christlike in every good man has grown in upon Hemingway since 1940, when the Christian Anselmo, another aged man, was established as the moral norm in *For Whom the Bell Tolls*. The ancient Santiago, stumbling out of his boat with dried blood on his face from a partly healed wound, and with the deep cord-cuts like stigmata on his hands, carries the mast over his shoulder up the hill. Sleeping exhaustedly face down on the spread newspapers that cover the springs of his bed, he lies cruciform, with arms out straight and palms turned upwards. *In hoc signo vinces*. He has entered the Masonic order of Christian heroes. In short, Hemingway has enhanced the native power of his tragic parable by engaging, though unobtrusively, the further power of Christian symbolism. Somewhere between its parabolical and its Christian meaning lies one important explanation of this book's power to move us.

The Old Man and the Sea is a great short novel, told with consummate artistry and destined to become a classic in its kind. It is a good kind of present for a man to give the world on or about his fifty-third birthday.

CARLOS BAKER

RAINTREE COUNTY, by Ross Lockridge, Jr. Houghton Mifflin Company, 1947.

Not since Thomas Wolfe's first novel appeared has there been a literary birth like this one. Here is a titantic endeavor to grasp American life in its entirety, to put on paper the vast legend which is the United States, to show in the life of one man how all that has gone into the making of the legend might be summed up in the loves, hates and vicissitudes that one man endured.

Like Wolfe (the parallel is inescapable), Ross Lockridge has reached too far, written too much, delved too deeply. There is even a Wolfian note in the story that he lugged a suitcase full of manuscript to the publisher's office, from which was sifted out a novel of 1,060 pages. Like Wolfe, too, is the author's habit of mingling passages of prose poetry with lusty, realistic pictures of the human comedy. And if, as with Wolfe, his reach has exceeded his grasp, he also, like Wolfe, has achieved something prodigious, beautiful, moving, and gripping.

It is the story of John Wickliff Shawnessy, who was born in Raintree County, Indiana, in the days when the Republic was young, grew to be a lad of great promise, fought and bled in the Civil War, and returned finally to his homeland to grow old as one of the solid citizens of his community. But that was not all, for, like Ulysses, much had he seen and known. Into the core of his existence were blended many friends and acquaintances, some from Raintree County and some not, who were figures of their times. At the periphery of his life were the historical personages he saw or met, all woven into the fabric of life in the United States.

But it is not simply the story of men and events, it is a story of man's ideals, of his ceaseless searching for a meaning in the pattern of his days.

In the rich and fruitful earth John Shawnessy hunted the key to the mystery—the mystery expressed by the legend of the

From the *Chicago Sunday Tribune Magazine of Books*, January 4, 1948. Reprinted by permission of the publishers.

raintree which gave the county its name. And in his loves, fulfilled and unfulfilled, John Shawnessy sought unendingly the
beauty and the magic which always seem so near yet are always
so elusive.

The novel is written in a stylized form that is both exciting
and irritating. It moves through a single day—July 4, 1892—
and by a series of flashbacks relates all that has gone before in
Shawnessy's lifetime. These are episodes, mostly of Shawnessy's
career, but also much concerned with the lives of others. It is
not hard to place each episode in time, and tell which is in the
past, and which is a part of that Fourth of July celebration of
1892. However, the episodes do not move in chronological
sequence, but jump about in time so that the reader—at least
this reader—is often confused in trying to relate them to one
another. Numerous verbal and typographical tricks make the
story different from anything one has read before, but do not
add to the ease of reading.

Nevertheless, the story has such power and momentum that
it carries the reader through page after page, if only to find out
what really happened to Shawnessy in his famous match race
with the county's champion runner—an event foreshadowed
and even referred to in the past tense long before it is related
in full.

Make no mistake about it, *Raintree County* is unique. If I
have compared it to the work of Thomas Wolfe, that was not
said in derogation. In many ways it is better than Wolfe. It
certainly comes closer to the heart of America, and it is less
distorted in its view of life than Wolfe often is. Ross Lockridge
is not Wolfe's successor, but in the exuberant vitality of his
story-telling, in the sweep and scope of his work, he belongs
in the same class. He well deserves to win the MGM award
and have his novel chosen by the Book-of-the-Month Club.

KELSEY GUILFOIL

THE MAN ON A DONKEY, by H. F. M. Prescott. The Macmillan Company, 1952.

England is a small island with a long memory and her writers are able to reach into the distant past as though it were yesterday. They have always excelled in historical novels and this is one of the best.

The Man on a Donkey tells the story of those difficult years when England was changing from a Roman Catholic nation to a Protestant one under Henry VIII. The book rises to its climax in that heroic, confused, and dignified rebellion, the Pilgrimage of Grace which had no effect except to hasten the pillaging of the religious houses by the King, and it mirrors a world of confused loyalties and divided allegiances that should seem familiar enough to any twentieth-century reader.

The story is told primarily through five people and in what the author calls a "chronicle" style. That is to say, she follows her five people month by month for almost thirty years. They are like five small boats, moving slowly through a changing sea and always getting nearer to the final whirlpool.

One of the five is Robert Aske, a London lawyer who entered the rising almost by accident. He could never resolve his twin dilemma, treason to his Church or treason to his King, and finally chose the latter with bitter reluctance, to become the hero of the Pilgrimage of Grace and to die in chains. There is also Lord Darcy, that fine old conservative who entered the Rising when he was seventy and hoped that the Lord of Hosts would count it equal to his death in a crusade. There is a young, wild girl who cared nothing for religion or politics and only longed to shelter Robert Aske from danger of pain. There is a self-conscious, self-tormenting priest who turned Protestant because he himself was poor and he hated the wealth of the Church. And there is a Prioress—the most brilliant portrait of the lot—who cared nothing about the rest of England so long as her sense of property and her own religious house were safe.

From the *New York Herald-Tribune Book Review*, September 14, 1952. Reprinted by permission of the author and publishers.

Behind these five moves a procession of the great and the small, people of the court, the towns and the countryside, each bent on his own problem; and apart from them all stands the serving woman, Malle, who possesses nothing and longs for nothing, and upon whose innocence descends the vision that gives the book its title. At one point in the book the vision becomes actual and the Savior becomes a visible man, "shaggy haired, in patched leather hosen," who talks to the Prioress' cook. The ground is not well laid for anything quite so explicit, and the success of the book on a mystical level will depend somewhat on the point of view of the individual reader.

On the historical side there is little to question, for Miss Prescott is a scholar and she has brought the crowded years to life as though she had lived in them herself. If anything, she has tied herself too closely to the actual documents in her description of the Rising, so that the Pilgrimage of Grace becomes a little muted. For instance, the most interesting moment in the Rising from the psychological point of view is the interview between its leader, Aske, and the king whom he is defying. The chroniclers could not record the interview since it took place behind closed doors, and Miss Prescott does not imagine it.

Yet perhaps, in a book of this kind, it is not the people that the reader will remember longest. It is the small flowers by the roadside, described so lovingly and minutely, the clear windy days of summer and the frost tracery of winter, the exact, sharp, jewel-like scenes of convent life. To read the book is for the most part to walk in pleasant leisure through a countryside that the English poets have loved for many centuries, and when Miss Prescott writes of that small beloved land she is not the least of these.

MARCHETTE CHUTE

THE SHORT STORIES OF KATHERINE MANSFIELD.
With an Introduction by J. Middleton Murry. Alfred A.
Knopf, 1937.

It is almost a decade and a half since an English reviewer, on
the occasion of the posthumous publication of Katherine Mansfield's *The Doves' Nest*, observed that "This book, too, has its
uncompleted promise," and touched gingerly upon "work of
a quality which invites one to compare it with that of the
masters and suggests that it may live." Since that time, literary
journalists in England, America, France, Italy, Canada, and
Australia have been contributing yearly to a long parade of
memoirs, tributes, translations and brief interpretative pieces, of
which her bibliographer, Ruth Elvish Mantz, had already com-
piled a formidable catalogue in 1931.

Through the influence of the late Hso Tzumo, Katherine
Mansfield has, more recently, attracted notice in China, where
of the forty-seven English writers translated in the last quarter
of a century, she is the only short-story writer. Five of her
volumes, including the *Letters* and *Journal*, had been published
in France by 1934, as well as a score of articles. . . . She has
since her death been the subject of a Lamont Lecture at Yale,
a valuable if vertiginous biography, a tribute in a notable history of Russian literature, and a memorial (a tram shelter!)
in New Zealand.

In a very real sense, however, Katherine Mansfield remains
still to be discovered, as a re-reading of her stories, handsomely
brought together in one volume for the first time, now vividly
reminds us. At least a dozen of these titles are to be found in
as many different anthologies, all of them cited as models of the
craft. Yet the processes of her technique have thus far resisted
appraisal both in their own right and in terms of what is today
comfortably designated "the modern short story."

Certainly it cannot be doubted that the reader who turns to
Katherine Mansfield for liberal helpings of fictive complication

From *The New York Times Book Review*, September 12, 1937. Reprinted by permission of the author and publisher.

and "the good, old-fashioned suspense," is sure to rise a hungry and hoodwinked man. On the contrary, he must be content with little, for the approach is largely in terms of "strange" relationships, in which broad outlines and contiguous acts are merely the receptacles for exposition of a different sort. Similarly, there is to be noted a constant probing, within the large time-units for the moment and the fraction of the moment— a narrowing down and splitting of the simple outlines of temperament into moods, and the moods into flashes of intuitive feeling, which, though they impinge only for a second upon time, have their repercussions throughout a lifetime. It is only in these moments of prophetic sixth sense, these stories would seem to argue, that the truth is brought closest to our understanding. They were, for Katherine Mansfield, experiences curiously sufficient in themselves, coming and going without regard for the familiar machinery of cause and effect, but with a portent of their own. "One just has glimpses, divine warnings— signs."

If, for example, one were to judge such a story as "Bliss" in terms of formal postulates merely, one would be compelled to return a mixed verdict. The plot is one which harassed critics have long damned with references to a geometrical symbol of three sides. It is, moreover, a story almost wholly devoid of action and suspense, and consequently without "form." We have no cause to believe Bertha Young's dinner party will solve any problems for us, for the very good reason that we are given no hint of any problem to solve. The key to the story, indeed, lies elsewhere—in the oblique and secret handling of that latent detail (the pear tree, the color of the sky, the garden beds) which for all its seeming "irrelevance" to the plot itself, opens up on moments of dazzling spiritual awareness and in the end stirs us most deeply of all. It is through them alone that the sense of an unfolding plot is kept in motion, for they, in effect, are the plot, suspense and climax, and determine the focus of narrative. This same indescribable complex of detail and mood may be traced through any of a number of the stories: the little lamp in "The Doll's House," the cooing birds in "Mr. and Mrs.

Dove," the ice-pudding in "Sun and Moon," and—very brilliantly—in the scrawled phrase on the scrap of blotting paper
in "Je Ne Parle Pas Français." In each of these stories details
are secretly but continuously at work; so that, viewed at close
range, a story by Katherine Mansefield is like the "motionless"
drop of water upon which a microscope has been trained. A
world of swarming molecular life springs into place below,
which, for all its fierce motion, has left the contour of the drop
undisturbed.

What is principally to be borne in mind by the reader of this
volume is the fact of its origin. For, as Mr. Murry points out,
it lies within the realm of poetry and must be so approached
and so judged. It would be patently absurd to approach an ode
of Keats with any importunate expectations of plot, development, and climax. Yet, reading the poem, one discovers that,
for all the absence of factual bulk, the experience of plot and
suspense and climax is there, and that truths are immediately
emergent. It is this quality of lyricism—which has too often
been misnamed a *technique* rather than a *Stimmung*—that
Katherine Mansfield absorbed from Chekhov and passed on into
the stream of the story, with a difference. Its first virtue has
been to make her work the medium for an extraordinary mood
of excitement; her errand is one of self-renewal and seeks its
truest nourishment not in fact but in astonishment and wonder.

This is perhaps another way of saying that the Mansfield
story is, above all things, an *act of creation*. She was, indeed,
continually reiterating that her method was dependent upon
what she termed a "process of becoming." "It isn't as though
one sits and watches the spectacle," she explained to her husband on one occasion. "That would be thrilling enough, God
knows. But one IS the spectacle for the time." In consequence
her art is characterized by an effect of improvisation, of flying
movement, that makes it appear artless, as the lyrics of Shelley
and Blake might seem artless. She possessed in abundance what
Chekhov lacked almost wholly—a secret of projection, of
making that "divine spring into the bounding outline of things"
(the phrase is employed by her), by virtue of which writer

and materials merge into almost chemical union with one another.

A story such as "Prelude," one might instance, takes shape very much as the recollection of a dream takes shape—in sudden shocks and flashes which burst for a moment above the horizon of the subconscious. A fragment is struck off from here, a detail from there, with increasing excitation and surety; and soon the entire consciousness has caught the infection and proceeds to send out to every side a sustained barrage of impression. Then, in her own words, the story "just unfolds and opens."

It is hardly necessary to urge that this genre of writing is not only impossible without an ordeal of painful preliminary adjustment but is perhaps the most volatile in all the range of art. It presupposes, in the first place, an individuality flexible enough to sound the gamut of human reaction and give back clear tones throughout. It requires likewise an unerring intuition, a quality of spiritual energy that can be neither depleted nor contaminated, but is inexhaustibly pure. Most important of all, however, it requires that this sensibility be in motion always. It must overtake, surprise and create with electric surety of touch, whirling out of its movement forward a solvent capable of assimilating all the "impurities" of form and fact that stand in its path.

Readers of Katherine Mansfield's letters and journals will not need to be reminded that she remained throughout her life one of the most restive and dissatisfied writers of her time. Only a week before her death at La Prieuré, near Fontainebleau, she professed disappointment with everything she had written, claiming to have evolved a "different" technique that alone would give back an untroubled image of the truth. With this judgment the world has not been willing to concur. One has only to turn to "Prelude," "Je Ne Parle Pas Français," "The Man Without a Temperament," "The Fly," "At the Bay," "Bliss," "The Doll's House," "Psychology," or "A Married Man's Story." And if, as Katherine Mansfield feared, these stories are indeed deficient in truth, let him who will stay for the answer, for the word has disowned its connotation.

BEN BELITT

JOHN BROWN'S BODY, by Stephen Vincent Benét. Doubleday and Company, 1928.

One of the several things for which Mr. Stephen Benét's poem is pleasantly remarkable is that it succeeds in reincarnating the American Civil War in the terms of the period and yet depicts the events within a well-projected perspective of the present day. That the poet fully realized the inherent difficulties and magnitude of his task, his almost prayerful invocation to the American Muse bears little less than a glorious witness. The author has accomplished, however, much more in *John Brown's Body* than an admirable literary *tour de force*. Here is a book that is poignantly and exhaustingly alive. It is neither a peep-show, a puppet theatre, nor a moving picture in type, for its fusion of life, art, and critical acumen in flights of lyric poetry with final dramatic effect offers its audience, at one and the same time, a vivid vicarious experience, and an important philosophic comment. This may be high praise, but so it is.

From a literary standpoint the thing which has interested this reviewer most is the author's skill in combining the classical implications of his intellectual point of view towards his material as a whole with his romantic method and lyrical style in expressing his emotional attitude towards his particulars. For categorically Mr. Benét's book cannot be conceived as anything less than a literary microcosm of the American Civil War in which the episodical parts of the narrative rest with a nice logical order and proper emotional emphasis within the classically conceived framework of the whole. In a major way, Mr. Benét has thus made an interesting departure in fusing the episodical technique of the "movie"—the crucial dramatic glimpse, the recurrence, and the flash-back—with the scheme

From *The Yale Review*, XVIII, 391-393 (December, 1928). Copyright, Yale University Press.

of the popular historical outline, and in avoiding the banalities of both. Luckily he knows not only dramatically how but philosophically why to choose his incidents, and humanly when and where to cut his film.

Historically Mr. Benét has divided his material into three parts: that comprising the general economic, political, and military facts of the period; the great or outstanding figures who shaped and controlled these forces; and a host of minor characters in all walks of life and from all sections of the country with whom and through whom the reader partakes in the events of the conflict. These last are the vigorous but subtly imagined creations of the author out of the rich human and environmental materials of the time. To the mind of this reviewer these men and women, that the poet's imagination has so brilliantly and prodigally evoked, constitute the chief merit of his work, and they should be, by any just method of criticism, not only recognized but proposed as a fine addition to the main body of American literature.

With the two remaining factors Mr. Benét has not been quite so successful. Although in this case the mortar between the stones of his edifice remains still only too plainly mortar, it has, nevertheless, been cunningly and colorfully used as an essential part of the masonry. What more can be done with mortar we do not know. In depicting his historical figures the author has been both brilliant and disappointing. John Brown is perhaps, perhaps, we say, allowed to remain too much of a symbol. Grant and Lee are woefully inadequate. On the other hand, we do not recall ever having seen anywhere more brilliant and concentrated portraits of Lincoln, Davis, and Benjamin than are to be met with here. These miniatures contain within them the voice and mind, the body and the times of those whom they depict. In addition to the personal, the romantic, and the picturesque colors of his period, the author is also fully aware of the economic drifts and of the cleavage and clash between the two types of society which confronted each other in arms.

These are some of the major excellences and minor weaknesses of what must be received all in all as a remarkable, fascinating, and essentially valuable book. Mr. Benét closes his volume with a movement in verse whose symbolism is prophetic. What has grown from John Brown's Body, that is, the industrial civilization in which we move, is *here*, the poet says. Weak deprecations of it are of no avail. On the other hand, there is nothing to prevent the soul of John Brown, who, we are also reminded, was a shepherd and a farmer, from marching on.

HERVEY ALLEN

WINGED CHARIOT, and Other Poems, by Walter de la Mare. The Viking Press, 1951.

At seventy-eight, Walter de la Mare seldom finds his right to be named England's foremost living writer called in question. As a poet he has been remarkable for his ability to produce profound and exquisite lyrics over a phenomenally long period, but his two greatest single achievements are the fruits of his old age. These are the long philosophical-narrative poem, *The Traveller*, published in 1946, and now this remarkable, 1600-line meditation upon Time, *Winged Chariot*, the greatest poem of its kind since *In Memoriam*, which his American publishers have just given us in a double-decker volume with the fifty-six lyrics which were published separately in England under the title *Inward Companion*.

The theme of Time—which involves Eternity—haunts beyond all others the modern creative imagination. In these musings Mr. de la Mare leaves few of its aspects unexamined, from his own obsession with clocks (a charming autobiographical passage), to the evocation of those moments in which, even here, we leap beyond Time. "One stricken glance" of a hitherto unknown face may do the business for a lifetime.

> And saddest of all earth's clocks is Others growing old:
> The silvering hair that once was palest gold.

An interesting bit of lagniappe in *Winged Chariot* is the

From the *Chicago Sunday Tribune Magazine of Books*, November 18, 1951. Reprinted by permission of the publishers.

series of brief quotations from older literature printed in the margins like so many epigraphs. These take the place of titles for the various sections.

The *Inward Companion* section involves all the favorite de la Mare themes: the beauties of earth and sky, and another world impinging upon this one; children, birds, beasts, insects, and flowers; literature in the form of thoughts upon the poet's craft and tributes to great writers; the glories and the terrors of human relationships.

To the poet, the face of a child twelve hours old is a chart which "maps secrets stranger than the seas'," nor does he cease to wonder that the departing swallow "knows where the coast of far mysterious sun-wild Africa hours." It is precisely because Mr. de la Mare has loved this world as few have ever loved it that he knows that the world cannot satisfy the needs of the human heart. Even now,

> It is the ghost in you I hold most dear.

And the greatest wonder of all creation is not the glory of the heavens but the fact that "in Time's small space," the heart itself "may hold in its span all night, all day!"

The de la Mare of this volume is a new de la Mare; he is the de la Mare we have always known and loved, grown old and wise but never tired. As daring in his freedom as any of the youngsters who make a cult of freedom because they are not free, he has lost none of the magic he knew in the days of *The Listeners* and *Peacock Pie*.

EDWARD WAGENKNECHT

ENDS AND MEANS, by Aldous Huxley. Harper and Brothers, 1937.

Aldous Huxley's *Ends and Means* is a volume certain to be discussed over intellectual dinner tables for many months to come. It is written with the lucidity and touches of the stylistic brilliance that we have come to expect of its author. A remark-

From *The New York Times Book Review*, December 12, 1937. Reprinted by permission of the author and the publishers.

able volume in its own right, its interest is heightened by the extraordinary transformation it reveals in Mr. Huxley's mental attitude. That transformation, foreshadowed in the last pages of *Eyeless in Gaza*, here becomes explicit. It is an example of what used to be called religious conversion. The intellectual libertine has become a holy man. The cynic has turned messiah.

But let us not exaggerate either the suddenness or the extent of the conversion. If Mr. Huxley's novels seem to be crowded with mental playboys and sex addicts, he has depicted them, not with tenderness, but with a sort of fascinated loathing. His essays, though they played with paradoxes, have always had a serious tinge, and have become increasingly serious in recent years. The present volume is so intensely earnest that paradoxes and witticisms are rarely to be found in it. Yet the overtones of mysticism are superimposed on a theme and a logic that are basically hard-headed.

Ends and Means rests on the premise implied by its title and already set forth in *Eyeless in Gaza* that the end cannot justify the means for the simple reason that the means employed inevitably determine the nature of the ends produced. Hence Huxley is opposed to all efforts to achieve a better world through the methods of violence, whether it is the violence of fascist revolution, of Communist revolution, of persecution of minorities, of armed resistance on the part of the democratic countries to the fascist countries, or of the so-called "international police force." The very "definition of democracy against fascism," he fears, will entail the transformation of democracy into fascism. In increasing their armaments to take a "firm stand" against fascist aggression, the democratic countries are gradually but systematically being transformed into the likeness of the fascist states they so much detest. "Those who prepare for war start up an armaments race and, in due course, get the war they prepare for."

This overpowering and increasing evil of war, in Mr. Huxley's opinion, is the central evil of our time. No means that involve war or lead to war can bear good fruit. It is no doubt true that the voters in every country desire peace. But he quotes from the *Imitation*: "All men desire peace, but very few desire those things which make for peace." In the modern world the things that make for peace are "disarmament, unilateral if necessary; renunciation of exclusive empires; abandonment of the policy of economic nationalism; determination in all circumstances to use the methods of non-violence; systematic training in such methods."

We cannot get rid of war unless we get rid, first of all, of its psychological causes. But these causes are extremely deepseated. They lie not merely with governments but with the individual voter; they begin with his earliest training. They are part of the whole modern philosophy of life. They are the fruits of the obsession with power, success, position. But this is merely to say that we must overhaul our whole system of education; that we must reconstruct the basic metaphysics that move mankind.

We cannot expect the work of reform, however, to be initiated by the rulers of a nation. Reform must begin at the periphery and work in toward the center. It must begin in the souls of individuals who are willing to remake themselves and willing, then, in turn, to form small groups to put into practice on a small scale the ideals which they advocate for society as a whole. These individuals will be fundamentally religious in their world view. They will discipline themselves ethically, recognizing for one thing that "chastity is the necessary pre-condition to any kind of moral life superior to that of the animal." They will be "non-attached," not merely to bodily sensations and lusts, but to the craving for fame and possessions. The two fundamental virtues for which they will strive will be love and awareness, charity and intelligence. And they will give themselves to meditation in the hope that they may achieve mystic insight.

This is the thesis that Mr. Huxley develops with persuasiveness and power. As one reader, I am prepared to accept a great deal of it, but I also have serious objections to offer at certain points. Two of these will do for illustration.

The first concerns Mr. Huxley's economic program. He is

against the "capitalistic system," or at least he thinks he is. In one passage he even lumps it with "imperialism, war, the use of torture, press censorship, tyranny" and other "iniquities." This is a fashionable attitude of literary intellectuals today. Yet he fails to realize how much more opposed he is to the real alternative to capitalism. Capitalism means the private ownership and control of the means of production. Socialism means the governmental ownership and control of the means of production. But this implies an enormous extension of the power of the State and of individual "enslavement" to it. This is one of the results that Huxley most fears. "State socialism," he recognizes explicitly at one point, "tends to produce a single centralized, totalitarian dictatorship, wielding absolute authority over all its subjects through a hierarchy of bureaucratic agents." The political road to a better society, he tells us, on the other hand, is "the road of decentralization and responsible self-government." But this comes pretty close to being a definition of private enterprise in the economic field. The confusion shows how far Mr. Huxley is from having thought this problem through.

I think Mr. Huxley is confused also in his metaphysics. He attacks the philosophy which maintains that the universe as a whole is without meaning or value. The world, he insists, has meaning, has value. In all this Mr. Huxley seems to me to be the victim of an even greater confusion of thought than those whose views he is attacking. The concepts of "meaning" and "value" (as well as those of "meaninglessness" and "valuelessness") are anthropopsychic concepts which cannot be applied to the universe as a whole. A thing "means" what it "expresses," what it "signifies," what it symbolizes, what it "stands for." But the universe as a whole cannot stand for or express anything more or less than itself. It does not "mean" anything absolutely, but only to us. Similarly, "value" is a relative term which implies a valuer. The universe has value *to whom?* If Mr. Huxley means to mankind, then again he is viewing the universe anthropocentrically. There would be no harm in this if Mr. Huxley recognized clearly that this is what he is doing, and did not attempt to attribute to the universe per se a quality which it has only in relation to a species of two-legged animal on one minor planet.

Mr. Huxley falls into a similar confusion, I think, when he discusses mysticism. It is one thing to insist on the reality of the mystical experience. It is quite another to maintain, as he does, that this experience gives an objectively valid insight into the nature of "ultimate reality" not attainable by science. If science can give only partial and symbolic knowledge, it does not follow that mysticism can penetrate to the heart of things. Some one, in any case, should reassure Mr. Huxley that he does not really *need* the dubious metaphysics by which he so often seeks to support his ethical beliefs. What is sound in those beliefs can stand on its own feet; it can be justified pragmatically and on eudemonistic grounds. Life can have whatever meaning and dignity men choose to give to it.

HENRY HAZLITT

THE MADWOMAN OF CHAILLOT, by Jean Giraudoux. Adapted by Maurice Valency. Presented by Alfred de Liagre, Jr. 1949.

It is a deep relief to those who like to make a distinction between theater and show business that *The Madwoman of Chaillot* is catching on. It looked at first as if the Belasco's macabre tenant might be caviar to the long run, and it is the sort of thing you want to keep around so that you can share it with special people. Even if you hold some reservations about the production, the play by the late Jean Giraudoux has imagination, tenderness and mordant wit; Martita Hunt is extraordinary in the title role; and Alfred de Liagre, Jr., did his good deed for the season when he imported Christian Bérard's brilliant settings and costumes—though by the curiosa of organized artistry he is forced to credit the red-bearded one in the back yard of the playbill.

From the *Chicago Daily Tribune*, February 15, 1949. Reprinted by permission of the publishers.

The play is a fable on the theme that the mad speak true. When the Madwoman discovers that the world through which she drifts in a dream is being ravished by the greedy, she baits a trap with the very wealth they would destroy Paris to confiscate, condemns them at a mock trial in their own image, and sends them to oblivion down a great flight of steps leading nowhere—a secret imparted by the king of the sewers, who can always count tomorrow on the flower given her today.

This is a godlike gesture, made in the dream of a better world. It is also made in a worldly wise and wearily witty play, so that you have it in counterpoint to the cynical shrug of aware acceptance. As the boldness of its theme takes possession of imagination, you say, "This is what could happen." As the theme recedes in retrospect, you say, "Did it happen, or was it a dream?" For the woman is certainly mad. Is the world to be saved by madmen? Or is it just that when they try to save us we call them mad? This is a fable, spun of logic and cobwebs. Spin your own solution, since Giraudoux is too adroit to do it for you, and his adapter, Maurice Valency, has left it at that.

I wish I had seen Jouvet's production in Paris, particularly if Bérard is the clue. The air and light of the sidewalk café, its slender façade at home in space, the texture and depth of the Madwoman's underground abode, the splendor, somehow both Jezebel and dowager, of her ragbag finery—these are more than pictures. They have resonance and dimensions.

So, too, does Miss Hunt's performance. As an exhibition of dementia on the grand scale she is both shattered and invincible. Under the counterfeit of chalk-white face and flaming wig, she is the woman she once saw in that lying mirror, the woman who prefers the newspaper of a certain day in 1904 when she last knew love. She lives in a dream but it is not soundproofed to suffering. It is a vulnerable dream from which distress must be banished. Hungry cats, unhappy people, a desperate world— how, unless she rescues them, can she cling to her own illusion?

There is no use pretending the whole production is thus resoundingly satisfactory. Such a play challenges all the theater can offer, and that challenge has not been fully met. This should be, and it is not, an overwhelming triumph. But it offers many fascinations: Estelle Winwood's haggard beauty at the mad tea party. The gentle sincerity of Leora Dana and Alan Shayne, who play the lovers. The lyricism of Martin Kosleck as the deaf mute. Clarence Derwent's precision as he states the philosophy of the spoilers. John Carradine's touch of rue as the ragpicker whose greeting is a lift of his topmost hat. The aura of kindness with which gentle people surround the woman life has driven to the refuge of madness.

This is a lot for one playgoing evening. If your imagination meets it even part way, *The Madwoman of Chaillot* can be wonderfully stimulating theater.

CLAUDIA CASSIDY

HAMLET (Two Cities). Adapted from the Play by William Shakespeare. Directed by Laurence Olivier. 1948.

Watching this motion-picture version [of *Hamlet*], one realizes first of all that Elsinore, both in sound and significance, has always been, for the reader and the spectator, no more—and no less—than a dark, rich, but unfigured setting which heightens the values of the play itself as the black rim of a volcano intensifies the brilliance and heat of the fires burning within. Mr. Olivier has made Elsinore a concrete castle in an actual landscape; and these tangible battlements and steps of stone, this actual wind and sea, dreamlike though they are, inevitably dissipate some of the intensity and continuity of the blaze of passions and of language that is *Hamlet*. As a result the play becomes, if I may throw more images, a sequence rather than a spiral, a stream rather than a maelstrom.

I am not at all sure that such plays as *Hamlet* or *Macbeth* or *Lear* can be translated into films of comparable power, but if it is possible then it could be done only by a director who was himself enough of a genius and enough of a revolutionary to

From *The Nation*, CLXVII, 468 (October 23, 1948). Reprinted by permission of the publishers.

disregard all the conventions either of film-making or of producing Shakespeare.

Mr. Olivier is not that director—as a matter of fact he falls, here, between the two sets of conventions—but I wish to add quickly that his *Hamlet* is nevertheless very much worth seeing and hearing. It is a serious and sincere and beautifully mounted production of a great play; and there are elements in it which might well be incorporated in that perfect film I have posited.

I am thinking particularly of Ophelia as she is created by Jean Simmons, under the direction, of course, of Mr. Olivier. I say created advisedly, for both in the play as written and as I have seen it produced—though I have not seen all of even the more recent productions—Ophelia has always seemed to me a two-dimensional lay figure who might have been taken over from allegory. Neither she nor her young love, her madness, and her death seemed real, or central to the story of Prince Hamlet. In this production Ophelia becomes a person in her own right; her suffering is not merely represented by gestures and costume but directly communicated. The performance is in itself very moving. And this realization of Ophelia has effects upon the play as a whole. For one thing, it points up the conflict of forces in the character of Hamlet by dramatizing the suffering it inflicts upon another and innocent human being. Again, since Ophelia is a character and not a lay figure, the role of Hamlet's mother is inevitably a little reduced. There are two women in the play, not one. And this effect is emphasized, whether by design or not, by the casting of Hamlet's mother not as the ripe matron of middle age, greedy for life and fearful of old age, but as a rather young woman whose relationship with her son is more than ever ambiguous.

Miss Simmons's and Mr. Olivier's interpretation of Ophelia may be "wrong," but it is an exciting and fresh interpretation and it does no violence to the text.

Olivier's Hamlet struck me as competent and faithful and a little shallow. He does not plumb the depths either of weakness or of strength in Hamlet's character. As the film opens we are told that *Hamlet* is "the story of a man who could not make up his mind," and at times this rather banal and quite inadequate description appears to have been Olivier's directive for his performance. I liked the device of presenting some of the soliloquies as thought—we hear the voice but the lips are still—though at times one has the impression merely of a close-up too long drawn out.

Of the rest of the cast, Polonius and Osric are very good; Horatio and Laertes are adequate; the King is inadequate but not disturbingly so. The gravedigger—there is only one—is funny, but his broad cockney sounds somewhat out of place in Elsinore. The cuts and telescopings, it seemed to me, have been done with care.

MARGARET MARSHALL

MEET ME IN ST. LOUIS (Metro-Goldwyn-Mayer). Screen Play by Irving Brecher and Frank Finklehoffe, after the stories by Sally Benson. Directed by Vincente Minelli. 1944.

... Most of [the] rather pretty new and old tunes [in *Meet Me in St. Louis*] are sung in an up-to-date chromium-and-glucose style which bitterly imposes on one's ability to believe that the year is 1903; and most of its sets and costumes and characters are too perfectly waxen to belong to that or any other year. Indeed, this habit of sumptuous idealization seriously reduces the value of even the few scenes on which I chiefly base my liking for this picture; but at the same time, and for that matter nearly all the time, it gives you, for once, something most unusually pretty to watch. I can't remember ever having seen studio-sealed Technicolor better used, and would like particularly to mention three shots: one in which a mother and four daughters, all in festal, cake-frosting white, stroll across their lawn in spring sunlight, so properly photographed that the dresses all but become halations; one of a fine black horse and buggy in a brisk and resonant autumn night—an atmosphere you can all but get the temperature and cider fragrance

From *The Nation*, CLIX, 670-671 (November 25, 1944). Reprinted by permission of the publishers.

and staidly spotty erotic tension of; and one of Hallowe'en, which I will speak of later.

I liked the general intention of the movie: to let its tunes and other musical-comedy aspects come as they may, and to concentrate rather on making the well-heeled middle-class life of some adolescent and little girls in St. Louis seem so beautiful that you can share their anguish when they are doomed to move to New York. I must confess I could have liked it much better still. For by a process of elementary reasoning on which I hold no patent and which, indeed, I would be only too happy to see appropriated by people in a better position to make use of it, I am persuaded that this very good because very real idea might have been adequately served only in proportion as the girls, and the visual and emotional climate they move in and are supposed to love, themselves approached and honored rather than flouted and improved on reality. The one member of the cast who proved my childishly blunt point by turning it, over and over again, into a heart-piercing sword was the incredibly vivid and eloquent Margaret O'Brien; many of her possibilities and glints of her achievement hypnotize me as thoroughly as anything since Garbo.

What she is playing here is still, as usual, safely glossed and thinned and sweetened; but someone has surrounded her with an air of generosity and ease and perfection in which she does some of her most satisfying work so far. (I imagine it may be the director, Vincente Minelli, especially if he is also responsible for a kind of graciousness and sense of joy in many of the shots, and sometimes in their succession, which seem to me Italian.) Her nicely cute acts, like her song, and her cakewalk, or her pleasure when she sits high beside a carriage driver, manage to mix stock cuteness with enchantment and with accurate psychology; the scene in which she is lugged in with her lip cut, screaming half-lies and gibberish, is about the most impressive and complex job of crying I have ever seen put on. I can hardly wait for her to be old enough to take on Hedwig's fearful jag in *The Wild Duck*—and can less than bear to realize what miraculous things she will almost certainly never get the chance to do between now and then.

Her annihilation of the snowmen she can't take to New York would have been terrifying if only she had had adequate support from the snowmen and if only the camera could have had the right to dare to move in close. Being only the well-meant best that professionals could design out of cornflakes or pulverized mothballs or heroin or whatever they are making snow out of just now, these statues were embarrassingly handicapped from their birth, and couldn't even reach you deeply by falling apart. Her walk on Hallowe'en, away from the bonfire into the deepening dark of the street, her fear and excitement intensifying as she approaches her destination (the insulting of the most frightening man in the neighborhood) and follows the camera (which withdraws a few feet ahead of her in a long soft curve) are a piece of acting, of lovely, simple camera movement, and of color control which combined, while they lasted, to make my hair stand on end. If the rest of the picture's autumn section, which is by far its best, had lived up to the best things about that shot, and the rest of the show, for all its prettiness, had been scrapped, *Meet Me in St. Louis* would have been, of all things on earth it can never have intended to be, a great moving picture—the first to be made in this country, so far as I can remember, since *Modern Times*.

JAMES AGEE

INDEX

Index

369

RENEWALS 458-4574

DATE DUE

MAY 1 2			
GAYLORD			PRINTED IN U.S.A.